The Good Citizen

A FOUR-STEP GUIDE TO GOSPEL-CENTERED CITIZENSHIP

JOSH HERSHBERGER

"Let your light so shine before men, that they may see your good works, and glorify your Father which is in heaven."
-Jesus Christ, King of Kings
Sermon on the Mount

"We are in fact of all men your best helpers and allies in securing good order."
-Justin Martyr, Roman Subject
First Apology to Emperor Antoninus Pius

"Whatever makes men [and women] good Christians, makes them good citizens."
-Daniel Webster, American Statesman
Plymouth Rock Oration

4 Steps to Gospel-Centered Citizenship

Step#1
Go over (review) your role as
citizen in light of Scripture.

Step #2
Offer prayer for and build relationships
with government officials.

Step#3
Offer solutions and partner with government
officials to solve key problems.

Step #4
Do the hard work of Christian citizenship
in the public square.

TABLE OF CONTENTS

1 INTRODUCTION: THE TROUBLED EXPERIMENT

T hanksgiving is my favorite American holiday. Now, please don't label me as "Scrooge" just yet. I still love Christmas. My wife puts up our Christmas tree no later than the first weekend in November, and I am fortunate if I do not hear Christmas music before October. But I still favor Thanksgiving. Why? Well, a few reasons. First, American culture has not figured out how to fully commercialize Thanksgiving. And this day, set aside for giving of thanks, also undermines our constant self-worship. It is quite difficult to sit with family in front of a Thanksgiving dinner and recite an ode to yourself.

Imagine giving this invocation before the family feast: "Oh vast and expanding universe of which I am the center, I want to thank myself for myself, for my endless knowledge and hard work and for the love and care that I endlessly bestow upon these blessed family members before me. May they be constantly mindful of my goodness and greatness now and forever. Amen." This prayer would be a great way to ensure that you do not host Thanksgiving next year or ever again.

So, Thanksgiving requires us to give thanks to God or at least to the other people that are important in our lives. And this tradition is a long and rich one in American history. From the Pilgrims to Lincoln to Obama to Trump, we, as a people, have often set aside times to give thanks to the Almighty.

But I must admit that I have a much less spiritual and much less mature reason for prizing Thanksgiving. You see, I was attacked by a turkey when I was a kid.

I was four or five years old, and I was walking down to a lake to go swimming. I had on blue shorts and those blown-up flotation devices on my arms to prevent me from drowning. But my carefully planned swimming attire was no match for what I was about to encounter.

On my way down to the lake, I noticed a turkey poult or chick. I thought something along the line of "oh, look, a cute little bird; I think I'll try to pet it." Suddenly, from the underbrush came a distinct rustle and an enraged gobble. Then, a monstrous, diabolical bird thundered from the underbrush and charged toward me!

Quick side note. Have you ever looked closely at a turkey? God's ways are higher than mine, but I honestly can't figure out what He was thinking when He made the turkey. Consider the majestic bald eagle, the vivid feather patterns of the Macaw parrot and the exotic beauty of the Peacock. So, what happened to the turkey? The turkey has impressive tail feathers and intricate plumage on its body. But its head resembles, well, the head of a demon! It's like an animal kingdom Lego set, and some jokester angel attached the wrong head to the bird's body! Just google "turkey head" if you need a reminder—and a nightmare.

Anyway, from the underbrush thundered this demon-headed birdzilla. I then looked it in the eye, stood like the Greeks at Thermopylae or the Texans at the Alamo and did battle with the fiendish beast. Actually, scratch that. I ran in terror while screaming like a little girl (with all due respect to little girls), but I wasn't fast enough to escape this foul fowl. It kept chasing me and pecking me on the back until I finally reached my mom, who scared the thing off and saved me from certain doom.

In the turkey's defense, it was just protecting its young from this very strange-looking little human with overinflated arms. In a sense, the baby turkey ran to its momma, and I ran to mine. But still, I was terrified by that enraged bird.

So, did I mention that I love Thanksgiving? In the closing weeks of November, I have my revenge on the extended family of that demon bird. Not so tough anymore, are you, turkey? Sweet potatoes? Nah. Pass me another slice of that very delicious and very deceased turkey. Actually, I am working on forgiving all turkeys. But turkey's still delicious.

Now, for all of you readers out there who are questioning my sanity or at least my need for intense therapy, please have sympathy. I'm sure you were never scared or traumatized by anything during your childhood. If I'm honest, I think (read this in a hushed tone) we're all a little bit crazy. This realization, perhaps more than any other, has helped me make sense of our shared human experience. So, now you know all the reasons Thanksgiving is my favorite American holiday.

In a similar way, the United States is my favorite country. This may be a bit controversial today; but, considering that most people on the planet would call their own country their favorite country, this is probably not a surprise.

The story of the United States has always inspired me. A group of colonies stood up to the might of the British Empire and won. America's first great general, when given the chance to make himself king, declined and returned to his farm like the great Roman general Cincinnatus before him. And the American people boldly set out to build a nation on largely untested ideas: freedom and self-government.

Our founding charter, the Declaration of Independence, sets out the components of those ideas. All people are created equal. As human beings created in God's image, we are entitled to protections or rights. Our rights come from God, not government. Limited government is critical because human beings tend to abuse power. And ordered liberty is the best way to chain our worst instincts and unchain our best ones.

America has not fully lived up to these ideas and probably never will. But this does not mean that we stop trying or that our fits and starts toward a free, just and equal society do not differ drastically from the checkered stories of nations that fill the pages of history.

Nor should church leaders and other committed Christians overlook the tremendous benefits the American experiment has brought to the American church. These benefits include tax exemptions, private property rights, an institutional separation of church and state, the rule of law, religious freedom, financial wealth, individual liberty and powerful technologies. The early church never even dreamed about some of these benefits, and they have unquestionably contributed to the spread of the gospel here and abroad.

But, then, something happened. The American church was like the younger version of myself happily enjoying the blessings of the American experiment when a divergent view of freedom unexpectedly raised its ominous head. Let me explain.

As mentioned above, the United States is synonymous with freedom and self-government. These ideas have been and continue to be our national identity. But, like the meaning of so many other words these days, the meaning of the word "freedom" is in dispute.[1] The freedom set out in the U.S. Constitution is an *ordered* liberty based on Judeo-Christian principles and moderate enlightenment ideas. But modern jurisprudence and cultural developments have turned that freedom from an ordered liberty into an open license to pursue a society of our own making.

This has made Christian citizenship, well, complicated. The church has always celebrated ordered liberty because of its strong Biblical foundation, but this new version of freedom smacks of the French Revolution and its deification of reason instead of the American War for Independence and its dependence on religion and morality.[2]

Rather than finding purpose in God's good design for us and our society and enjoying the *freedom to* work, create and dream within that framework, we have shaken our fists at heaven and declared a *freedom from* God's design so that we can please ourselves and pursue our own vision of humanity's purpose and future.

Stated differently, the United States is no longer "One Nation Under God." Rather, we are "One Nation Over God," as in we are <u>over</u> the idea of an all-powerful, all-loving God who created all things having anything to say about our lives, communities or nation.

This divergent view of freedom is much more than a political or cultural theory, for American courts have established an orthodoxy in secular humanism and relegated the Judeo-Christian viewpoint to minority status. The first commandment of this religion, "You shall have no other gods before yourself," is largely unquestioned by law and culture and is enforced as a dogma. This expressive individualism or personal autonomy is the reigning first principle in American culture and is at the core of the hot button issues of the day.

This divergent view of freedom ambushed the unsuspecting church. Within a short period of time, the Christian sexual ethic changed from the hard but right choice to the "hateful" choice of the "hard right." The church's refusal to affirm this new-found freedom from authority and tradition was and is viewed as hateful and even dangerous. And the church's core exclusive claim concerning truth and eternal salvation rings like the tyrannical proclamation of a distant and ancient king. So, in these early decades of a new century, the church finds the power and genius of the American experiment coopted and turned against it.

In response to these seismic changes, the church has employed two primary strategies. First, from about 1920 to 1970, the church withdrew. Surely, the gospel could be preserved and the church's influence protected if Christians extracted themselves from educational institutions, entertainment, big business, media, and, especially, politics. In summary, that didn't work. By the 1970s, Christians realized that they were losing their cultural influence and came roaring back into public life.[3]

Movements like the Moral Majority would solve the problem and restore the church's central role in American law and culture. Though the term "culture war" has a negative connotation among many Christians, I have read the cases from that time period and have met several of the primary figures (or at least their successors) in that movement. I am convinced that the motives of these leaders were primarily Biblical and proper. However, the political arena is filled with traps and tensions, and it is very easy to be coopted by the lure of power or to engage in public life out of fear and self-preservation.

Now, the pendulum is swinging back. Many Christians and especially young church leaders have determined the best way to preserve the gospel is to simply withdraw from anything related to public life.

But, as noted above, we have already tried that strategy! And it failed. We live in a participatory democratic republic. So, if we do not participate in public life, we should not be surprised when our religious liberty is abridged, when public policy reflects unbiblical and harmful ideas and when culture worships principles that undermine our gospel message.

In sum, our model for citizenship isn't working. The church has a strong and comprehensive teaching on how to live out our faith at work, at school, and at home and how to apply our faith to technology, relationships, our sexuality and much more. But then we come to the arena of politics—and que the crickets.

Church leaders say very little about the political sphere. In fact, a recent survey from Lifeway Research and the Billy Graham Center at Wheaton College found that 60% of Christians receive little to no "political discipleship" from their churches.[4] That may seem like a good thing at first, but is it?

Christians will find guidance on this topic somewhere and will be influenced by someone. Can we agree that it is unhealthy for Christians to be catechized in their role as citizens by political candidates, political parties or the media? I do not mean to disparage any of these institutions or people, but their goals are often quite straightforward: power and influence.

We lament the rise of political tribalism in our churches, but then provide no alternate model. We are quick to point out the loss of civility in public life, but then question the sanity and even humanity of our political opponents. We applaud the concept of reaching out to ideological enemies in our weekly gatherings but then retire to our social media echo chambers to blast the "left-wing libtards" or the "right-wing Nazis."

There are two possible explanations for the scarcity of "political discipleship" or strong Biblical teaching on citizenship and the intersection of faith and public life. The first explanation is that Scripture has nothing to say about this area of our lives. Perhaps Christians, who are so clearly called to be Christ's disciples in every other area of their lives, have a free pass to act like secluded hermits or Machiavellian devils in the arena of politics. The second possibility is that Scripture provides guiding principles in this area, and we have just neglected to teach and live them out because they can be controversial and require time and attention to apply well.

Thankfully, the truth on this matter does not take a rocket scientist or even a political scientist to figure out! Of course, Scripture speaks to citizenship as it does to every other area of our lives. Therefore, we simply need to recover or create a gospel-centered model for citizenship.

And we need to do so quickly. Why? Because, absent a major spiritual awakening or renewal in the United States, the pressure to either withdraw or culture war out of fear and self-preservation will only intensify in the coming years.

I am writing this in the lead up to the 2020 presidential election. In the last few years, several key U.S. Supreme Court cases have swung in favor of religious liberty. But this brief hiatus may not last. The part of America that is <u>over</u> God is keen to remove Biblical principles from public life and to consign the church to an ever-shrinking sacred bubble.

The temptation will be great in coming years to jeopardize the gospel for political gain, as if a century or more of cultural developments and the stubborn evil of the human heart can be stopped by simply electing the right person to the White House, selecting the right party to control Congress and appointing the right judges to the Supreme Court.

And the temptation will be just as great to quietly withdraw, as if we have no responsibility to this constitutional republic, no neighbors to serve and no ideological enemies that wish to see the gospel and Biblical truth erased from the cultural conversation.

For these reasons, we must develop an unnatural or, should I say, supernatural ability. Like the Jews who helped Nehemiah build the wall around Jerusalem, we must learn to build with one hand (think building relationships with elected officials and serving our neighborhoods and cities) while remaining vigilant and ready to defend with the other (think elections, comments on public policy and religious liberty litigation).

If we neglect to build, we will appear defensive and uncaring. And, if we neglect to guard our liberties, we will lose significant opportunities to spread the gospel and impact our communities. So, as John Stonestreet says, "We need to learn how to walk and chew gum at the same time."[5]

Most church leaders I speak to agree with the general analysis set forth above. But then comes the billion-dollar question (that's a million-dollar question adjusted for inflation): "So, how exactly are we supposed to do that?"

Church leaders with budgets to balance, deacons or elders to consider, young converts to lead and politically divided congregations to address are right to be cautious about the intersection of faith and public life. And other committed Christians with jobs to keep, kids to feed, lives to live and neighbors to reach with the gospel are right to scratch their head about how to do this well.

This is why we need to revisit our story about and strategy for citizenship. We need to review what Scripture states about this issue, nail down those guiding principles or bright-line rules (and, by implication, identify areas where Christians can disagree without violating Scripture) and then identify action steps that are working now.

Here's another way to think about this. Many people are familiar with Dave Ramsey and how he has distilled Biblical principles about finances into action or "baby steps" and guided a movement of people toward financial freedom. Well, we need something similar for public life. We need guiding principles and practical steps for becoming gospel-centered citizens in a polarized and increasingly plural America.

That, in a nutshell, is the purpose of this book. What follows is not an academic tome. There are other great resources and books that set out a comprehensive study of Scripture and public theology. This book is intended to be a practical, Thom Rainer or Dave Ramsey-style guide to addressing this thorny issue and to impacting your community, state and the nation.

As I have worked in church leadership, litigated religious liberty cases, advocated for Christian ideas in public life and observed other successful Christians in the public square, I have developed four practical steps to help church leaders and other committed Christ-followers think through and then engage their role as citizen in an increasingly polarized and plural America.

Those steps are as follows, and they spell "GOOD," as in "good citizen." We should all be good citizens, so: (1) G - go over or review your role as citizen in light of Biblical principles and examples, (2) O –

offer prayer for and build relationships with elected officials, (3) O – offer solutions and partner with government officials to solve key community problems and (4) D – do the hard work of Christian citizenship in the public square. These steps form the basic outline of the book.

Whenever I study a topic, the first thing I want to know is what Scripture says about the topic (rather than what the author thinks). I am sure you apply the same filter. So, let's start there. Step #1 is all about reviewing what God says about government and applying those principles to our form of government in this cultural moment. Let's jump right in.

STEP #1 GO OVER (REVIEW) YOUR ROLE AS CITIZEN IN LIGHT OF SCRIPTURE

2 REVIEW BIBLICAL PRINCIPLES

I almost laughed while being sworn in to practice law in the Commonwealth of Kentucky. Now, there was nothing overtly funny about the experience. The chambers of the Kentucky Supreme Court, where the ceremony occurred, are ornate but formal with dark-stained wood and an aura of authority. And Kentucky Chief Justice John D. Minton administered the oath to the soon-to-be attorneys with all the gravity that the moment deserved.

So, why did I almost laugh? Because the oath, required by Section 228 of the Kentucky Constitution, includes the following statement: "I do further solemnly swear (or affirm) that ...I have not fought a duel with deadly weapons within this State nor out of it, nor have I sent or accepted a challenge to fight a duel with deadly weapons, nor have I acted as second in carrying a challenge, nor aided or assisted any person thus offending, so help me God."[6]

So, yes, I struggled with keeping a straight face while being sworn in to practice law. For the record, I looked around and noticed that I was not the only one struggling with solemnly swearing this solemn oath. Why did I almost laugh? Well, I can't say that I have ever been tempted to settle my disputes by lining up back to back with an implacable foe, counting several paces while trusting my opponent not to get that mixed up (oh, was that five paces instead of four? My bad...), then turning and firing a pistol at another not-so-gentle gentleman at close range. And, none of my friends, who have asked me a lot of strange questions, have ever asked, "Hey, Josh, I'm dueling that dishonorable scoundrel down at the steamboat landing tomorrow. Will you be my second?" All of this, of course, begs this question: why is the oath in the Kentucky Constitution?

Here's my best explanation. Dueling, which originated in Europe as a means to settle disputes over romance or honor, evolved in the United States into a means for settling political differences. Alexander Hamilton, a leading American statesman and major author of *The Federalist Papers*, and his son both died in duels. Andrew Jackson participated in several duels, and Abraham Lincoln was even challenged to a duel (he considered fighting with a sword because his long arms would have given him an advantage, but he eventually decided against the duel). This practice of dueling, which was largely limited to the wealthier classes, worked as a sort of "brain drain" because it killed off so many prominent landowners and government officials.

Eventually, the people of Kentucky noticed that their leading citizens were engaging in a fashionable but wasteful form of conflict resolution and put an end to it. Their point? Dueling, no matter how fashionable or "gentlemanly," is just plain dumb.

Here's my point in sharing this bit of historical folly. The oath in section 228 of the Kentucky Constitution points to a much deeper issue: our human tendency of putting our cultural habits and practices on autopilot without full consideration of the origin or consequences of those practices. Sometimes, we need to stop and review even well-accepted norms to ensure that they are healthy and helpful.

As I explained in the introduction, Christian citizenship is one of those habits or practices that has the tendency of being put on autopilot. We all pick up our political ideology and public theology somewhere (home, political party, friends, etc.), and we often engage politics the same way as our family and friends.

But when was the last time you stopped and thought deeply about your role as citizen in light of God's Word? And when was the last time you revisited this in light of our quickly changing culture and the shifting political landscape?

That's why the first step to becoming or remaining a gospel-centered citizen is to review or rethink your role as citizen. Before we jump on social media to comment on the president's latest tweet or allow the busyness of life to overwhelm us until the night before we vote (nobody actually does that, right?), we need to stop and think about how we should engage in this area of our lives.

Because this is a complicated task, I will spend several chapters on this question before moving on to more practical steps and ideas for engaging as gospel-centered citizens. To begin our review, let's take a look at Biblical principles about government.

5 Key Biblical Principles about Government

So, what does Scripture say about the role of government and our relationship to it? Though there are many principles about government listed in Scripture, I will focus on five key principles about government that every Christian should know: (1) government is God's idea, (2) government isn't God, (3) government needs a guide, (4) government guards good works and (5) government will go away. We will study each of these key principles in turn.

#1 Government Is God's Idea.

Given the complicated relationship between church and state and the fact that governments have historically abridged religious liberty and even persecuted the church, it is important to remember that government is one of the three institutions created by God: the family (Gen. 2:18), the church (Matt. 16:18; Acts 2; I Tim. 3:15) and government (Gen. 9; Rom. 13).

In Romans 13, we are commanded by God to be subject to governing authorities because those authorities are appointed by God. Further, Romans 13 states that governing authorities are God's servants or ministers for our good and that they should praise and promote good works.

However, that is not government's only role. Government is also tasked with bearing or wielding a sword to execute God's wrath on those that do evil (Rom. 13:4). Where's a surprised or astonished face emoji when you need one? That's strong medicine for a modern society! So, why did God institute government? Here's the summary: God instituted government to punish evil and promote good.

This summary is seconded by I Peter 2:13-14, "Submit yourselves to every ordinance of man for the Lord's sake: whether it be to the king, as supreme; or unto governors, as unto them that are sent by him for the punishment of evildoers, and for the praise of them that do well."[7]

Now, it is important to remember that these passages were not written in the context of a democratic republic or even a benevolent dictator. Rather, these words were penned under the tyrannical reign of the Roman emperor Nero, who ordered the death of his political rivals, many early Christians and even his own mother (really, who does that?)! Still, Scripture states that ruling authorities are appointed by God and are his servants tasked with punishing evil and promoting good.

So, yes, government is God's idea. He created the idea of government and tasked government officials with punishing evil and promoting good.

Now, what does this principle mean practically?

Here are a couple of thoughts. This principle clearly undermines the notion that politics or government is categorically dirty and must be avoided by mature Christians at all costs. Government is not the construct of a pagan chieftain, a medieval monarch or an atheist thinker. Government is God's idea, and we should relate to and influence that institution with His principles.

Further, this principle has a profound message for any clown with a crown (or an elected office) that consciously or even subconsciously attempts to usurp the authority of the kingdom of heaven. The greatest emperors in history and the great leaders of our day had and have only delegated authority from our eternal King.

In summary, this principle means that Christians should not treat the state as categorically unholy. And this means that we should, from time to time, remind ourselves and our elected officials that we would have no power unless given by God.

#2 Government Isn't God.

Jesus stated this principle clearly in Matthew 22. In that passage, the Pharisees sent several of their disciples to test Jesus; and these disciples asked Jesus if the Jews should pay tribute to Caesar. Jesus asked for a denarius (the common Roman coin of the period) and asked whose image was on it. They responded, "Caesar's." Jesus then made this profound statement, "Render therefore unto Caesar the things which are Caesar's; and unto God the things that are God's" (Matt 22:21).

Because Jesus asked for and then commented on the denarius, it is important to note the symbols and inscriptions on the coin itself. On the front side of the denarius was the likeness of the emperor and the inscription, "Tiberius Caesar Augustus, son of the divine Augustus." On the back side of the denarius was the image of Tiberius' mother, depicted as the goddess of peace, along with the inscription "highest priest."[8]

So, Jesus apparently considered the political claims of the front side of the coin to be in line with His teachings. As Christians, we owe to government our general civic obedience and respect, which includes paying taxes and avoiding criminal activity.

But the back side of the coin was a different matter, for its spiritual symbolism and inscription demanded worship of the Roman state and especially the emperor. What was Christ's point? Only one King is worthy of ultimate allegiance and worship, and Caesar is not that King.

So, what does this mean practically?

The most apparent application of this principle is that our ultimate allegiance must be to heaven and that we should not bow to a government interpretation of morality that contravenes the clear teaching of Scripture.

But there is a key corollary to this principle. You see, if government isn't God, then politics isn't religion. For Americans just a century ago, this concept of politics as religion would have been quite unthinkable. But most church leaders I speak to today consider this a problem.

This principle is first a reminder to the church and then a critique of our current political practices. The fact that politics has become religion is not a new observation. In the 1960s, Lesslie Newbigin, a missionary who spent much of his adult life in India, returned to Britain and was simply dumbfounded. While he was away, Britain had secularized. In his book, *Honest Religion for a Secular Man*, he noted that, when men replace God, all of the sacred orders fall way.[9] And he theorized that people in secular societies would eventually return to what he termed the "political religions." That prediction turned out to be prophetic.

More recently, columnist Peggy Noonan observed, "For more and more Americans, politics has become a religion. People find their meaning in it. They define themselves by their stands...When politics becomes a religion, then simple disagreements become apostasies, heresies. And you know what we do with heretics."[10]

As I mentioned, this is primarily a reminder to the church. As followers of Jesus, we must find our identity in Christ rather than in our political tribe such as conservative Republican or liberal Democrat.

Next, this principle is a strong critique of our current political climate. Americans do politics like we used to do religion. Religion has traditionally provided community, a moral framework and meaning. Now, many Americans find community in their political tribe, base morality on whatever feels right to the most people and pursue meaning and legacy through political activism. In contrast, Scripture teaches that government was never meant to be the arbiter of ultimate truth and politics was never meant to be the primary purpose of our lives.

So, in review, government isn't God. God deserves our ultimate allegiance and worship no matter who or what claims otherwise, and politics is a shallow and dangerous replacement for true religion.

#3 Government Needs a Guide.

In Romans 13, Scripture states that government authorities are "...not a terror to good works, but to...evil." And, in 2 Peter 2:15,

Scripture states that government is ordained by God "...for the punishment of evildoers, and for the praise of them that do well."

These verses are fairly straightforward, but they do raise an important question. If government is charged with punishing evil and rewarding good, how exactly does government determine what is evil and what is good? Is government itself the source of morality? Haven't many kings bloodied chapters of history with a morality that appeared remarkably similar to their own self-interest and greed? And if government is not a good source of morality, then who or what is?

As Christians, we have an easy answer to that. Government is God's idea, and He designed government to punish evil and promote good as He defined those terms (Rom. 13). Contrary to popular opinion, we can't magically create our own truth, and neither can a president or a judge. Rather, from a Biblical perspective, government's job is to pursue justice and to reward good as defined in Scripture.

This is, of course, controversial and complicated by the fact that we live in an increasingly plural democratic republic. In a later chapter, I will address how this principle practically works out. But, for now, remember that we are studying Biblical principles and not just my opinion. Romans 13 and similar passages are very clear: government needs a moral guide.

The book of Deuteronomy contains a powerful example of this principle. In Chapter 17, God instructed future Jewish kings to write a personal copy of God's law in a book:

> And it [the copy of God's law] shall be with him, and he shall read therein all the days of his life: that he may learn to fear the Lord his God, to keep all the words of this law and these statutes, to do them: That his heart be not lifted up above his brethren, and that he turn not aside from the commandment, to the right hand, or to the left: to the end that he may prolong his days in his kingdom, he, and his children, in the midst of Israel (Duet. 17:18-20).

The message here is simple. Government officials are ultimately appointed by God and should govern according to God's principles.

This lesson is apparent throughout Scripture. Many of the stories of kings and rulers in the Bible include another key character. If you have watched movies portraying ancient and medieval courts, you might expect that key character to be a court jester, a wise magician or a capable general. But, aside from a few important generals and a few Egyptian magicians, such figures are absent from the Biblical narrative.

Instead, a priest, prophet or prophetess stood beside or opposite rulers. Think of Moses and Pharaoh, Deborah and Barack, Samuel and Saul, Nathan and David, Elijah and Ahab, Micaiah and Jehoshaphat, Ahijah and Jeroboam, Jeremiah and Zedekiah, Esther and Ahasuerus, Daniel and Nebuchadnezzar, Daniel and Cyrus, John the Baptist and Herod, Jesus and Pilate, and Paul and Nero.

These representatives of God's kingdom were not token religious advisors that blessed political machinations with a sprinkle of holy water and misapplied Scripture. Instead, many of these priests and prophets condemned their prospective rulers for idolatry and adultery, often reminded them of God's commandments and even paid with their lives for their bold witness.

This principle (government needs a guide) was also clearly practiced in early American history. Many colonial and early American legislatures asked ministers to give "election sermons" to elected officials. For example, on May 26, 1790, Reverend Daniel Foster preached an election sermon to Governor John Hancock (also a famous signer of the Declaration of Independence), Lieutenant Governor John Adams (a future President of the United States), and the full Senate and House of Representatives of Massachusetts.

Pastor Foster's text was Proverbs 8:16, in which wisdom (personified in the chapter) states: "By me princes rule, and nobles, even all the judges of the earth." And here is a key excerpt from that sermon:

> In compliance with the laudable example of our pious Ancestors, on such joyful anniversary occasions as this day presents us with we have assembled in the House of God, to offer our devout praises to him for what he has done for them, and for us, their children; *to seek his direction and blessing upon our Political Fathers here present*, in

the discharge of the important trust reposed in them, and his smiles on this confederate rising Republic [emphasis added]...

He continued:

And as it has fallen to one of the least of the Ambassadors of Christ, to perform so essential a part of the exercise of the day, it will not be expected that he turn Statesman in this sacred place, or wander into all the affairs of government: But, in compliance with his character as a Minister, make such observations from the sacred text, as may be profitable for direction and encouragement, that the men of God here present, may be furnished to every good work.[11]

This is an excellent example of a pastor providing encouragement and moral guidance to government. Now, let's fast-forward to more modern times.

Martin Luther King, Jr. powerfully summarized this Biblical principle and the historical role of the American church as follows: "The church must be reminded that it is not the master or the servant of the state, but rather the conscience of the state. It must be the guide and the critic of the state, and never its tool. If the church does not recapture its prophetic zeal, it will become an irrelevant social club without moral or spiritual authority."[12]

So, in sum, government needs a guide or conscience. And, the church, as the pillar and ground of the truth (I Tim. 3:15) is the best guide.

Now, I imagine most Christians would agree with the above principle, but the application of that principle is the tricky part (no joke, Sherlock!). So, what does this mean practically? Are we trying to build a theocracy? How should this principle be applied in an increasingly plural democratic republic?

The first and fairly straightforward application of this principle is that church leaders should courageously speak truth to power. Who will warn our society about the atomizing effects of new technology (such as social media), the dangers of genetically engineered super-humans, the consequences of the sexual revolution, the breakdown of the nuclear family, the pursuit of profit over human flourishing, the dangers of all-powerful government and other developing threats in the coming years? Will it be Big Tech? Will it be scientists? Will it be Wall Street? Will it be Congress? I doubt it.

Though voices in these communities or industries may raise an alarm from time to time, it falls to the church to stand athwart (possibly my favorite word) the whirling, pounding forces of advanced modernity and declare, "This is right, and this is wrong." In short, as our society careens back and forth between dangerous and dark chasms on our way to an unknown future, the church should embrace its God-given role as moral guide.

Here's another, more controversial application of this principle: the proper, institutional separation of church and state. In review, the state's role is to punish evil and promote good. And the church's primary role is to fulfill the Great Commission by making disciples of Jesus among all nations (Matt. 28:16-20).

Let me illustrate these roles. In Romans 13, Scripture uses a sword to exemplify the state's authority and political power. And, in Matthew and Revelation, Scripture uses a light or candlestick to exemplify the church's spiritual influence (Luke 8:16; Rev. 1). God intended for these sources of influence or power to be independent but complementary. However, humans, always lusting after power, discovered that wielding the power of the state and the influence of the church together could create fear and control people. I mean, what moves people to action (or inaction) better than threatening them with losing their heads and their souls!

Here's how this played out in history. Rulers who wielded the sword (political power) coopted the church's light or candlestick (spiritual influence) to further their own ends. The Roman Empire and most empires throughout history and their demands of emperor-worship or king-worship are a perfect example of this. And the European idea of the divine right of kings also perpetuated this misapplication of Scriptural principles.

On the other hand, the Christian church and other religious leaders have, at times, "borrowed" the state's sword in an effort to further its spiritual influence and coerce converts. The medieval Catholic church and its relationship to European monarchs is an example of this. When Martin Luther was tried for heresy after he posted the Ninety-Five Theses, who presided over the trial? The Pope? Nope. Luther was tried before Charles V, the emperor of the Holy Roman Empire.

So, what do you get when you put a light and a sword together? Well, you get a *lightsaber*, a weapon of immense and devastating power. Now, I am way too clumsy to wield one of these imaginary weapons (hey, I accidently sliced off my left arm in that practice session today, let's try jumping and spinning with this sizzling laser weapon tomorrow!), but they certainly appear to be terrifying weapons. So, no ruler or (human) church leader should ever be allowed to wield the punishing force of the state's sword and the transforming influence of the church's light combined into the tyrant's weapon of choice: the lightsaber.

Fortunately, the American founders recognized these historical lessons and established an institutional separation of church and state. The religion clause in the First Amendment states the following: "Congress shall make no law respecting an establishment of religion, or prohibiting the free exercise thereof..." The intent was simple. Congress may not establish a national or state-recognized religion. Why was this intent so clear and apparent to the founding generation? Because nine of the thirteen colonies had established religions, and this system led to coercion of Baptists and other dissidents because they refused to support the state-established church.[13]

In sum, the founders intended to separate the institutions of church and state; but they did not intend to remove religion's key influence in public life. Consider the practice of election sermons described above and George Washington's admonition in his farewell address: "Of all the dispositions and habits which lead to political prosperity, religion and morality are indispensable supports."[14] Professor Bruce Riley Ashford concisely states this principle as follows: "We must separate church and state, but we cannot (due to human nature) separate religion from politics."[15]

Today, the church has a healthy concern about coopting the state's political authority to further its spiritual aims, and this principle should remain front and center in our efforts in the public square. But, in my experience, the state has little qualms with subconsciously and perhaps consciously coopting the church's spiritual authority to accomplish its political ends. This is a strong and perhaps controversial statement, so let me explain.

Secular humanism is advertised as neutral. Our jurisprudence and political dialogue assume that general, secular principles are devoid of religious bias. But secularism has smuggled in the concept of neutrality, for secularism still makes religious or at least quasi-religious claims upon its adherents. Just considers the secular dogmas of personal autonomy, sexual freedom and reproductive rights. And, by pressing its claims of secular orthodoxy, the state or at least the state in conjunction with culture has wrested control of the light of spiritual authority and now points it and the sword of political power at American culture to bend culture to its will.

Stated differently, the state now wields an especially powerful and dangerous lightsaber that is being used to direct American culture toward a progressive secular vision. As highlighted by this principle, this arrangement is out of order. The church should guide the state on moral issues, not vice versa.

Let me summarize when it comes to the Biblical principle that government needs a guide. Christianity was never officially the religion of the United States. But there is strong evidence that Christian principles deeply influenced the founding generation and the formation of the American republic.[16] And this is a healthy template for the church now. We should respect the institutional separation of church and state but provide first principles and moral guidance to citizens and government.

#4 Government Guards Good Works.

Throughout the New Testament, the church is repeatedly commanded to "do good" (Matt. 5:16; Titus 3:1-2; Gal. 6:10; Eph. 2:10; I Peter 2:15). For example, in Matthew 5:16, Christ states: "Let your light so shine before men, that they may see your good works, and glorify your Father which is in heaven." Also, consider Titus 3:1-2, "Put them in mind to be subject to principalities and powers, to obey magistrates, to be ready to every good work, to speak evil of no man, to be no brawlers, but gentle, shewing all meekness unto all men."

Quick side note. These verses inspired the title of this book and the name of The Good Citizen Project. The New Testament is replete with commands to "do good" to those outside the church and in our role as citizen. Therefore, we should be "good citizens" of a Biblical sort.

If government is doing its job of punishing evil and promoting good, we as Christians will be able to lead "...a quiet and peaceable life in all godliness and honesty" (I Tim. 2:2)—we will be free and secure in proclaiming the gospel and doing good works. Here's that principle stated in a more concise way: government should guard and commend the good works of the church.

What does this mean practically? Well, for starters, we should not shrug off the fact that American government has largely but imperfectly fulfilled this role throughout America's brief history. We should be grateful for and mindful of the tremendous benefits (listed in the introduction) the American experiment has brought to the American church.

Many Christians consider government an opponent. Due to slavery, segregation, government discrimination, the culture wars, religious liberty litigation and coercive government mandates, I certainly understand this perspective. However, according to Scripture, government and the church should not be opponents. Rather, these two institutions should be partners in carrying out their Biblical and complementary roles.

I acknowledge that there will always be tension in this space. But, in the context of some of our most complex problems such as the drug crisis, the foster care crisis, racial injustice, and the general breakdown of the nuclear family, there are numerous opportunities for church and state to work together for the common good.

Remember the three God-ordained institutions: the family (Gen. 2:18), the church (Matt. 16:18; Acts 2; I Tim. 3:15) and government (Gen. 9; Rom. 13)? As the family has broken down and the church has shifted its focus inward, government is left trying to maintain order and promote a flourishing society. So, we can complain about big government. Or, we can work on restoring the other two institutions while reminding government of its proper, limited role.

In summary, government's job is to guard and promote good works, and it's our job as the church to do the good works that point people to Jesus and solve societal problems. It's time to treat government more like a partner than an opponent.

#5 Government Will Go Away.

Fifth and finally, government will go away. One of my favorite examples of this principle is Christ's conversation with Pontius Pilate. For context, Pilate was the prefect or governor of the small but troublesome Roman province of Judea, and he was the agent of the Roman emperor Tiberius. At that time, Rome was the greatest empire the world had yet seen (the Chinese Han dynasty probably rivaled or exceeded Rome's territorial reach but arguably not its military power) and stretched from the British channel to the African desert to the Euphrates river in the Middle East.[17] Jesus, by all appearances, was an impoverished carpenter from a small city named Nazareth.

Pilate and Jesus had two conversations in John 18 and 19. In the first exchange, Pilate asked Jesus if he was Kings of the Jews. And Jesus responded with this curious statement, "...My kingdom is not of this world: if my kingdom were of this world, then would my servants fight..." (John 18:36). After this exchange, Pilate returned to the Jews and declared Christ's innocence.

The Jews, for their part, demanded that Jesus be crucified anyway. The consummate politician, Pilate had his innocent (according to his own analysis) prisoner flogged. While beating Christ, the Roman soldiers placed a crown of thorns on Christ's head, put a purple royal robe on Him, and sarcastically hailed Him as "King of the Jews."

Pilate, who seemed conflicted by the situation but needed to pacify his subjects, brought the bloodied Jesus out to the crowd and prepared to turn Him over for crucifixion. Then, the Jews yelled out something that caught Pilate's attention.

They screamed that Jesus must die because He claimed to be the Son of God (and not just King of the Jews). This supernatural claim gave Pilate pause and even scared him (John 19:8), and he brought Jesus back into the Praetorium (Pilate's residence) for further questioning.

As recorded in John 19, Pilate asked Jesus where He was from. In response, Jesus said absolutely nothing. Oh, to be a fly on the wall! Can you imagine the pompous glare that Pilate gave Jesus? Pilate was the governor. He wielded the power and might of imperial Rome, the "eternal city" and "capital of the world." And Jesus, who was beaten, crowned with a mock crown and faced death, dared to defy him! Pilate, like many an upset judge to a defiant defendant, demanded an answer and reminded Christ that he, Pilate, had the power of life and death.

At this, Jesus finally broke his silence. He did not argue. That would have implied a parity between the kingdom of Rome and the kingdom of heaven. And He did not question Pilate as He so often did by responding to a question with a question. That would have signaled an ongoing conversation about authority.

No, in this moment, Jesus spoke like as a King pronouncing a decree. No questions. No argument. Just truth. Christ told Pilate he would "…have no power at all against me, except it were given…from above" (John 19:11).

Boom! What? Drop the mic! There, in the Praetorium, an age ago and half-a-planet away from the coffee shop in which I am writing this, King Jesus gave the prefect of Judea a one-sentence reminder of the order of the universe. Rome, the so-called eternal city and capital of the world whose mighty legions controlled their known world, wielded nothing but delegated power from the throne room of heaven. Imperial power could do nothing but bow before eternal power that ruled all. These words apparently stunned Pilate, for he said nothing in response and immediately sought Christ's release.

This story gets better. Remember when Jesus said His kingdom was not of this world? Well, someday soon, that will change. Have you ever considered the political implications of Philippians 2:10-11, "That at the name of Jesus every knee should bow, of things in heaven, and things in earth, and things under the earth; and that every tongue should confess that Jesus Christ is Lord, to the glory of God the Father."

You read that right. Jesus Christ is Lord! And, just in case there was any confusion about what kind of Lord He is, Scripture further explains that Christ is King of kings and Lord of lords (I Tim. 6:15; Rev. 19:16). Remember the *Hallelujah Chorus*? Here are the words:

The kingdom of this world
Is become the kingdom of our Lord,
And of His Christ, and of His Christ;
And He shall reign for ever and ever,
For ever and ever, forever and ever,

King of kings, and Lord of lords,
|: King of kings, and Lord of lords, :|
And Lord of lords,
And He shall reign,
And He shall reign forever and ever,
King of kings, forever and ever,
And Lord of lords,
Hallelujah! Hallelujah!

Hallelujah and amen! Jesus isn't just the King of the Jews. He is the high King of the universe who arrived in a manger to inaugurate his redemptive and revolutionary reign and will return on a white horse with a host of heaven behind him to destroy evil and make all things new.

Christians, we worship that King and that Lord! And we look for the day when evil will be judged, pain will end, suffering will be banished and death itself will die. And we long for the day when we will bow before our eternal King and join Him as the servant kings and queens of the universe (Rev. 22:5).

I don't know about you, but I'm getting my worship on up in here! "Thine, O Lord, is the greatness, and the power, and the glory, and the victory, and the majesty: for all that is in the heaven and in the earth is thine; thine is the kingdom, O Lord, and thou art exalted as head above all" (I Chron. 29:11).

So, what does this principle mean practically?

Simply put, government (or at least as we think of it now) will go away someday. When Christ returns, He will rule and reign; and there will be no need for government in the traditional, human sense. We, the citizens of another republic much younger and even more powerful than Rome, must remind ourselves and our elected officials of the same principle that Pilate heard in the Praetorium. We, the people of the United States, would have no power unless given to us from above.

But we aren't there yet, are we? So, what does this mean now? This principle makes us good citizens of heaven, but it also makes us good citizens of the United States.

Many government officials down through the centuries have viewed this allegiance to Christ as disobedience or at least a lack of loyalty to the state. But, this higher allegiance to God and his principles actually equips Christians to be the best kind of citizens. Why? Because we are compelled by Scripture to participate in civic life, to serve our fellow man and to obey our rulers within the bounds of their authority.

Here's just one example: sociologist and religious demographer Rodney Stark points out that, during the Plague of Cyprian in the 3rd century, "...death rates in cities with Christian communities may have been just half that of other cities..." due to the Christian commitment to care for the sick.[18] Non-Christians can, of course, be good citizens too. But Christian dual citizenship is an asset to our cities and country rather than a liability.

That said, our ultimate allegiance is never to a politician, a political system or even a particular flag. Christians served Rome but could not bow to Caesar's supernatural and eventually destructive claims. And we should faithfully serve the United States; but we cannot bow to our culture's and, at times, our government's ever-changing and harmful demands about self-worship, sexual autonomy and liberty as license.

This view of citizenship equips American Christians to be loyal but prophetic, engaged but uncorrupted and practical yet visionary. I would argue that the United States needs exactly this kind of citizens these days.

Remember the public life pendulum I mentioned earlier in the book (withdrawal to culture warring back to withdrawal)? There always has been and always will be a tension between evangelism and engagement in public life.

Some will argue that we should just preach the Good News about eternal life in anticipation of Christ's return and avoid engagement in public life. This approach puts the gospel in a building-shaped box, deemphasizes full-life discipleship, ignores the comprehensive commands of Scripture and plays right into the secular playbook of a sacred/secular split (Matt. 28:16-20).

And some will argue (even if this message is implicit rather than explicit) that we should focus much of our energy on high-stakes political engagement while deemphasizing the church's primary priority of making disciples of all nations. This approach neglects the Great Commission, frames people rather than ideas as our enemies, marries the church's public witness to a party or politician and attempts to bring in the kingdom of God through the ballot box or a judge's gavel.

The fact that government will go away provides a solution to this dilemma. Government was instituted by God and is important, so we should do good works and engage government according to Biblical principles. But government and politics is not ultimate.

So, we should engage government with the ultimate purpose of pointing people to the truth and beauty of the gospel with the understanding that ultimate justice and peace will elude us until eternity. In other words, what Jesus said in Matthew 5:16: "Let your light so shine before men, that they may see your good works, and glorify your Father which is in heaven."

Like so many issues in life and especially the Christian life, we want to "solve" the issue of citizenship by abdicating our role or simply doing it like everyone else. But Christian citizenship is more like a habit to be formed and maintained than a problem to be solved. Why can't we just accept that? It's like weight control, budgeting and relationships. These things take time and attention to manage well, and we need to dedicate ourselves to mastering this discipline in turbulent times.

In sum, the fact that government will go away gives us a great template for citizenship. We should engage in public life for the common good in the here and now but look to the hereafter for ultimate peace, justice and vindication.

In review, here are the five key Biblical principles about government: (1) government is God's idea, (2) government isn't God, (3) government needs a guide, (4) government guards good works, and (5) government will go away. Next, let's review Old Testament and New Testament examples of citizenship.

3 REVIEW BIBLICAL EXAMPLES

I would like to "have a word" with the engineer that designed our SUV. Why? Well, the battery died without warning while the vehicle was parked on the side of the street in a busy downtown neighborhood. Now, I am sure there was some failure on my part to check said battery, but who's accepting responsibility these days?

Further, I tend to leave car repairs to the professionals. But, changing a battery is not that hard—unless the battery is inaccessible from the engine compartment and is behind a wheel well. Further, the SUV was parked driver-side out, so I had to dodge traffic while attempting the repair.

Again, I would like to have a word with the engineer and the vehicle company. In the six-hour ordeal that followed, which involved me hazarding my life and almost jeopardizing my Christian testimony, I walked to and from a store in search of tools, removed a tire and numerous rusty bolts, and lost some blood and a lot of patience.

I first consulted the vehicle manual, and this manual explained the general workings of a car battery and the location of the battery (very helpful, indeed!). But I am not a mechanic. So, I did what any self-respecting millennial man would do in such a crisis. I consulted YouTube prior to telling everyone how I "figured it out on my own" (just kidding). I found a video that showed me step-by-step how to replace the battery and what everyone else in the world thought about the battery placement. For example, one of the first comments on the video exclaimed that the engineers, "…should be hung by their pinky toes over a pit of crocodiles." Alrighty then. That's quite creative, but I am a little worried about the future of civilization!

In sum, the principles in the manual were helpful, but a video showing me how to apply those principles assisted my efforts and gave me confidence that I was completing the task correctly. By the way, next time, I am just paying the towing fee.

As we consider how to navigate citizenship in our times, it is important to know and understand key Biblical principles. But we should also review Biblical examples. These individuals navigated many of the same tensions we experience even if they lived in a different cultural context, so let's learn from their example.

Abram

Consider Abram (a.k.a. Abraham after Genesis 17), who often interacted with kings and even rescued Lot after he was taken captive by a king named Chedorlaomer. For the record, King Chedorlaomer and his army had just decimated the Rephaims, the Zuzims, the Emims, the Horites, the Amalekites, the Amorites, and an allied army of 5 kings, including the king of Sodom (Gen. 14). What did Abram do in the face of such unjust pillaging and kidnapping? Did he just think to himself, "Lot should have listened to ol' Uncle Abram" and then hold a quiet prayer vigil for his doomed relative? No. He organized his 318 commando-servants, planned a daring rescue and defeated this steamroller of an army in a night raid.

Shortly after this battle, a curious priest named Melchizedek (who some consider a prefigure of Christ) showed up, blessed Abram and praised God for delivering Chedorlaomer into Abram's hand. In sum, Abram, a man of deep faith, did not stand by in the face of injustice and oppression. He hazarded his life to set things right, rescued a wayward relative and was praised by God for it. I point out Abram's story because, from the very beginning of Scripture, those that followed the way of Jehovah (and Jesus) were holy in that they were set apart by God for His work. But they were not hermits in that they engaged the deep brokenness of their times.

Moses

Consider Moses, who stood before Pharaoh and commanded him to let God's people go (Ex. 5). What was Pharaoh's response? He proclaimed, "Who is the Lord, that I should obey his voice to let Israel go? I know not the Lord, neither will I let Israel go (Ex. 5:2)." This Pharaoh, probably Ramses II or Amenhotep I,[19] was a "god-king" (remember the lightsaber) that claimed to be divine and ruled one of the most powerful kingdoms in the ancient Near East.[20] And he scoffed at the notion that the God of his slaves would demand their release.

But Pharaoh was about to learn a thing or ten about authority and power. God told Moses and Aaron: "And the Egyptians shall know that I am the Lord, when I stretch forth mine hand upon Egypt, and bring out the children of Israel from among them" (Ex. 7:5).

God sent ten plagues among the Egyptians and led His people out of Egypt by a pillar of cloud and a pillar of fire. Yet, despite the devastation of the plagues, Pharaoh could not let his slave labor force just walk out of Egypt. So, Pharaoh led his army in pursuit of the Jews and caught up with the children of Israel as they camped by the Red Sea.

At that moment, all seemed lost. But God had other plans. He commanded Moses to stretch out his hand over the sea to divide it.

I am a curious person, and this is one of the Biblical stories that piques my interest. My daughter recently asked me if there is such a thing as "the force" similar to what is portrayed in Star Wars. I told her "no" generally but explained that God has, at times, used human instruments to accomplish his purposes in miraculous ways. So, maybe the better answer is "kind of." Wow, what a rush! Can you imagine holding out your rod and your hand over the sea and watching it divide? And then reaching back out and watching it close? After that, what do you do with the rest of your life? But I digress.

God destroyed the Egyptian army in the waters of the Red Sea, and Moses led the children of Israel on toward the promised land.

Moses, as God's representative, proclaimed God's Word to the most powerful ruler of his day. And he eventually defied that ruler while trusting in God's supernatural guidance and protection. Moses' story highlights a common story or theme among Biblical characters: a prophetic individual with little to no real power standing before the splendor and power of an earthly throne with a prophetic message.

Deborah

Consider Deborah, who led the children of Israel to victory against their Canaanite oppressors. Deborah was a warrior, judge, prophetess and poet; and she encouraged her fearful general Barack to take on the Canaanite army led by Sisera. No big deal, right? Right. Except for the fact that Sisera's army fielded nine hundred iron chariots (the equivalent of a modern battle tank) to Israel's chariot force of exactly zero. After Israel won this battle and Jael dispatched Sisera with a tent spike, Deborah penned a profound worship song to Jehovah (Judg. 4-5).

Here's an excerpt: "In the days of Shamgar the son of Anath, in the days of Jael, the highways were unoccupied, and the travelers walked through byways. The inhabitants of the villages ceased, they ceased in Israel, until that I Deborah arose, that I arose a mother in Israel."

Deborah summed up the reason for Israel's victory as follows: "They that are delivered from the noise of archers in the places of drawing water, there shall they rehearse the righteous acts of the Lord, even the righteous acts toward the inhabitants of his villages in Israel: then shall the people of the Lord go down to the gates."

What a story! In the face of insurmountable military odds and despite a grim fear shared even by her top general, Deborah led the children of Israel to victory and pointed them back to their mighty King. Deborah's story highlights another common theme throughout Scripture: God often called His faithful servants to lead His people against impossible odds to prove God's strength and power.

Saul

Consider Saul, who was appointed by God to be Israel's first king. Though he initially followed God's principles and commands, Saul disobeyed God and forfeited his kingship. And the circumstances of that forfeiture are important to our study on citizenship.

After Samuel anointed Saul as king, he commanded Saul to go to Gilgal and wait seven days (I Sam. 10). Samuel told the new king that he (Samuel) would perform a sacrifice and give Saul further guidance when he arrived. At first, Saul complied. But, when Samuel did not show up after seven days, Saul became nervous (I Sam. 13: 8-9).

And it's hard to blame Saul for this. He was facing 30,000 chariots, 6,000 horsemen and a massive army of Philistine foot soldiers. And his soldiers did not even have swords or spears! Because of this, Saul decided to get on with things and performed a burnt offering to God. When Samuel arrived, he rebuked Saul and told him that his kingdom would be taken from him.

Why was this such a problem? First, Saul disobeyed a direct command from God (speaking through Samuel) and displayed a self-reliance and disobedience in the process (I Sam. 10:8). Next, Saul was a king, not a priest. As a member of the tribe of Benjamin, he could not legally offer up a burnt sacrifice or offering. Yet, he disregarded this clear separation of authority and offered the sacrifice as if he was God's spiritual representative to the Israelites rather than their legal authority.

Saul's story speaks in stark terms to me personally. How often have I grown impatient or fearful and decided to attempt to build God's kingdom in my own way? How often have I looked at the overwhelming odds stacked against truth or the church and decided that God's timetable and strategy is inadequate given the urgency of the times?

Saul's story also speaks strongly to the institutional separation of church and state. Saul was to listen to God's guidance, rely on His strength and wait for Samuel to come to Gilgal to offer a sacrifice. Yet, Saul wrongly took up the mantle of priest and offered the sacrifice.

Through the ages, kings have often fallen into this trap of conflating God's voice and authority with their own. And such misadventures have always result in disaster. This mistake cost Saul his kingdom and remains a dire warning to all that wield power today. Government is not God. May we learn that lesson from Gilgal.

Jeremiah

Consider Jeremiah, the weeping prophet who pleaded with Judah to turn back to God prior to its conquest by Babylon. Here's the historical setting: approximately 900 years passed from the time of God's covenant with Israel at Sinai to the fall of Jerusalem. In comparison, the United States is a young upstart, with less than 250 years in its history books. And Jeremiah lived at the very end of Israel's physical rule over the promised land.

The ten tribes of the nation of Israel, which had broken away from Judah in the time of Jeroboam, had already been destroyed by Assyria. Judah was all that was left of the physical kingdom of God's chosen people. The might of David and the splendor of Solomon had fallen into decay and ruin, and Judah was threatened by ancient Egypt and a rising Babylon.

In this moment of peril, God called Jeremiah to rally his people like Deborah or Hezekiah to crush their overwhelming foes and restore the glory of God's people Israel. Except that's not what God called Jeremiah to do.

Rather, God called Jeremiah from before he was born to call out the evils of Judah and to call God's people to repentance (Jer. 1:5). And God told Jeremiah that the people of Judah would not listen to him (Jer. 7:27) and that they would be sent into captivity (Jer. 9:16). Jeremiah's message, which broke his own heart (Jer. 9:1), was that God's boiling cauldron of judgment would, at long last, boil over with terrible but just consequences.

During the reign of Zedekiah, the Babylonians besieged Jerusalem but eventually withdrew to contend with an Egyptian army. Despite this apparent victory, God told Jeremiah that the Babylonians would come again, "...and fight against this city, and take it and burn it with fire" (Jer. 37:8). As you might imagine, this message was considered treasonous by the already besieged Judean king and earned Jeremiah a trip to a muddy dungeon where he was left to die.

Finally, Jerusalem fell. Can you imagine a foreign army marching down the streets of Washington, D.C., razing the Washington Monument and raising their foreign flag above the U.S. Capitol?

This was the type of soul-rending national moment that Jeremiah lived and ministered in. Yet, he faithfully proclaimed God's Word to his hard-hearted people. And, when the people of Judah were taken to Babylon, Jeremiah sent them a letter encouraging them to leave their Jewish enclave and to seek the peace and prosperity of their new city (Jer. 29).

Here's the powerful lesson from Jeremiah's life: be faithful to proclaim God's truth no matter the response or consequences. The Jewish religious leaders rejected Jeremiah, the political leaders imprisoned him and the people disregarded his message. Then, Jeremiah watched as the walls of Jerusalem were battered down and the people of God were scattered to foreign lands. Yet, he faithfully and boldly proclaimed God's Word even though he knew his people would not turn.

God may call us to a similar role in our times, though I pray this is not the case. Therefore, we should commit ourselves to speaking the truth, praying for mercy and trusting God no matter the response or consequences.

Daniel

Consider Daniel, the Old Testament prophet and statesman, that prayed for and provided wisdom to four kings in two competing and diverse empires. To begin, Daniel and his three friends were taken as captives in the first of three Babylonian campaigns (probably around 605 B.C) that eventually destroyed Judah. Can you imagine Daniel's internal dialogue during his trudge to Babylon? He was a Jew, raised in a society that followed Jehovah and assumed protection by Him. Then, suddenly, he was walking as a captive of a gentile power that openly defied his God. Can you imagine the small-town-kid-comes-to-the-big-city type of awe that Daniel felt when he walked into Babylon and viewed its massive double walls and the beginnings of the awe-inspiring Hanging Gardens?

Surely, Daniel experienced some doubts about his faith. During a time when gods were judged by how well they protected worshippers, Daniel was a captive in a rich and pagan city. Despite these questions and despite being a teenager according to our standards, Daniel passed his first test of faith. You know the story. When given the "king's meat," which must have included food prohibited by Jewish dietary laws, Daniel purposed in his heart not to eat the meat (Dan. 1:8). In doing so, he followed the way of Jehovah and set an example for respectful requests or petitions for religious accommodation.

Daniel also built relationships with rulers (Dan.1:9), prayed fervently for his own people (Dan. 9:18-22; Dan. 10:11-14), displayed knowledge and wisdom that far surpassed his contemporaries (Dan. 1:17-20), spoke truth to power (Dan. 4:19-23), courageously stood for religious principle when he knew it could cost him his life (Dan. 6), and pointed two emperors and their empires to the one, true King (Dan. 4, 6:25-28).

Since most of the readers of this book are familiar with Daniel's story, I will highlight two key themes: engagement and wisdom.

First, in my opinion, Daniel, Esther, and Nehemiah are, other than Christ, the best Biblical parallels for citizenship in the American republic. Let me explain. The example of Israel in the Old Testament includes first a theocracy and then kings who often received direct revelation from God and ruled a very religiously and culturally uniform society. And New Testament figures lived under a pagan, authoritarian regime that allowed precious few opportunities to participate. In contrast, Daniel, Esther and Nehemiah participated in the government or at least the leadership of culturally and religiously diverse empires.

In this unfamiliar context (especially to Daniel, who was exiled rather than born in exile), Daniel did not withdraw like the Jews taken to Babylon later (Jer. 29). Rather, he participated in the life and governance of the Babylonian and later Persian empires; and, in so doing, exhibited wisdom, proclaimed truth and even changed the hearts of kings.

Next, wisdom is a persistent theme throughout the book of Daniel. His wisdom, which was a gift from God, was ten times better than all the academics and scientists of the Babylonian empire (Dan. 1:17-20).

And he used this wisdom to win religious accommodations, interpret Nebuchadnezzar's dream, and explain hard truths.

Most American Christians are aware that we need courage in our turbulent times, and most of us look to Daniel as an example of courage. But we also need wisdom to navigate citizenship in an increasingly secular, participatory democracy. And that is a key lesson from his life.

God has placed us in our own version of Babylon, a multicultural, religiously diverse melting pot with great power in the world and a god (ourselves) we cannot worship. So, what should we do? Like the old Sunday school song suggests, we should dare to be a Daniel.

Esther

Consider Esther, the Jewish exile that became queen of the Persian Empire and saved her people from genocide. The Persian Empire arguably ruled a greater percentage of the world's population (about 44%) than any other empire in world history and stretched from modern-day Pakistan to Greece.[21] To reach the same level of power, a modern regime would need to rule approximately 3.4 billion people.

It is important to note that the story of Esther occurred in and around the Greco-Persian campaigns of Ahasuerus (Xerxes I), which ended in a pyrrhic victory at Thermopylae (remember the 300 Spartans?), a crushing naval defeat at Salamis, and a decisive land defeat at Plataea.[22]

I imagine you are familiar with the book of Esther, so I will focus on a few key elements of the story. Esther was an exiled and orphaned Jew raised by her Cousin Mordecai, and King Ahasuerus chose her as queen after deposing Queen Vashti for refusing to appear at a drunken party.

Though Esther is the star of this story, don't miss the actions of Mordecai. He acted as Esther's guide and encouraged her to do the right thing by staying silent and enjoying her position of safety and prestige while she had it. Oh, wait, that's not how the story goes! Mordecai encouraged her to use her God-given position of influence to save her people and hypothesized that God had raised her up for "...such a time as this." (Est. 4:14).

Then, it was up to Esther. She called for a fast and left the results up to God as indicated by her statement: "If I perish, I perish." Esther then hazarded her life for her people. The king's court in Persia was closely guarded, was wrapped in an aura of deity and power, and was not commonly open to women in this very patriarchal society.

Further, Esther must have been mindful of the king's previous record of putting his power and prestige above the interests of his wife. He had banned Vashti for challenging his authority and had not "sent for" (note the power dynamic) Esther in thirty days. What would Ahasuerus do if Esther showed up without a request? How would that reflect on the king's control of his own household and, therefore, his empire?

Fortunately, the king extended his scepter. And Esther showed remarkable wisdom in requesting two different banquets and guarding her identity until just the right time. Then, she displayed incredible courage and conviction in stating, "The adversary and enemy is this wicked Haman" (Est. 7:6). By the way, Haman engineered the genocide, but King Ahasuerus authorized it. The following awkward conversation just might have occurred between Esther and Ahasuerus, "Hey, honey, would you pick up your socks—oh wait, I mean, would stop trying to exterminate me and my entire people group!"

And Esther did not stop there. She continued to petition the king to reverse his death decree, but the king opined that his decree to kill the Jews could not be reversed (seems like a dumb policy to me!). So, she won the right to self-defense instead. In all of this, Esther displayed a dependence on God, a fearless determination to engage the great injustice and (simply put) racism of her day, and skill in navigating the unpredictable ego of her husband-king and the complicated politics of the Persian empire. All I have to say is "wow."

And don't miss the most critical verses of the book. In Esther 8, right after the Jews are authorized to resist the genocide, Scripture states, "The Jews had light, and gladness, and joy, and honor...[a]nd many of the people of the land became Jews; for the fear of the Jews fell upon them" (Est. 8:16-17). Though I cannot say that all of these "conversions" were true religious conversions rather than conversions of convenience or fear, I know this: Esther's influence, just like that of

Daniel and his friend, pointed the people of this massive empire to the one, true King.

There are so many lessons here! Most Christians draw from this story the sense of providence and destiny at work in our lives, the importance of courage in key moments, and God's ultimate protection. These are all important and valuable lessons, but I want to focus on something else. When given the opportunity to participate in government, Esther did not shrink back out of fear or a sense of impropriety. Rather, she saw her position as a divine appointment and engaged as a follower of Jehovah. And it was this engagement (rather than a quiet withdrawal) that eventually pointed the Persian empire to the truth.

Nehemiah

Consider Nehemiah, the cupbearer to King Artaxerxes and governor of the province of Judah that rebuilt the walls of Jerusalem. Don't miss the fact that Nehemiah, a Jew, was serving in the high court of Persian King Artaxerxes (the son of Ahasuerus/Xerxes I and stepson of Esther). This is probably due to the influence of Daniel and Esther, who preceded Nehemiah in government service.

We have already discussed the remarkable extent and power of the Persian Empire, but the empire is remarkable for another reason as well: religious toleration. As noted in the "Cyrus Cylinder," an ancient declaration of religious freedom by King Cyrus, the Persians respected cultural and religious differences or, in more modern terms, religious liberty. And Nehemiah relied on this policy while Governor of Judea.[23]

While serving King Artaxerxes, Nehemiah received the terrible news that the walls of Jerusalem were broken down and the gates were burned with fire. In the parlance of the ancient Near East, this meant that the crown jewel of Israel and the location of the temple had been reduced to ruin and doomed to insignificance. Simply put, walls were critical to any city's survival and flourishing due to near-continuous conflict among competing empires and local rulers.

Nehemiah requested and received an appointment as governor of the province of Judah and then returned to Jerusalem to rebuild the wall. He requested supplies from government stores; and he weathered an impending invasion, internal conflict, death threats and blackmail to lead the reconstruction of the city walls in an astonishing fifty-two days (Neh. 1-6).

But the story doesn't end there. While the priest Ezra led a religious revival in Jerusalem (Neh. 8-9), Nehemiah set out to reform Jewish society according to Biblical principles. He demanded that the wealthy stop profiteering and charging high interest rates during the crisis (chapter 5), kicked his old enemy Tobiah and his household belongings out of a grand room in the temple (sounds a little bit like Jesus cleansing the temple), encouraged the practice of tithing, and enforced the observance of the Sabbath (Neh. 13). The book closes with a simple prayer by Nehemiah, "Remember me, O my God, for good (Neh. 13:31)."

Similar to Daniel and Esther before him, Nehemiah governed as a Persian official. And he used this authority to rebuild the walls of Jerusalem and to reform Jewish society. Don't miss the intriguing pattern that occurred under the reign of Josiah and then again under the leadership of Nehemiah: spiritual revival was followed by cultural reform. The spiritual renewal of God's people naturally leads to a change in civic practices to reflect Biblical principles.

As a follower of Jehovah serving as a government official of a foreign kingdom, Nehemiah displayed incredible faith, wisdom and determination to accomplish all that God had put on his heart. And he prayed that his eternal legacy with the King of heaven (apparently the audience Nehemiah was most concerned about) would be the great good he had accomplished in His name.

New Testament Examples

Next, let's consider New Testament examples of citizenship. Most readers are familiar with the Roman Empire and the fact that its rule extended to Palestine during the time of Christ. But we should zoom in a bit to better understand the political system of the day. Here are the three primary working parts of the political structure of ancient Palestine at the time of Christ: (1) the Herods, (2) Rome and (3) the high priest and Sanhedrin. We will review each in turn. First, to the Herods.

When Christ was born, Palestine was ruled by a Roman client king named Herod, a.k.a. Herod the Great (c.75 - 4 B.C.). Though Rome maintained legions in Syria to the north and Egypt to the south, Rome, in a sense, delegated the rule of Palestine to Herod as long as he remained loyal to Rome and maintained order in the area. Herod was known for massive building projects, an arbitrary ruthlessness, and paranoia. Need an example? Well, he killed all of the male children in Bethlehem out of fear of an ancient prophecy that he misinterpreted (Matt. 2).

But Herod the Great is not the only Herod in the New Testament. I lived in Arkansas during high school, and (no offense to the beautiful Natural State) we used to joke about every male at a hillbilly family reunion being named "Darrell." Well, it seems that almost every ruler in the New Testament is named "Herod." So, it may take a little work to keep them all straight.

Here's a list of the important Herods: (1) Herod the Great was the key figure in the Christmas story, (2) Herod Archelaus was the son of Herod the Great deposed by the Romans and replaced with Pontius Pilate, (3) Herod Antipas was another son of Herod the Great that killed John the Baptist and earned a reprimand from Christ, (4) Herod Agrippa I was the grandson of Herod the Great that arrested Peter and was eaten of worms, and (5) Herod Agrippa II was the great-grandson of Herod the Great that conversed with Paul and almost became a Christian.[24] Don't worry about nailing down that list right now because I will point out the relevant Herod in each Biblical account.

Next, Rome played a key role in politics in Palestine. When Herod the Great died shortly after Christ's birth, his kingdom was separated into five parts. For our purposes, we will focus on two of those parts. His son Herod Archelaus became the ruler of Judea and Samaria, and his son Herod Antipas became the ruler of Galilee and Perea. The Romans deposed Herod Archelaus in A.D. 6 for ruthless and reckless behavior, turned Judea and Samaria into a Roman province and installed a Roman official called a prefect or procurator to govern the area. The prefect during the ministry of Christ was named, you guessed it, Pontius Pilate.

Even though Rome assimilated the province of Judea directly into its empire, Pontius Pilate ruled indirectly through local leadership.

Pilate had about 3,000 Roman soldiers at his disposal and lived in Caesarea, about a two-day march from Jerusalem.

In sum, in the New Testament, the province of Judea was controlled by Rome through Pontius Pilate, and the province of Galilee was controlled by a client king named Herod Antipas and often referred to as simply "Herod." Many of the events in the Gospels occurred in these two provinces.

Finally, the Jewish high priest and the Sanhedrin played a role in governing the area. Though Pontius Pilate officially ruled Judea, Rome delegated to the Jewish high priest and the Jewish Sanhedrin the day-to-day governance of Jerusalem and Judea and, especially, the tasks of maintaining order and ensuring that taxes and tribute were paid.[25]

The high priest and the Sanhedrin come up numerous times in opposition to Jesus and then the apostles. The Sanhedrin originated with God's command to Moses to gather seventy elders of the people of Israel to help Moses bear the weight of governing (Num. 11:16-17). And, by the time of Christ, the Sanhedrin was composed of 71 (think Moses plus 70) elders and served as the supreme religious, legislative and judicial body for the Jews in Palestine.[26]

Further, the high priest was recognized by the Romans as the political leader of the Jews.[27] Though the high priest and the Sanhedrin possessed significant authority to rule Jerusalem and Judea, their authority was not total. For example, the Sanhedrin could not decree the death penalty during the time of Christ (John 18:31).

This tentative arrangement between Rome and the Jews in Palestine did not last long after Christ's death and resurrection. The hostility between the Jews and the Romans that is evident throughout the Gospels soon erupted into a revolt. The Romans crushed the rebellion, destroyed the temple in A.D. 70 and overwhelmed the final Jewish stronghold at Masada in A.D. 73.

John the Baptist

First, let's consider John the Baptist, the locust-eating, camel cloth-wearing forerunner of Christ. John's core message was one of repentance, and he proclaimed, "...the kingdom of Heaven is at hand"

(Matt. 3:2). This talk of another kingdom and a coming king intrigued and then troubled the Roman tetrarch Herod Antipas.

I imagine you are very familiar with John the Baptist's call to repentance and salvation, but don't miss his encouragement to the people, publicans and soldiers after he baptized them.

When the people asked him "[w]hat shall we do?," John responded that they should give one of their coats and half of their meat to the poor. When the publicans (tax collectors) asked John what they should do, he told them to take no more than the official Roman tax rate (publicans were infamous for tacking on extra taxes to increase their individual wealth). And, when the soldiers asked him what they should do, John told them, "[d]o violence to no man, neither accuse any falsely; and be content with your wages" (Luke 3:10-14). So, John the Baptist called people to repentance and salvation and then, in a sense, called them to good citizenship.

Apparently, even Herod Antipas took notice of this. According to Mark 6:20, "…Herod feared John, knowing that he was a just man and an holy, and observed him; and when he heard him, he did many things, and heard him gladly."

But this cordial relationship did not last long. John did not equivocate on Biblical truth and did not separate public and private morality. Instead, John publicly denounced Herod for living in adultery with and marrying his brother's wife, Herodias (Mark 6:18). This proclamation appears to have enraged Herodias much more than Herod, and Herodias orchestrated a lewd scheme that eventually led to John the Baptist's martyrdom.

In summary, John's message was one of full-life devotion to the teachings of the coming King, Jesus. And this message had real-life application for the common people, the Pharisees, publicans, soldiers and even high government officials. He did not split his ministry into the sacred and secular, and he fearlessly spoke truth to power no matter the cost.

Did Jesus rebuke John for stepping out of his spiritual role to dabble in political matters? No, while John was in prison, Jesus called John the greatest man born to date (Matt. 11:11).

May we follow John's example in our time.

Peter

Many Christians, including this one, find encouragement in the impulsive but devoted ministry of Peter. He followed Jesus with his whole heart and soul—even if didn't always engage his mind in the process.

But, Peter's water-walking, ear-hacking, boat-jumping, Christ-denying and prison-breaking story is a powerful example and lesson to all of us who imperfectly but passionately follow Christ. As you might expect, Peter's interactions with government officials were as remarkable as the other aspects of his ministry.

To begin, Peter didn't quite "get" Christ's explanation that He, "…must go unto Jerusalem, and suffer many things of the elders and chief priests and scribes, and be killed, and be raised again the third day" (Matt 16:21). When Judas came to arrest Jesus with soldiers from the chief priest, Peter drew his sword, attempted to defend Jesus and cut off Malchus' ear. (Matt. 26:47-51). Jesus then healed Malchus' ear and reprimanded Peter, who must have been incredulous. Christ told Peter that He could easily call down reinforcements of twelve legions of angels but that such an action would cut against God's purpose and plan (Matt. 26:53).

Christ's statement about 12 legions of angels has always intrigued me. Perhaps heaven's army is organized differently, but a Roman legion totaled approximately 6,000 men. So, Jesus was saying that He could request approximately 72,000 angels to come to his defense.[28] Further, I have never seen an angel fight, but I imagine they are pretty hardcore—maybe like Thor in the Marvel movies or Legolas in *The Lord of the Rings*?

Regardless, that number fascinates me because the Roman army that sacked Jerusalem in 70 A.D. was approximately 70,000 strong.[29] In other words, this force of angels could have challenged mighty Rome and certainly could have handled the Jewish officials. But military and physical might was not the issue. Rather, Jesus was calling Peter to put down his sword and to join Him in pursuing a supernatural strategy designed to save humankind from an eternal destiny much worse than Roman domination.

Josh Hershberger

Peter then denied Christ three times. This is a well-known story, but it is important to note where this happened—in the courtyard before the high priest's house (Luke 22:54-62). This is the same official that will play an important role in the next chapter of Peter's life.

In Acts 4, Peter and John were arrested by the Jewish authorities for healing a lame man and preaching about the resurrection of Christ. When Peter and John appeared before the high priest and the Sanhedrin the next day, the high priest and the other Jewish rulers, "...commanded them not to speak at all nor teach in the name of Jesus" (Acts 4:20). To this, Peter and John responded bluntly, "...we cannot but speak the things which we have seen and heard."

I love this! Here's the richly dressed, smug religious leader telling the poor Galilean fishermen to just shut up about all things related to Jesus Christ. And what did they say? A respectful but firm "No." In this exchange, Peter and John stood firmly on Biblical principle and on what we might term today free speech and religious liberty claims. And the Jewish leaders backed down because they feared the people.

In Acts 5, Peter was arrested again for, you guessed it, preaching about Jesus. That night, an angel opened the prison doors and commanded the apostles to preach in the temple. The next morning, the Jewish authorities found the prison empty and started frantically searching for the missing prisoners.

Where were they? Hiding out? Nope. They were back in the temple preaching, of course! So, the Jewish authorities arrested the apostles, hauled them back before the council and reprimanded them for preaching about Jesus *again*. What was the apostle's response? You know it: "We ought to obey God rather than men" (Acts 5:29).

Next, Herod arrested Peter as part of a persecution of the early church that had already cost James his life. So, this was no laughing matter, and Peter probably expected to be martyred. Perhaps Herod had heard about Peter's remarkable penchant for escaping prison (just call him Houdini!), so Herod handed him over to 16 soldiers. And the soldiers literally chained Peter to two of their group! No matter. An angel showed up that night, removed the chains and opened the doors to allow Peter to go free (Acts 12:5-11). Thus, Peter escaped custody three different times.

Peter also set out one of the key tensions of Christian citizenship. He told the high priest, "We ought to obey God rather than men," and then later encouraged the church to, "Submit yourselves to every ordinance of man for the Lord's sake: whether it be to the king, as supreme; or unto governors, as unto them that are sent by him for the punishment of evildoers, and for the praise of them that do well..." (I Pet. 2:13-14).

Don't those statements seem contradictory? Yes, but they are explained by the life of an apostle reprimanded for defending Christ from an unjust arrest, praised for his stand on Scripture, rescued by angels, and eventually martyred for his devotion to Jesus. Per Peter's example, we are not to be rabble-rousers. We are to be good and respectful citizens. But, when the likes of Herod or the high priest commands a Christian to violate Scripture, our prior command is clear: we must obey God rather than men. Peter was, at first, uncertain in his application of these principles. But he became a worthy example of Christian citizenship throughout the remainder of his ministry.

In all of his encounters with governing officials, Peter must have been mindful of Jesus' statement that he, Peter, would one day die in Christ's service. Remember the passage where Jesus asked Peter if Peter loved Him? At the conclusion of that line of questioning, Jesus told Peter that he would one day die by spreading out his hands (probably an allusion to crucifixion; John 21:18-20). Scripture does not record Peter's response to this ominous prophecy. Rather, Scripture only records Jesus' next statement to Peter, "Follow me."

And that, in a nutshell, is the lesson from Peter's citizenship. He went from the reckless and fearful fisherman to courageous and wise church leader because he followed Jesus.

Paul

The apostle Paul is a unique case study in citizenship because, unlike the other disciples, he possessed a unique credential that he put to good use: *Civitas* or Roman citizenship.

Civitas was a highly prized privilege in the ancient Roman world. *Civitas* granted an individual (among other rights) the right to sue at law; the right to stand trial; the right to appeal to Caesar and a prohibition on torture, scourging or death without a trial.[30] We take such rights for granted these days, but legally recognized protections and a civilization powerful and advanced enough to administer and enforce them were exceedingly rare in the ancient world.

Roman citizenship could be obtained as follows: (1) by birth; (2) by winning the right via military service or other significant service to the empire; (3) by an act of the emperor; or (4) by purchasing the right, though this was not common and often involved some form of bribery.[31]

Saul (who was renamed Paul after his conversion) was born in Tarsus, a city in Cilicia (Acts 22:3) in the Roman province of Syria. So, Paul was a Roman citizen by birth.

Before his conversion, Saul worked on behalf of the high priest (who, as we have studied, also wielded political power) to imprison and kill followers of Christ. Then, once converted, he carefully and strategically exercised his citizenship to further his ministry. Paul's actions at Philippi, at Jerusalem, before Agrippa and in Rome are great examples of this.

At Philippi, Paul and Silas were beaten and cast into prison because they cast a demon out of young girl and exposed a satanic and exploitative get-rich scheme (Acts 16:16-40). The magistrates sent officials to release Paul and Silas the next day, so this imprisonment appears to have been little more than a politically motivated attempt to "get rid" of Paul and Silas. While in prison, Paul and Silas put on an uplifting prayer and praise session followed by an earthquake and the conversion of the jailer.

This story intrigues me. Paul and Silas did not reveal their Roman citizenship to prevent a flogging and imprisonment without a trial. When the whip came out, I probably would have whipped out my Roman citizenship! Perhaps Paul and Silas were not given an opportunity to speak; or, their words were disregarded by the guards.

Paul and Silas did, however, raise the issue when the magistrates attempted to secretly evict them from the city as if they were common criminals. Paul reminded the magistrates of his Roman citizenship, and he demanded that the magistrates personally come and release them. Paul and Silas then publicly visited Lydia and the other believers to comfort them before leaving the city. In sum, in Acts 16, Paul appears to have strategically used his Roman citizenship to protect the public witness of the young church he had just started.

Next, in Jerusalem, Paul was assaulted by a Jewish audience for taking a gentile into the temple area, and he would have been killed if the Roman garrison had not intervened (Acts 21). Before being escorted inside the fortress Antonia (which adjoined the temple courtyard), Paul asked for an opportunity to speak to the people. The commander consented and the mob listened for a time until Paul mentioned that God had called him to preach to the gentiles. The mention of that word "gentiles" sent the crowd into a murderous frenzy.

At this point, the Roman commander, who was most concerned about maintaining public order, retreated into the fortress and defaulted to the ol' "beat it out of the prisoner" approach to finding the truth in the situation.

As the Roman soldiers prepared to beat Paul, Paul asked simply, "Is it lawful for you to scourge a man that is a Roman, and uncondemned?" The Roman commander immediately stopped the beating and mentioned that he purchased his citizenship with a significant sum. Paul replied that he was born as a Roman, which apparently carried greater weight.

Why did Paul use his citizenship in this way? Though the facts of this story are a bit complicated, Paul's motivation and plan are clear throughout. He was ready to be bound and to die at Jerusalem for the cause of Christ (Acts 21:13), but he did not intend to die quietly or to give up his freedom without benefit to the gospel. Rather, he carefully and strategically used each event to further his gospel message.

Christ later appeared to Paul and confirmed his actions. Christ stated that Paul had testified about Him in Jerusalem and must bear witness of the gospel in Rome (Acts 23:11).

Next, Paul appeared before Felix, the Roman governor or procurator. Felix held the same role as Pontius Pilate during the trial of Christ and proved to be a greedy and cruel official. He left Paul in prison for two years in hopes that he would receive a bribe. When Paul was finally given an opportunity to speak to Felix and his wife Drusilla, Paul "…reasoned of righteousness, temperance and judgment to come" (Acts 24:25).

Once again, we see a follower of Jesus disregarding our more modern and enlightenment-influenced conception of the sacred and secular. Paul reasoned with this Roman governor about righteousness, self-control and eternal judgment, and this conversation surely included a conversation about Felix's actions as a Roman governor as well as in his personal life. At the conclusion of this conversation, Felix trembled. Apparently, Paul's words left a deep impression on the Roman official.

Felix was eventually replaced by a Roman official named Festus, and this new appointment gave both the Jews and Paul an opportunity to revisit the matter of his imprisonment. Festus, who wanted to do the Jews a favor, asked if Paul would consent to a hearing or trial in Jerusalem. Paul probably thought about that for all of two seconds and replied, "…I appeal unto Caesar." Here, Paul must have known that injustice and even death waited at Jerusalem, so he sought a trial in Rome.

King Herod Agrippa II, the great grandson of Herod the Great and the son of the Herod Agrippa I that enslaved Peter, came to visit Festus. And Festus invited Agrippa to hear from Paul. After Paul's famous sermon and Agrippa's near conversion, Agrippa and Festus agreed that Paul had done nothing worthy of death or imprisonment and sent him to Rome.

Paul was imprisoned in Rome for two years, and it appears that his legal case ended in a default and freedom. The book of Acts does not include the description of a trial, and Paul's letters to Timothy and Titus refer to a later ministry in and around the Aegean Sea.

At some point, Paul was arrested again by Roman authorities, which interpreted his belief in and proclamation of the gospel as treason to their polytheistic state and "deified" emperor. And he was probably martyred on Nero's order around or after the time of the great fire in A.D. 64.[32]

In Paul's second letter to Timothy, Paul gave one last ringing reminder about his Roman citizenship. Though he faced execution, Paul confidently stated, "And the Lord shall deliver me from every evil work, and will preserve me unto his heavenly kingdom, to whom be glory for ever and ever. Amen. (2 Tim. 2:18)."

This may seem like a spiritually rich but politically insignificant salutation. But, if Paul was imprisoned in Rome (as church history suggests) prior to his execution, he would have been surrounded by the might and majesty of the "eternal" city and crown jewel of the known world. And he went to his death by decree of a Roman god-king. Yet, before the sword fell, Paul saw past this façade and glanced over Rome's fleeting glory to a just and eternal kingdom that would never end.

From Paul, I draw several lessons. First, I note what Paul did not do. He did not denounce the Roman state and attempt to incite a slave revolt or rally fellow Roman citizens to defy Nero. By the time Paul was born around the time of Christ, the Roman republic was dead. Brutus and Cassius lost their attempt to save the Roman republic at the battle of Philippi, and the ascendence of Octavian as emperor in 27 B.C. marked the beginning of the Roman empire.[33] By Paul's time, the right to vote inherent in *civitas* was illusory, and the Jewish revolt against the Romans ended in the destruction of Jerusalem in A.D. 70. So, politically, Paul lived under an authoritarian regime and possessed no power and precious little influence on the public life of the empire. So, he focused on preaching the gospel and on spiritual transformation.

Next, I will note what he did do. Paul was apparently well-informed about citizenship and legal standards. He used his rights as a Roman citizen to further his ministry in Acts 16 and Acts 22, and he used his knowledge of Roman criminal appellate procedure to procure an audience in Rome in Acts 25. Further, he objected to unjust punishment, refused to quietly leave Philippi, requested protection from a Roman solider when threatened by the Jews, reasoned with elected officials about righteousness and judgment, and took the gospel to the center of the Roman world.

And these efforts eventually produced remarkable results in the spiritual and civic life of the Roman state, including the end of gladiatorial games and the practice of infanticide.

So, the key lesson from Paul's ministry (as it relates to citizenship) is that he applied his *civitas* to further his gospel ministry. Rather than downplaying it or avoiding it as non-spiritual, Paul put his citizenship to work. And we should do the same. We should use the law as a tool

Josh Hershberger

rather than an excuse, and we should exercise our citizenship in this country while pointing our fellow citizens to another, more eternal kingdom.

Jesus

I previously explained Christ's interaction with Pilate and his teaching in Matthew 22. But there are additional lessons about citizenship to be learned from the King of kings. Here are three.

On Power

First, Christ's birth critiqued the earthly concept of power. Kings and governments throughout history have attempted to impress their subjects and illustrate their power through grand palaces and awe-inspiring public throne rooms or government halls. For example, I once accompanied a client from a rural area into a federal courthouse for the first time. He was absolutely mesmerized by the gold leaf, brilliant hues and Neo-classical architecture of the place. The architects had done their job of emphasizing the power and reach of the federal government and casting an aura of authority. That is the way that kings and governments have always operated.

Yet, as we all celebrate at Christmas time, King Jesus was born in the equivalent of a barn in a humble town and laid in an animal trough instead of a cradle (Matt. 2). This sits well with our democratic sensibilities. This communicates that Christ is like us in a sense and came to be with us through the incarnation.

But we shouldn't take that too far. This was not in any sense an abdication of Christ's authority; rather, this was a coronation in a cradle. And wise men from the east emphasized this truth in the Christmas narrative by bringing regal gifts and worshipping this monarch in the manger.

As Christ grew and started his earthly ministry, he emphasized this principle further. Though Christ had ultimate power, he wielded it humbly and sacrificially. While other rulers built armies and sought glory and domination, Christ called a group of disciples around him and sought to ease suffering and change the hearts of those that would listen to him.

He had no palace or even home; and, when given the opportunity to march triumphantly into Jerusalem, he chose the workman's donkey rather than a warrior's stallion (Matt. 21). While most monarchs of the day ordered servants to meet their every need, Jesus washed the dirty feet of His disciples. And he wore no crown except the mock crown of thorns forced onto His head prior to His execution.

The kings and queens that have ruled humanity throughout history would not have recognized the significance of His reign any more than Herod or Pilate; and, yet, it is Christ's kingdom that has stood and will stand the test of time and eternity.

Christ's kingdom is different from every other earthly kingdom. I am reluctant to admit this, but I did not study the word "kingdom" in depth until recently. That word is everywhere in the New Testament—162 times by one count.[34] For example, in Mark 1:15, Jesus said, "The time is fulfilled, and the kingdom of God is at hand." Further, Jesus told his disciples to heal the sick and to proclaim, "...the kingdom of God is come nigh unto you (Luke 10:8-9)." And, of course, there is the popular verse that commands us to seek first, "...the kingdom of God (Matt. 5:33)."

Christ came to die for us to give us the opportunity for everlasting life (John 3:16). But Christ also came to inaugurate his kingdom, his redemptive and revolutionary reign, which will one day culminate in Christians becoming co-regents as kings and queens of the universe (2 Tim. 2:12; Rev. 22:5). The kingdom is both (1) here and (2) not yet in the sense that it will not be fully realized until Christ returns on a white horse followed by the armies of heaven.

So, what does this mean for Christians in the United States? To be clear, Christ's example concerning power does not change the state's role of punishing evil and promoting good. But it does emphasize the church's primary responsibility of transforming hearts and minds through the power of the gospel rather than the force of government.

And it stands as a strong example and a stark warning to us as we enter the ballot box, petition our government and take up elected office. As followers of Jesus, we should never seek power for the sake of power. And, though we should promote that which is right, true and beautiful via public policy, we should be mindful that conversion comes through a relationship with Jesus Christ and not the force of law.

In this way, Christian citizens and Christian public servants should be marked by confidence in what is right, by concern about the lure of power, and by service to their fellow citizens. By His manner of birth, His ministry and His death, Christ critiqued the age-old use and abuse of power.

On Persuasion

Christ's use of persuasion rather than force is a corollary of His treatment of power, but this principle is worth noting separately. Christ could have called down a legion of angels to free Him and crush the Jewish hypocrites and Romans oppressors, but He willingly went to the cross.

One day, Christ will rule and reign with a rod of iron as the King of Kings and Lord of Lords (Rev. 2:27; 19:15); but that was not the model of his earthly ministry or His command to the church for this time in history. Rather, Christ focused on persuading hearts and minds through his words and actions.

For example, instead of condemning the woman caught in adultery (which was a capital punishment under the Mosaic law), he wrote in the sand and remarked that the man without sin should cast the first stone (John 8). Instead of shunning the woman at the well, He deftly navigated her cultural biases to lead her to an eternal truth beyond the tyranny of Roman rule, ethnoreligious squabbles, and impulsive desires (John 4). And, instead of fomenting a rebellion against Rome like many observers hoped or expected, He declared spiritual independence from the hypocritical Jewish leaders and the evil that inhabits every human heart (John 8:36).

You see, rulers throughout history have employed one primary strategy in dealing with opposition: destruction. Human, worldly power must crush or destroy anyone or anything that stands in its way. But, in the end, power can only win over us. It cannot win us over.

In contrast, persuasion dignifies and cares for the rebel. Human rulers throughout history have dealt with insurrection by removing rebel heads, but Christ dealt with it by reaching rebel hearts. The cross is, therefore, the ultimate symbol and argument for persuasion. Instead of threatening humanity to bend to His will, God sent His son to die for us. And, in giving up His life, Christ's offered a better way to live, lead, and inspire.

In summary, Christ's current kingdom is upside-down and inside-out. It is immensely powerful, but in a righteously subversive sort-of way. The gospel moves men and women by changing the heart, not cracking the whip. And Christ's plan for changing the world was to go into all the world and preach the gospel—not go into all the world and conquer the locals. So, we should take note. Persuasion rather than blunt power should be our default mode of engagement in public life.

On Public Life

In contrast to visions of an exiled or monastic church with little to say about the great events of the day, Christ lived a very public life and engaged a wide range of issues. For example, Jesus addressed proper taxation (Matt. 22:21), poverty (Luke 14:14), power (John 19:11), marriage laws and family structure (Jewish religious and civil authority were bound together; Matt. 19:3-9), unbiblical racial pride (Luke 10:25-37), religious hypocrisy (Matt. 23:27), and unbalanced Sabbath regulations (Luke 14:5). And he often critiqued harmful social mores through his actions. For example, he ate a meal with a publican (Luke 19:8-9), ministered to a Samaritan woman (John 4), cleansed the temple (Matt. 21:12-17), healed lepers (Matt. 8), and spent most of his time with a ragtag set of disciples rather than kings and religious rulers.

And He even publicly critiqued a Roman client-king for overstepping his authority. While Jesus was ministering in Galilee, the Pharisees warned Jesus that Herod wanted to kill Him. Just so we are keeping our Herods straight, this was Herod Antipas, who ordered the beheading of John the Baptist and eventually handed Jesus over to Pilate for trial.

The Pharisees were not big fans of Herod Antipas either because he built his new capital Tiberius on an old Jewish cemetery (whoops!), divorced his first wife to marry his sister-in-law and niece Herodias, and requested or at least allowed his step-daughter to dance in public (no pious Jew would allow that).[35] But, despite this mutual distrust, the Pharisees appear to be in league with Herod in this passage.

Jesus responded to the Pharisee's warning by telling them to give Herod a message (Luke 13:31-35). Jesus said, "Go…tell that fox, Behold, I cast out devils, and I do cures today and tomorrow, and the third day I shall be perfected. Nevertheless I must walk to day, and tomorrow, and the day following: for it cannot be that a prophet perish out of Jerusalem."

The term "fox" is a profound critique of Herod. I have heard Christians use this passage as justification for political name-calling or at least strong negative descriptions of political leaders. Though Christ sometimes used strong metaphors (such as a fox in this passage or "whitewashed tombs" "full of dead men's bones" in describing the Pharisees), they were truthful and designed to prove a point. In this passage, his use of the word "fox" is quite rich. Here's what I mean.

When we think of a fox, we think of a crafty or cunning animal because we have grown up with sayings like "sly as a fox" and folktales like Br'er Fox and Br'er Rabbit. And, certainly, the fox's natural craftiness is implied here. But Scripture attributes a second meaning to foxes: they are small, powerless and insignificant animals. In Nehemiah 4:3, Tobiah mocks the wall at Jerusalem, stating that "…if a fox go up, he shall even break down their stone wall." In Ezekiel 13:4, the prophets of Israel were compared to "foxes in the desert" and reprimanded for not protecting the children of Israel. And, in Matthew 8:20, Jesus noted that "…foxes have holes, and the birds of the air have nests…" but He did not have a home in the traditional sense. So, Jesus used the fox as an example of a small and insignificant animal. And, in Jewish society, foxes were sometimes contrasted with lions, as follows: "There are lions before you, and you ask foxes?"[36]

So, when Jesus called Herod a fox, He was not just commenting on his craftiness. Jesus was also communicated something along these lines: "You, Herod, are neither honorable nor great. You claim to be lion, but you are a fox. You are powerless and insignificant, and you do not know whom you threaten."[37]

Don't miss the power of this moment. In this exchange, the fox met the Lion. This insignificant and petty client-king of Rome dared to threaten the purpose and life of the Lion of the Tribe of Judah, and

Jesus told Him in no uncertain terms that Herod could not touch or control Him!

In sum, though Jesus focused on teaching and preaching the Good News of eternal salvation, He did not limit his ministry to more "sacred" activities (as we think of them) or to sacred spaces like synagogues. He met physical needs, preached to crowds outdoors, reprimanded and called out leaders for fraudulent or hypocritical behavior, critiqued unjust or burdensome laws, smashed cultural and racial stereotypes with His words and actions and stood up to the political leaders of the day when they overstepped their proper authority.

No, Jesus did not foment revolution against Rome or the Jewish council; rather, he worked to break the chain around every human heart and to win true freedom for us all (John 8:36). May the world see in us a reflection of Him.

This concludes our survey of citizenship in Scripture. Next, we will turn to some historical examples of Christian citizenship.

4 REVIEW HISTORICAL EXAMPLES

I try not to be a snob—except when it comes to coffee. I know I should be frugal and content with the muddy water served at some fast-food restaurants. But it's hard. And don't even get me started on church lobby coffee. I am even convinced that strong coffee is somehow linked to sound doctrine. I don't have chapter and verse; but, if the former is weak, I start worrying about the latter. Kidding aside, what's the point of life without access to a quality dark roast from some exotic place in the bean belt?

Please don't judge me too hard on this one. You're probably a coffee snob too, or a car snob, or a computer snob. I am going to stop right now before I alienate everyone on the planet. But I think you get my point. Most of us have our "thing" that we highly value and refuse to insult through the use of a generic version.

So, maybe it's okay to be a coffee snob or a Mac fanatic, but let's not be chronological snobs. Many Christians (this one included) can be cited for this. We fall into the trap of thinking that the swift pace of technological change makes us unique in all of church and human history and disqualifies the great lives and minds of the past from teaching us anything important now. Well, that's rubbish. In a multitude of counselors, there is safety (Prov. 11:14). And Christians have been navigating the tensions of citizenship long before George Washington didn't chop down a cherry tree.

So, let's look back to some helpful examples of citizenship in the Christian past.

A few notes before we begin. I have included primarily positive examples of Christian citizenship. I acknowledge that the church, like any other significant movement in history, has had its share of bad actors. Those that claimed the name of Christ have, at times, committed terrible acts or failed to stand up to the evil of their time. But there are many helpful works explaining the Crusade massacres, the Spanish Inquisition and the hypocrisy of Christian slaveholders in the American South. The point of this book is to find a way forward and to encourage good citizenship, so I have focused on positive examples.

Further, the purpose of this book is to study Christian citizenship. American Christians often focus on just American or British examples of citizenship because, well, we are American citizens and draw from a shared history with Great Britain. But Christianity is an historic and global faith, and we should also learn from the followers of Jesus before our times and outside our borders.

For these reasons, I have included a number of key American citizens, but I have also included example citizens that emphasize the church's incredible story across continents and ages. This exercise helped me unwrap the Bible from the American flag and focus on being a Christian first, and I hope it will do the same for you.

With all that said, let's jump in. Here are some key historical examples of citizenship you should know about.

The Church in Rome

Consider the church in Rome, which grew from a marginalized and persecuted group of believers to the dominant religious influence in the Roman empire and then the Western world.

Early Christians were initially seen as radical and even dangerous by Roman society. Christians refused to participate in pagan events and feasts, and Romans even accused Christians of cannibalism due to a misunderstanding of the Lord's supper. Christians believed in one God instead of many gods. And, Romans, especially Roman males, found the Christian sexual ethic oppressive because it condemned adultery (prostitution and sex with slaves was common and acceptable in Roman culture), homosexuality and pederasty (sex with boys).[38]

I regularly have conversations with church leaders about the complexity of following Jesus in our increasingly secular culture. But our dilemmas seem quite tame when compared to those of the Roman Christians. For example, Scripture prohibits making or bowing down to idols and commands Christians to worship God alone (Ex. 20:3-4). But this was not an easy task in a culture filled with pagan symbolism and ceremonies.

Idolatry was pervasive in Roman business, politics, ceremonies and most other aspects of public life. The Roman senate was always held in a temple, and every senator was expected to place wine or frankincense on the altar before attending to the business of the empire. Games (including gladiatorial combat), feasts and spectacles were considered an essential element of Roman religion; and even marriages and funerals were filled with pagan symbolism and worship. For further reading on this topic, consider Paul's extended discussion of pervasive idolatry and the dilemma of food offered to idols (I Cor. 8:1-13).

On the lighter side, the common response to a sneeze was "Jupiter bless you." This may seem innocent enough, but one early church father exhorted Christians to respond to this simple salutation with an explanation that Jesus, not Jupiter is God. In sum, early Christians had to navigate complex issues of conscience, and many withdrew from a number of activities in Roman life because they could not participate without practicing idolatry.[39]

The Christian refusal to worship Roman gods probably raised eyebrows because it smacked of sacrilege, but the Christian refusal to bow down to Caesar raised imperial ire because it whiffed of treason. As I mentioned above, Roman emperors were sacro-monarchs that claimed legal and spiritual authority over the Roman people. And, when early Christians refused to worship Caesar, they challenged the power and control of the Roman state.

For example, Roman officials encouraged early church father Polycarp to simply state "Caesar is Lord" in exchange for his life, but he refused. In the arena, Polycarp was asked to simply swear an oath by the "luck of Caesar" in exchange for his life; but, again, he again refused. His punishment? He was burned at the stake.

This same terrible drama unfolded again and again during the persecution of the church. Roman authorities demanded that Christians worship Caesar, the Christians refused, and the authorities executed them for their beliefs. But, these public executions and burnings, designed to scare people into submission, backfired on the Roman state. When the superstitious and martial Romans observed Christians going resolutely and joyfully to their terrible deaths, they wondered at the faith that inspired such hope and courage. In fact, Edward Gibbon, in his classic *The Decline and Fall of the Roman Empire*, cites this confident hope at death's door as one of the key factors that persuaded Romans to consider Christ's claims.[40]

Further, despite cultural censure and deadly persecution, Roman Christians selflessly served their neighbors. They rescued young children left to die (infanticide was common); helped the sick during plagues; dignified and protected women, slaves and children; protested the violent gladiatorial games and otherwise advocated for cultural reforms that reflected equal human dignity.

And, in the end, Christ won over Caesar. Many historians will point to the conversion of Constantine in A.D. 312 as the watershed moment when Christianity triumphed over pagan religions. But this is incorrect or at least an oversimplification.[41] The Edict of Milan, which ended the persecution of Christians, was a signpost of an incredible transformation; but it was not the cause of that transformation.

Instead, we should focus on the fact that a small group of believers who were persecuted, maligned and often killed shook and then transformed the greatest empire in the ancient Western world.

Through their bold witness, their sacrificial service, and their eternal hope, these followers of Jesus turned the Roman gaze from their "eternal city" to eternity. Though the names of several church fathers have been passed down to us, this movement had no figurehead other than Christ. This was a movement of slaves, women, the poor, and the foreigner long before it moved the heart of the emperor. And perhaps the greatest testament to the early church came from the lips of Emperor Julian, who attempted to return the empire to its pagan roots. As the story goes, while Julian lay dying on a battlefield, he pointed toward heaven and groaned, "You have conquered, O Galilean."[42]

Notice that this lament did not focus on the institutional church or those who called themselves Christians. Rather, Julian specifically called out the one who inspired these individuals and whose teachings had overcome the religion of the Caesars—Jesus, the humble Carpenter from Galilee.

Augustine of Hippo

Consider Augustine (A.D. 354-430), who defended the Christian faith as the Roman empire fell, advocated against slavery and wrote *The City of God*, a classic treatise on the relationship between the church and the state. Augustine was born to a Christian mother and a pagan father, and he experimented with a number of philosophies and lifestyles before converting to Christianity in A.D. 354. In A.D. 410, the Visigoths under King Alaric sacked the city of Rome. Though Rome was of little strategic importance by that time (the Eastern Roman Empire's capital was in Constantinople, and the Western Roman Empire's capital was in Ravenna), the sacking of the eternal city was a cataclysmic and symbolic end to Roman dominance.

The emotional and societal toll of this event was enormous. Rome, mighty Rome, had fallen, and many who still followed the traditional Roman gods blamed Christianity for its fall. Did not Christ, the head of the established Roman religion, have a responsibility to defend the walls of the city?

In response to these arguments, Augustine wrote a twenty-two-volume work titled *The City of God*. He pointed out that Rome's pagan gods had not prevented Roman calamities in the past, that the worship of these gods had led to a slow fall from virtue and corresponding societal decline, and that misfortune falls on the righteous and unrighteous alike.

But Augustine did not stop there. He also set out a philosophy of history and society that recognized two distinct cities: the "City of God" and the "City of Man." He said, "Mankind is divided into two sorts: such as live according to man, and such as live according to God. These we call the two cities... The Heavenly City outshines Rome. There, instead of victory, is truth."[43]

Augustine did not directly link the City of God to the institutional church and the City of Man to the state. Rather, Augustine's concept of the City of God is more akin to what Jesus called the "kingdom" and what we might think of when we hear the term "Big C" Church. Augustine's City of God is a movement of believers spread across continents and disciplines fulfilling the Great Commission and the great commandment. This is a pilgrim city in a strange land working to accomplish the will of its eternal King. And Augustine's City of Man is what we might term the "world" in the sense that it is made up of individuals working across disciplines against God's design and purpose. This City of Man is a movement of individuals who have crowned themselves and who are working to accomplish their own will. Unfortunately, even Christians lend effort to the City of Man when they give in to their base desires or seek their own selfish ends.

Note that Augustine avoided the separation of the sacred and secular taught by Plato, modern secular scholars, and some religious figures. Rather, he spread the Good News and emphasized good works by engaging in politics and civic life.[44]

Stated differently, his faith urged him to live out the principles of the City of God in every area of his life, including the political life of his city. Unfortunately, medieval popes took this principle too far by citing Augustine for papal authority over human rulers. But Augustine did not consider the Bishop of Rome as the head of his City of God, and medieval church doctrine related to papal supremacy appears to be a misapplication of his writings.[45]

In sum, we should know the basics of Augustine's writings. We are members of the City of God and should work to build a comprehensive counter-society that reflects God's principles. But, more importantly, we should not miss the key lesson from his life and ministry: Rome was not eternal or ultimate.

People in the ancient world put their hope and trust in mighty Rome; and, when she fell, Christians and non-Christians alike found themselves in a state of panic and despair. In *The City of God*, Augustine masterfully turned his audience's attention away from the smoldering ruins of Rome and pointed them to God's glorious, everlasting kingdom.

This is a message that American Christians need to hear right now. The United States still occupies a unique position on the world stage, and we should carefully steward that influence. But we should not tie the cause of the gospel to the future of the American republic. Why? This sentiment does little to strengthen our nation and reverse its societal decline (more on that later). And, as Christians, we've seen the end of such a story. If the American eagle, like Rome's, slowly falls from prominence, it will be a grave tragedy. But our hope is found elsewhere—in an eternal kingdom that will never end. This is Augustine's profound example and message to our times.

Frumentius

Consider Frumentius (c. 383), a slave who impacted the Kingdom of Aksum (modern-day Ethiopia), led its king to Christ, and established a church movement that continues to this day.

Frumentius was born in Tyre, a region in modern-day Lebanon, and his uncle encouraged Frumentius and his cousin Edesius to travel with him on a trip to see Arabia. Tragically, all of the ship's crew and passengers except Frumentius and Edesius were killed in a brawl or in a shipwreck. Either way, the two became slaves and soon found themselves in the court of Aksum, a key empire in eastern Africa. The King of Aksum was impressed with their bearing and knowledge and pressed them into government service as a cupbearer and a secretary. During this period, both Frumentius and Edesius encountered Roman merchants and became followers of Christ.[46]

Before the Aksumite king died, he granted Frumentius and Edesius their freedom. However, at the queen's request, they remained in Aksum to educate the prince, named Ezana, and to help rule Aksum until the prince came of age. When Ezana took the throne, both Frumentius and Edesius left the kingdom and traveled to Alexandria in Egypt.

After a period of time, Frumentius petitioned Athanasius (who most famously stood against the Arian heresy that questioned the deity of Christ) to appoint a bishop or missionary to Ethiopia. And

Athanasius thought it was such a great idea that he encouraged Frumentius to return to the country that enslaved him (don't you love it when the "somebody" in "hey, somebody should do something" turns out to be you!).

Frumentius did, in fact, return to Ethiopia (Edesius returned to Tyre and is responsible for recording this story). And Frumentius soon led King Ezana to Christ, started and organized the Ethiopian church and launched missionary efforts into Nubia and Yemen. When Emperor Constantine of Rome demanded that Frumentius be replaced with a bishop that favored the Arian heresy, King Ezana refused. Frumentius' efforts to disciple the king had apparently taken root.

Sometimes, it is difficult to measure the effectiveness of individuals who lived and ministered in the distant past. But Frumentius is not one of them. The Kingdom of Aksum was one of the most influential ancient civilizations and was a conduit of trade between the Roman Empire and the cities along the Indian Ocean.[47] Frumentius educated and then led its king to Christ. And this conversion so deeply impacted the culture of the empire that pagan inscriptions soon disappeared from the kingdom's coinage and were replaced by Christian symbols.

Most importantly, the Ethiopian church flourished, weathered long centuries of Muslim wars of conquest that captured all of the surrounding region, and survives to this day in the form of the Ethiopian Orthodox Tewahedo Church, with more than 30 million adherents.[48]

Thomas Aquinas

Consider Thomas Aquinas (1225-1274), a brilliant theologian and scholar who wrote prolifically on the intersection of faith and public life. Though his nickname was "The Dumb Ox," Aquinas' work is dumbfounding in its breadth, insight and continued relevance. And his writings, such as *Summa Theologica*, have secured his place as the greatest Christian thinker of the millennium spanning from A.D. 500 to 1500.

Aquinas lived and wrote during a time when Aristotle's philosophy had only recently been rediscovered and was highly prized. However, Aquinas interpreted Aristotle's philosophy in light of the gospel instead of accepting it wholesale or elevating it above Scripture.[49] He stated, "In sacred theology, all things are treated from the standpoint of God."[50] In sum, he saw benefit in reason but believed that God's Revelation in the Scriptures was ultimate truth.

You may be wondering why I have included a theologian and philosopher in a list of example citizens. I mean, aren't we studying examples of Christians that <u>did</u> something rather than just wrote massive treatises? Well, as the saying goes, "The pen is mightier than the sword."[51] What we think about faith and its application in public life will deeply influence how we apply that faith in public life. And Aquinas is an early and seminal figure who studied the same problem we are studying: how to faithfully apply Biblical principles to our cultural moment and government. Here are a few key points:

First, Aquinas noted that politics is a part of the human experience. He explained that humans are inclined to "live in society" and that we cannot escape the exercise or at least the effects of politics and governance. In addition to being a good mother, father, farmer or teacher, he encouraged Christians to be good citizens and to seek the common good of their cities and nations.[52]

Next, Aquinas formulated a concept known as "natural law." Aquinas argued that God has stamped his law on our consciences, our planet and reality itself (Rom. 2:14-15). And His law is universal, unchangeable and indestructible. No matter how hard we try to erase it or disregard it, God's law remains. And we should build our lives and societies around those eternal principles.

Aquinas also set out a framework for human legislation and justice that reflects Romans 13 and government's role of punishing evil and promoting good. More specifically, he saw peace, virtue, and justice as necessary for the common good. For example, Aquinas decried usury, the practice of charging enormous interest rates on loans to the poor.[53]

Finally, Aquinas recognized limits on the state. Though Aquinas treated political life as a good and necessary part of the human experience, he noted that politics is not our greatest purpose. Rather, he explained that human beings can only find ultimate fulfillment, community, and justice in God's kingdom.

As I mentioned, Aquinas was a prolific and skilled writer. A current collection of his work includes over 50 volumes and 20,000 pages covering most major theological topics.[54] And he wrote it all before his early death at the age of 49!

Despite his importance and prolific productivity, Aquinas remained mindful of God's purpose for him. Near the end of his life, Aquinas put down his pen after reportedly seeing a vision, and he refused to take it up again. When begged to resume writing, he responded, "I cannot. Such things have been revealed to me that what I have written seems but straw."[55]

I have drawn many lessons from the teachings of Aquinas, but his most important reminder to American Christians is, in my opinion, the final principle I explained above: politics is important, but it is not ultimate. We should not give in to political idolatry or find our identity in our political tribe. We should engage in public life, promote God's principles evident in creation and woven into our consciences but look to God's kingdom for ultimate purpose and hope.[56]

Martin Luther

Consider Martin Luther (1483-1546), the Augustinian friar turned reformer who sparked the Protest Reformation and quite literally changed the course of the Western world.

Luther was born 120 miles southwest of modern Berlin and entered the University of Erfurt to study law at the age of 13. There, he proved to be an excellent student, and he graduated in the shortest time possible.

When he was 21, Luther was caught in a thunderstorm, and a bolt of lightning struck the ground near him. This near-death experience terrified him, and he promised to become a monk if God spared his life. He lived, and he kept his oath.

Luther dedicated himself to the ascetic life of a monk, denying himself basic comforts, confessing every errant thought and even whipping himself as penance for his sin. Despite these efforts, his soul found no rest until he read Romans 1:17 and realized that righteousness comes by faith in God and not by man's flawed efforts to live a sinless life.[57]

This conversion and a continued study of Scripture as a professor of the Bible at the University of Wittenberg soon led him to rethink many of the teachings and practices of the medieval church. Then, an event near Luther clarified this conflict and drove him to action.

A local church official named Albrecht borrowed the princely sum of 23,000 ducats and paid it to Pope Leo X in exchange for an appointment as the Archbishop of Mainz. Nothing, apparently, clarifies God's will like a wheelbarrow of gold. And how did Albrecht plan on repaying this massive loan? He planned on selling indulgences, a spiritual scheme that promised to ease the eternal suffering of the departed in exchange for money. If this sounds like a greasy way to fleece the faithful, you are right. Albrecht's actions infuriated Luther, and he responded by posting his Ninety-Five Theses to the door of the church in Wittenberg.

It is important to note that Luther did not intend to spark a reformation. Rather, his famous theses were written in the form of an invitation to an academic debate about a number of topics, including indulgences. And he wrote them in Latin instead of German.

No one showed up at the scheduled time, so Luther decided to send his theses to Archbishop Albrecht and to a few academic friends. A printer named Christopher Scheurl managed to obtain a copy, was impressed by what he read and republished the theses without asking for permission from Luther. From there, in our parlance, Luther's words went "viral." Luther posted his theses on the Wittenberg Church door in October of 1517; and, by the spring of 1518, King Henry VIII of England had a copy. In short order, Luther's words were read by the nobility and the common people across the continent of Europe.[58]

A firestorm ensued. Luther's plainly stated Biblical principles and clear application threatened the church and the very power structure of medieval Europe. But, when threatened, Luther did not back down. He defended his position in public debates and through written works, including *The Address to the Christian Nobility*, *The Babylonian Captivity of the Church*, and *On the Freedom of a Christian*. In 1521, Luther received a summons to appear before Charles V, the newly elected Holy Roman Emperor, for an assembly that Luther thought was a debate. But, when he arrived, the Diet of Worms quickly turned into a trial over Luther's "heresy," and Luther was instructed in no uncertain terms to recant his views.

Luther refused. Instead, he resolutely stood before Charles V and declared, "...I cannot and will not recant, because it is neither safe nor wise to act against conscience...Here I stand. I can do no other. God help me! Amen." This statement emboldened the Protestant Reformation, sent shock waves through medieval power structures and earned Luther an imperial edict condemning him as a heretic.

If you have read much history, you know that individuals like Martin Luther do not normally live to see retirement. But, Luther's stand on Scripture influenced and even procured the protection of governing officials (this is why Luther is sometimes referred to as a Magisterial Reformer).[59] A German prince named Frederick III staged Luther's kidnapping and hid him in Wartburg Castle under the alias of "*Junker* Jörg" (Knight George).

After remaining in hiding for ten months, Luther returned to Wittenberg and resumed his work in strengthening and guiding the reformation. He later married a former nun, Katharina von Bora, who he helped escape from a convent via a fish barrel (does this story get any better?).

That said, Luther's life and ministry were not without complications. The German peasants (citing Luther's work) rose in a bloody revolt against the German princes, and Luther sided with the princes in reasserting their authority. And, in his later years, the often ill and ill-tempered Luther employed vulgar and hateful language toward his opponents and Jews. These statements were later used by the Third Reich to justify, in part, the horrors of the Holocaust.[60]

Despite these failures, Luther's legacy is monumental. He pointed Christians back to Scripture as their ultimate source of authority, refused to bow when church and state officials demanded he recant his views, and sparked and led a reformation of the church. Further, his actions helped launch Europe from the Middle Ages into early modernity and laid the groundwork for what we now understand as the right of conscience.

The Holy Roman Empire fell apart with the retirement of Charles V, and the imperial palace which hosted the Diet of Worms was destroyed by a French army in 1689. So, the power and even the palace where Luther made his famous stand and statement, "Here I stand, I can do no other," no longer exist. A simple stone marks the approximate location where this history-shaking event occurred, and the stone carries a brief, simple inscription:

Hier Stand
Vor Kaiser Und Reich
Martin Luther
1521

In English, the monument reads: "Here Stood Before King and Empire Martin Luther 1521."[61] I can think of no better summary of this giant of the faith who stood steadfastly before king and empire to proclaim the truth about Christ and His everlasting kingdom.

John Calvin

Consider John Calvin (1509-1564), the theologian and "ecclesiastical statesman" (he had authority in both the church and civil government) who helped lead the Protestant Reformation and applied Biblical principles in the life and leadership of Geneva, Switzerland.

Calvin was born in France, and he initially studied philosophy and theology in hopes of becoming a scholar. However, with his father's urging, he changed his focus to law and completed his legal studies at the University of Orleans.

During this period, Luther's teachings reached France and eventually persuaded Calvin of the importance and truth of his views. Calvin was marked as a "Lutheran" due to his participation in a public statement on theological principles, and he fled catholic France for a more tolerant Basel, Switzerland. There, he wrote the first edition of *The Institutes of the Christian Religion*, his masterwork on the basics of the Christian faith and how to apply them in everyday life. He wrote on church leadership, salvation, Christian liberty, personal discipline, and even politics.[62]

In Chapter 20 of Volume IV the *Institutes*, Calvin addressed civil government at length, including many of the same questions we face today. He concluded that government is ordained by God, that the church and state have separate but complementary roles, that government's role is to punish evil and promote good, that Christians should participate in civil government for the good of their neighbors while prioritizing their status as pilgrims and citizens of heaven, that all laws should be just, and that Christian must obey God rather than government when government passes a law contrary to Scripture.[63]

In 1536, while passing through Geneva, Switzerland, a church leader named William Farel quite forcefully encouraged Calvin to minister in Geneva. Calvin reluctantly agreed to stay, but he and Farel were "run out of town" just eighteen months later due to a disagreement with the city council. After a three-year ministry in Strasbourg, France, Calvin returned at the request of the Genevan city council and set out to reform the city in light of Scriptural principles.

Calvin was not the ruler of Geneva, though he was appointed by and paid by the city council. Rather, he was primarily a church leader that exercised moral and spiritual influence on the city and tirelessly participated in its life and functions, including work on the city constitution, drains and even heating appliances. His reforms included strict moral standards as well as care for the poor and the redress of various social ills. At one point, these reforms were so successful that Geneva recorded no beggars.

Like Luther's, Calvin's legacy is not without controversy. In 1553, Michael Servetus, a preacher who denied the Trinity, fled to Geneva for protection from Catholic authorities. But he found no refuge in Geneva. The city council condemned Servetus to death and burned him at the stake with the full support of Calvin. I will note that death by burning was the common punishment for such beliefs in Europe in the 1500s, but that does not excuse Calvin from scrutiny and censure. In promoting that which is right, true and beautiful, Calvin went too far and participated in the execution of a man who simply held a different religious view.[64]

By the end of his life, Calvin's books, sermons and reforms had deeply impacted Geneva and had helped propel the Protestant Reformation into a movement that still impacts us today. And his work in public life positively affected our concepts of economics, individual rights and even democracy.[65]

Roger Williams

Consider Roger Williams (c.1603-1683), a Puritan pastor who founded Rhode Island, influenced British parliament, and laid the groundwork for religious liberty in the United States.

Williams' story started in not-so-merry old England right before the English Civil War. Williams was educated at Cambridge and established himself as a minister and scholar. Then, he became an aide to Sir Edward Coke, one of the greatest if not the greatest English jurist of all time. Williams accompanied Coke to his work at parliament, to English courts and even to meetings with the crown. These experiences would prove invaluable in the years to come.[66]

When King Charles dissolved parliament in 1629, he instituted a period of authoritarian rule and cracked down on religious dissent. The Puritans, who were working to reform or purify the Church of England, decided to leave England to avoid persecution. A Puritan leader named John Winthrop, Roger Williams, and approximately 1,000 other Puritans sailed to the new world and established the Massachusetts Bay Company. As Winthrop framed it, Massachusetts was to be a "City on a Hill," a community fashioned after God's principles.

Williams assisted in the founding of Massachusetts Bay, but he quickly grew disillusioned with the colony's insistence on religious conformity. He pointed out that the Puritans had just literally crossed an ocean to avoid government persecution. Then, when given the opportunity to set up a government, they had established their own version of conscience control!

Due to these concerns, Williams turned down the pastorate of the church in Boston (the most prestigious pulpit on this side of the Atlantic) and eventually became the pastor of a church in Salem. There, he routinely criticized the colonial leadership for their hypocritical crackdown on religious dissent, and the General Court of the Massachusetts Bay eventually banished him from the colony. In January 1636, colonial officials sent soldiers to arrest Williams and send him back to England, where he faced, at best, life imprisonment.

Fortunately, Governor Winthrop warned Williams, and he fled into the wilderness with little more than the clothes on his back and some corn paste for food. Many years later, he described the perilous cold he experienced during his escape as the "snow wch I feele yet." He would have died without the aid of local Indians, who fed and sheltered him.

Williams then moved north and purchased a piece of land from the Narragansett Indians and founded his own settlement, stating: "having, of a sense of God's merciful providence unto me in my distress, [I] called the place PROVIDENCE, I desired it might be for a shelter for persons distressed for conscience." When families from his church in Salem joined him, he drafted a political charter and formed a colony that formally recognized religious freedom. This sounds normal to us, but it was novel at the time.

As you might imagine, the leaders of the Massachusetts Bay Colony were not pleased with Williams' experiment in toleration. And Massachusetts officials claimed land close to Providence and even marched soldiers through its streets. When Williams' objections were ignored, he sailed for England to take up the matter with parliament.

When he arrived, England was gripped in a civil war between the king and parliament; and Williams faced strong political opponents as well as almost unanimous intellectual disapproval of religious liberty. But this did not deter him from seeking formal recognition of his colony and its principles. He met with all of his former connections in parliament, worked to win the favor of key leaders and even procured a winter's supply of firewood for London (no easy feat) in an effort to garner support.

He also wrote a pamphlet explaining his experiences and arguing for what he called "Soul Libertie," the right to worship and live according to one's own conscience. Eventually, a committee of parliament relented and granted his request. Williams sailed back to the New World with a remarkable formal charter recognizing religious liberty.

Williams' big idea deeply influenced the charters of New Jersey and the Carolinas and the minds of John Milton and John Locke. Locke, in turn, heavily influenced Madison, Jefferson and the other architects of the U.S. Constitution.

In sum, when I began this study, I knew Roger Williams founded Rhode Island and championed religious liberty; but I had overlooked just how significantly this Puritan preacher influenced American government and especially the First Amendment. Perhaps the greatest praise for Williams comes from the pen of a historian who downplayed his contribution to the American experiment by claiming that he relied too heavily on Scripture. Emil Oberholzer, Jr. stated: "When Jefferson advocated religious liberty, he did it as a child of the Enlightenment; his motive was political and social. With Williams, the child of a theological age, the motive was wholly religious."[67] Not a bad legacy for a Christian citizen. Not bad at all.

John Leland

Consider John Leland (1754-1841), the Baptist pastor who championed religious freedom and secured the First Amendment to the U.S. Constitution. Before I explain the rest of his work, I must point out that Leland was a pastor first and foremost. During his ministry, he preached 8,000 sermons, baptized over 1,500 people, wrote pamphlets and music and spoke to audiences all over the young United States as an itinerant or circuit-riding preacher.

Born in Massachusetts, he was deeply troubled by the authority of the established state church and moved to Virginia to plant a ministry in 1775.[68] Unfortunately, he discovered a similar problem there. The established Anglican church strongly opposed Baptists and other religious sects. And Virginia authorities jailed a number of Baptist ministers for the following reasons: not obtaining a preaching license, violating the terms of that license by preaching outside church buildings, and refusing to comply with a Virginia law that required all citizens to attend and pay tithes to the Anglican church. Further, Baptist pastors were often heckled, threatened and even beaten by angry individuals and mobs.

These developments steeled Leland's resolve to extinguish the notion of state churches and to advocate for religious liberty.[69] Leland became a leader among the Virginia Baptists and worked with Thomas Jefferson and James Madison to promote the Virginia Statute for Religious Freedom, which disestablished the Anglican church in Virginia in 1786.

When the U.S. Constitution was proposed in 1787, Leland spoke up about his grave concern that the new Constitution did not sufficiently protect religious liberty. James Madison, who had helped draft the document, predictably disagreed. But Madison was keenly aware that Leland had more votes than Madison for a seat at the Virginia convention on ratifying the U.S. Constitution. So, Madison met with Leland to discuss the matter.

Though hesitant at first, Leland finally agreed to withdraw his name from consideration on one condition: Madison's promise to introduce an amendment protecting religious liberty. Madison kept his word, and we now have the First Amendment to the U.S. Constitution.

And Leland did not stop there. He later moved back to Massachusetts and assisted in disestablishing the state religion of Connecticut in 1818 and in Massachusetts in 1833. He also promoted his views on religious liberty in a book, *A Chronicle of His Time in Virginia.* He stated, "...Government should protect every man in thinking and speaking freely, and see that one does not abuse another. The liberty I contend for is more than toleration. The very idea of toleration is despicable; it supposes that some have a pre-eminence above the rest to grant indulgence, whereas all should be equally free, Jews, Turks [Muslims], Pagans and Christians."[70]

Though Leland strongly advocated for an institutional separation of church and state, he set a strong example of remaining engaged in public life while focusing on the gospel. Leland was a strong advocate for religious liberty, but he also spoke out on the issue of slavery.

Leland also had a flair for the dramatic. He entered the national imagination by delivering a 1,235-pound wheel of cheese measuring 13 feet in circumference and 4 feet in height to the newly elected President Thomas Jefferson. He gathered milk from 900 cows (he refused milk from "Federalist cows" owned by members of the more elite and now defunct Federalist party), made the cheese, and then transported it all the way from Massachusetts to Washington, D.C. in the dead of winter. Etched into the cheese's red crust was one of Jefferson's favorite sayings, "Rebellion to tyrants is obedience to God." Ladies and gentlemen, nothing says "Murica" like a tyrant-defying massive wheel of cheese! The cheese understandably drew attention and even light-hearted ridicule, was dubbed the "mammoth cheese" and even earned a poem. Here's a line from the "Ode to the Mammoth Cheese," which is just fantastic: "O! May no traitor to his country's cause / E'er have a piece of thee between his jaws."[71]

Jefferson graciously accepted this unique gift and then invited Leland to give a Sunday sermon in the chamber of the House of Representatives on January 3, 1802. Leland also preached numerous times on the way to Washington, D.C. and back, so the mammoth cheese can properly be considered a sermon prop.

Leland passed away in 1841, and his tombstone sums up his life and influence as follows: "Here lies the body of John Leland, who labored 67 years to promote piety and vindicate the civil and religious rights of all men."

Olaudah Equiano

Consider the example of Olaudah Equiano (c.1745-1797), who purchased his freedom from slavery, traveled the globe, and advocated for the end of slavery in the British empire.

Though there is some uncertainty about his early life, Equiano appears to have been born in southern Nigeria. He was kidnapped by slavers at the age of 11 and transported across the Atlantic to the Caribbean and then to Virginia. He was sold to a British Royal Navy officer, then a ship captain in London, and finally to a merchant on the island of Monserrat in the Caribbean. During this period, he learned to read and became a Christian.

Eventually, he earned enough money to buy his freedom. After traveling the world (including the Arctic), he returned to England and joined the "Sons of Africa," a group of twelve black men who worked to end the slave trade. As part of this effort, he wrote his autobiography, *The Interesting Narrative of the Life of Olaudah Equiano or Gustavus Vassa, the African*,[72] which became immensely popular and went through nine editions during his lifetime. His personal description of the horrors and inhumanity of the slave trade stirred the British conscience and assisted in the passage of the Slave Trade Act of 1807, which abolished the buying and selling of slaves in the British Empire. The full abolition of slave ownership came in 1833.[73]

Hannah Moore

Hannah Moore (1745-1833) was born in Bristol, England and rose to early literary fame in London.[74] She even befriended the key English writer Samuel Johnson and joined the Bluestockings, a group of women intellectuals. In 1787, she turned her literary talents to the issue of the slave trade and published her poem "Slavery," which includes these powerful lines,

Shall Britain, where the soul of Freedom reigns,
Forge chains for others she herself disdains?
Forbid it, Heaven! O let the nations know
The liberty she tastes she will bestow;
Not to herself the glorious gift confined,
She spreads the blessing wide as human kind;[75]

Also, in 1787, she met William Wilberforce, who shared her Christian beliefs and her fierce determination to end slavery, and they joined forces in the cultural and legal campaign against the institution. Hannah also noticed the intense poverty of English children in the working class, and she worked tirelessly to establish schools to teach children to read. Hannah died in 1833, but not before she had witnessed the abolition of slavery in the British Empire.[76]

William Wilberforce

Many American Christians are already familiar with the life and work of William Wilberforce (1759-1833), but I have found it helpful to review his legacy in light of what we have studied thus far. William was born to a wealthy family and won a seat in parliament in 1780 at the age of 21. William quickly found his ambitious and pretentious life rather empty, and he became a Christian in 1786.

Wilberforce famously wrestled with his purpose in parliament until a key conversation with John Newton, the slaver turned minister and author of the song "Amazing Grace." Newton encouraged Wilberforce to "serve God where he was" and to apply his Christian principles in public life.[77] Wilberforce heeded this advice and soon turned his attention to the slave trade and other civil ills.

Concerning the slave trade, Wilberforce stated, "So enormous, so dreadful, so irremediable did the trade's wickedness appear that my own mind was completely made up for abolition. Let the consequences be what they would: I from this time determined that I would never rest until I had effected its abolition."[78] With the help of abolitionist Thomas Clarkson, Wilberforce introduced twelve different resolutions to end the slave trade. They all failed, but Wilberforce persevered.

In time, he joined the Clapham Sect, a fellowship of prominent Christians (including Hannah Moore) that worked tirelessly to better working conditions, protect children, and reform prisons.

Wilberforce suffered from poor health and even developed an addiction to opium, which was a new drug with unknown side effects. But he continued his work against the slave trade and for the common good.

In 1807, the British Empire banned the slave trade. And, in 1833, three days before his death, Wilberforce learned that his life's work was complete. A remarkable group of Christians, led by this small and often feeble member of parliament, had overcome the wealth and influence of pro-slavery forces to abolish the ownership of slaves in the world's first globe-spanning empire.[79]

Harriet Tubman

Next, let's move across the Atlantic to the abolition movement in the United States.

Harriet Tubman (c.1820-1913) was born on a plantation in Maryland. At the age of 12, she protected a fellow slave by stepping in front of a heavy weight thrown by a slave master. The weight cracked her skull and caused her to experience headaches, drowsiness and hallucinations for the rest of her life.

Harriet escaped north in 1849, but she was not satisfied with her own freedom. She returned to the South at least 13 different times, personally leading more than 70 slaves to freedom via harrowing trips on the "underground railroad." And she proudly noted that she "never lost a passenger."[80]

In response to the growing number of escaped slaves, Congress passed the Fugitive Slave Act, which allowed slaveholders to pursue and arrest escaped slaves in northern states.[81] This lengthened the long trek to freedom, and Harriet began escorting her passengers all the way to Canada.

Infuriated slaveholders responded by posting a reward for the capture of "Moses," her new nickname. But she courageously continued her efforts with the motto "I can't die but once."[82] In all of this, Harriet was strengthened by her devout faith in God. She daily asked God for guidance and relied on His strength during her dangerous treks to and from the South. She said, "I always tole God, I'm gwine [going] to hole stiddy on you, an' you've got to see me through."[83]

Harriet befriended other abolitionist leaders, including Frederick Douglass and Thomas Garrett, and worked with them to advocate for the end of slavery in the United States.

During the Civil War, she served as a nurse and then as the head of an espionage ring. She provided critical intelligence about Confederate roads and supply lines, assisted escaping slaves and encouraged the formation of black regiments in the Union Army.

After the war, she moved to Auburn, New York, and eventually joined forces with Susan B. Anthony to advocate for women's suffrage. In 1896, she established the Harriet Tubman Home for Aged and Indigent Colored People.[84] She entered the promised land in 1913.

In sum, Harriet guided a number of escaping slaves on their long and harrowing trek north, and she helped lead the United States on its long and bloody journey to abolish slavery. Harriet's remarkable courage, ingenuity, strength and reliance on God is an example to us all.

Frederick Douglass

Frederick Douglass (c.1817-1895) was born on one of the wealthiest slave plantations in Maryland, and he observed the brutal whipping of his 15-year-old Aunt Hester while still a young boy. In 1826, his owners sent him to Baltimore to live with a couple named Hugh and Sophia Auld, and Sophia taught Douglass the alphabet.

When Hugh discovered and stopped Sophia's illegal instruction, Douglass covertly continued his studies and taught himself how to read and write. During this period, Douglass came to Christ under the teaching of the African Methodist Episcopal Church.

Douglass escaped north to Massachusetts in 1833, and he quickly joined the abolitionist cause. By 1841, he was speaking on the anti-slavery circuit around the nation. And, by 1845, he had published his first autobiography, *Narrative of the Life of Frederick Douglass, an American Slave.* Like Olaudah Equiano's autobiography in England, Douglass' story became an instant sensation, selling 30,000 copies in five years.

Douglass' speeches and book railed against the hypocrisy and evils of slavery in the United States. He declared, "Between the Christianity of this land, and the Christianity of Christ, I recognize the widest possible difference."[85] And he reserved his strongest words for pastors in the South, stating "The man who wields the blood-clotted cowskin during the week fills the pulpit on Sunday and claims to be a minister of the meek and lowly Jesus."[86]

Frederick also traveled to and spoke in Ireland and Great Britain, and he gave one of his greatest speeches—the "London Reception Speech"—during this tour. When he returned to the United States in 1847, he started his own paper, *The North Star,* which focused on abolition and women's suffrage.

In 1852, he delivered his famous speech, "What to a slave is the 4th of July?" He thundered:

> What, to the American slave, is your 4th of July? I answer: a day that reveals to him, more than all other days in the year, the gross injustice and cruelty to which he is the constant victim. To him, your celebration is a sham; your boasted liberty, an unholy license; your national greatness, swelling vanity; your sounds of rejoicing are empty and heartless; your denunciations of tyrants, brass fronted impudence; your shouts of liberty and equality, hollow mockery; your prayers and hymns, your sermons and thanksgivings, with all your religious parade, and solemnity, are, to him, mere bombast, fraud, deception, impiety, and hypocrisy — a

thin veil to cover up crimes which would disgrace a nation of savages. There is not a nation on the earth guilty of practices more shocking and bloody than are the people of the United States, at this very hour...

He continued:

...Allow me to say, in conclusion, notwithstanding the dark picture I have this day presented, of the state of the nation, I do not despair of this country. There are forces in operation which must inevitably work the downfall of slavery. "The arm of the Lord is not shortened," and the doom of slavery is certain. I, therefore, leave off where I began, with hope. While drawing encouragement from "the Declaration of Independence," the great principles it contains, and the genius of American Institutions, my spirit is also cheered by the obvious tendencies of the age.[87]

Remember our discussion about the Old Testament prophets encouraging and challenging Israelite kings? Well, Douglass played a similar role with President Abraham Lincoln. He assisted the war effort by recruiting black soldiers (including his sons Charlie and Lewis) for the Union cause. And, in 1863, he appeared at the White House uninvited to protest the President's silence on the abuse and execution of captured black soldiers at the hands of the Confederacy. President Lincoln immediately received him, stating, "I know who you are, Mr. Douglass."[88] Though the President did not grant all of Douglass' demands, this meeting started a strong relationship between the two leaders.

Lincoln invited Douglass to the White House twice more and to his Second Inaugural Address. Right before that famous speech, Lincoln noticed Douglass and even pointed him out to Vice President Johnson. Lincoln then turned to give his masterful address, which was largely a theodicy of the American Civil War and a hopeful vision for the future. Lincoln stated:

Fondly do we hope—fervently do we pray—that this mighty scourge of war may speedily pass away. Yet, if God wills that it continue, until all the wealth piled by the bond-man's two hundred and fifty years of unrequited toil shall be sunk, and until every drop of blood drawn with the lash, shall be paid by another drawn with the sword, as was said three thousand years ago, so still it must be said "the judgments of the Lord are true and righteous altogether."[89]

Can you imagine Douglass' perception of these words? The President had heard Douglass, and Lincoln framed the war in theological terms as a bloody but necessary crusade to end the evil institution. After the speech, Douglass met the President in a reception line, and Lincoln took Douglass aside to ask him about his opinion of the speech. Douglass replied that it was a "sacred effort."[90]

One of the great "what ifs" of American history is this: how would the story of reconstruction, discrimination and Jim Crow be different if Lincoln had lived and partnered with Douglass to create the "...just, and lasting peace..." Lincoln so eloquently described in his address? Unfortunately, we will never know.

Lincoln lived long enough to see the ratification of the 13th Amendment, which abolished slavery, and a Union victory in our great Civil War. But his life was cut short by an assassin's bullet. And he was replaced by Andrew Johnson, a former slave owner and former Governor of Tennessee.

Slavery had ended, but its ghost remained. Because of this, Douglass continued his advocacy, denouncing Jim Crow laws, unjust economic arrangements such as sharecropping, and the all-too-common public lynchings of black men. As he neared the end of his life, Douglass opined that the "malignant prejudice of race...still poisoned the fountains of justice, and defiled the altars of religion." And he pleaded with Americans to build a better society on the "...broad foundation laid by the Bible itself, that God has made of one blood all nations of men to dwell on all the face of the earth."[91]

In summary, Frederick Douglass was a modern-day prophet[92] who stirred the American conscience, decried the grave hypocrisy of the

Christian church on the issue of slavery, and challenged and encouraged President Abraham Lincoln to lead the United States to abolish slavery. Douglass remains a key example to us as we work to build the society he envisioned but never experienced.

John Mackenzie

Consider John Mackenzie (1835-1899), the British missionary and statesman who championed the rights of Africans during European colonization and helped secure the existence of modern-day Botswana.

Before I jump into Mackenzie's life and legacy, let's do a quick review of the often-dark history of Western colonization and conquest. True, migration and conquest has been common through human history and across cultures; but this does not absolve Western nations for subjugating foreign nations and tribes for wealth and power.

That said, I would also note that lumping all colonial powers together is imprecise. For example, British and Belgian colonial practices were markedly different. But, comparing body counts, the scope of land grabs, and the treatment of indigenous peoples does not change the moral determination of right and wrong. Many Western "Christian" nations simply did not see the inherent Biblical and moral conflict in the Age of Exploration's three-fold maxim: "God, gold and glory."

Here's a working summary of Western colonialism. For a few short centuries, Europeans possessed powerful weaponry and technology that the rest of the world did not. And the alluring prospect of wealth and empire proved too strong to resist. Further, this technological and military superiority led to a belief in racial superiority. Though this unbiblical belief was deeply influenced by social Darwinism, the church should have done more to stand against these forces. Sadly, even Christian missionaries sometimes conflated missions work with colonial expansion.

For example, in the United States, missionaries often worked alongside government officials in encouraging Indian leaders to sign away their land. And, when U.S. troops mowed down Sioux men, women and children with the equivalent of machine guns at the Battle/Massacre of Wounded Knee, the survivors were taken to an

Episcopalian mission. The battle occurred a few days after Christmas, and the wounded Indians that gathered in the Episcopalian mission long remembered the Christmas greenery and a crude banner near the pulpit that declared: "Peace on Earth; Good Will toward Men."[93] Our national hypocrisy has rarely been so stark.

That said, the narrative of colonial oppression aided by missionaries is not the only or even the primary story. Missionaries during the colonial era were often critical of colonization. For example, British missionaries John and Alice Harris exposed atrocities in the Belgian Congo. And colonial-era missionaries were a driving force in the collapse of monarchy as the reigning system of government and the rise of modern democracies.[94] In part due to their efforts, less than thirty of the approximately 195 nations in the world maintain monarchies, and only a handful of those monarchs wield significant power.[95]

John Mackenzie is a helpful example of this counterpoint to the general discussion about the church's role in European colonialism, so let's briefly review his life and ministry. Mackenzie was a missionary of the London Missionary Society and went to South Africa in 1858 to build on the work of Missionaries Robert Moffat and David Livingstone.

Mackenzie primarily ministered to the Tswana people in Bechuanaland, and he intervened when Boers (colonists of Dutch descent) from the Republic of Transvaal began encroaching on Tswana land. Mackenzie was concerned about land grabs, but he was primarily concerned about the Boer practice of *apartheid*, a strict form of racial segregation and discrimination.[96]

Mackenzie believed that a British protectorate was necessary to prevent Boer usurpation of Bechuanaland and oppression of the Tswana people. And he procured that protectorate in 1884 in partnership with Khama III, a Tswana chieftain. John even served as the deputy commissioner of the protectorate until replaced by another British official.

In 1885, Mackenzie assisted in procuring another protectorate for the land north of Bechuanaland; and this protectorate eventually became modern-day Botswana. John also aided Khama III and other Tswana chieftains in 1895 as they traveled to Great Britain, held rallies, launched petitions and even met with Queen Victoria in a successful effort to prevent Bechuanaland from becoming a possession of the British South Africa Company.[97]

In sum, Mackenzie preached the gospel to the Tswana people, but he could not overlook the physical and political danger they faced from colonial expansion and overt racism. So, he intervened as a citizen of Great Britain, advocated for protectorates, helped defend those protectorates from British commercial interests and procured the existence of modern-day Botswana.

Abraham Kuyper

Consider Abraham Kuyper (1837-1920), the Dutch pastor, theologian, journalist and politician who tirelessly lived out his faith in public life and modeled Christian citizenship in a modern participatory democracy.

Kuyper was born in a pastor's home in 1837 and made a profession of faith at age 10. A bright student, he attended the University of Leiden (the leading Dutch university at the time) and obtained his doctorate in theology by the age of 26.

Though Kuyper subscribed to theological liberalism for a short time after his graduation, he recommitted himself to an orthodox view of the faith after reading Scripture and the book *The Heir of Redclyffe*. In 1863, he moved to the small village of Beesd to pastor a church. But the people in Beesd ended up pastoring Kuyper! Kuyper was accustomed to an academic and conceptual Christianity; but these Christians showed Kuyper a practical, every day, whole-life devotion to Jesus. This experience deeply motivated Kuyper and awakened him to the desperate need for reform in the Dutch church. In 1870, he became the pastor of the largest church in the Netherlands, the Reformed Church of Amsterdam, and served there until his election to Dutch parliament.[98]

In 1872, Kuyper founded a newspaper, *De Standaard*, which provided commentary on public events. And, in 1874, he was elected to Dutch parliament. In 1878, he formed a political party, the Anti-Revolutionary Party, which mobilized the lower-middle classes around orthodox religious views and related social policies. In 1880, he founded the Free University at Amsterdam to provide theological training to pastors. In 1892, he led a movement of believers out of the existing Reformed Church of the Netherlands (which Kuyper viewed as too progressive and aristocratic) and founded a new church or denomination, the Reformed Church in the Netherlands. No wonder his adversaries called him "an opponent of ten heads and a hundred hands."[99]

In Dutch parliament, Kuyper championed private, religious schools and universities. And he eventually formed a coalition of parties and became the Prime Minister of the Netherlands from 1901-1905. During this time, he negotiated with Great Britain during the Boer War and advocated for an expanded franchise or right to vote. He remained in Dutch parliament until his death in 1920.[100]

Though Kuyper led an impressive political career, his greatest legacy remains his books, lectures and example of living out the Christian faith in public life. And he is remembered for promoting three key concepts: common grace, sphere sovereignty and worldview.

In Kuyper's book titled *Common Grace*, he argued that God extends undeserved blessings and favor to all people, regardless of whether or not they believe in Him. For example, God sends rain on the just and the unjust (Matt. 5:45), maintains order in the universe that allows for medical and scientific advancements, establishes governments to restrain evil and establish general civic order (Rom. 13) and writes His laws on the hearts of all people (Rom. 2:14-15).

Next, he developed the concept of sphere sovereignty, which posits that God created separate spheres (such as the home, the church and the state) that should act independently according to their Biblical roles under the headship of Christ.

And, finally, he promoted a concept we often term "worldview." In 1898, he traveled to Princeton University in the United States to deliver his famous Stone Lectures, a series of presentations on how Christianity impacts all of life, including religion, politics, science, art and the future. He saw modernism as an all-encompassing ideology to be opposed by a comprehensive Christian *Weltanschauung*, or worldview. He famously summarized this teaching by stating, "There is not a square inch in the whole domain of our human existence over which Christ, who is Sovereign over all, does not cry, 'Mine!'"[101]

In sum, Kuyper worked to renew the church and his nation by living out his faith in numerous spheres of influence.[102] He believed in the Biblical centrality of the church and worked tirelessly to serve and reform it. But he also believed that Christians should live out their faith in public life and should dramatically influence their nations for Christ. He eloquently described his life's purpose as follows:

> One desire has been the ruling passion of my life. One high motive has acted like a spur upon my mind and soul. And sooner than that I should seek escape from the sacred necessity that this is laid upon me, let the breath of life fail me. It is this: That in spite of all worldly opposition, God's holy ordinances shall be established again in the home, in the school and in the State for the good of the people; to carve as it were into the conscience of the nation the ordinances of the Lord, to which the Bible and Creation bear witness, until the nation pays homage again to God.[103]

This tireless theologian and statesman is now at rest, and his purpose became his legacy.

Frances Willard

Consider Frances Willard (1839-1898), an early advocate for temperance, educational reforms for women and women's suffrage.

Willard was born in upstate New York to a Methodist family, and her family eventually settled near Chicago, Illinois. In 1858, she enrolled at North Western Female College and trained to be a teacher. After graduating in 1859, she taught in one-room schoolhouses in Illinois and then in larger schools in Pennsylvania and New York. In 1871, she returned to Illinois and took a role as president of Evanston College for Ladies and then as the first Dean of Women at Northwestern University.

During this period, she became involved in Dwight L. Moody's evangelistic campaigns and in the growing women's temperance movement. This movement to end the sale and consumption of alcohol was sparked primarily by women who protested the pervasive abuse of hard alcohol and resulting domestic violence against women and children.

The Temperance Movement and the eventual 18th Amendment (Prohibition) to the U.S. Constitution sound like unnecessary and problematic bits of moralism to many modern Christians. But, the consumption of hard, high proof alcohol during this period was destructive to many families, and Prohibition did produce a hard reset on America's relationship with alcohol.[104] Further, the temperance movement was the first major political movement among American women and ran parallel to the women's suffrage movement.

Willard worked to broaden the temperance movement into a more comprehensive social reform movement that advocated for causes such as women's suffrage and against numerous social ills or inequalities. Her efforts proved successful, and she was elected as president of the national Women's Christian Temperance Union (WCTU) in 1879.

During this time, she became known for her oratorical skills, oversaw the construction of a modern office building in downtown Chicago (to be used as the WCTU's office) and developed a national and even international reputation. By 1890, the WCTU had become the largest women's political reform movement of the 19th century, claiming more than 100,000 members.[105]

Willard instituted a "do everything" policy at the WCTU and developed departments to advocate for causes such as women's suffrage, workforce safety, an eight-hour workday, fair treatment of women in the workforce, kindergartens for the poor, prison reforms, and an end to public lynchings. This comprehensive approach expanded the reach of WCTU and created significant change, but this policy also stretched the organization's resources and reputation thin. In later years, the strong-willed Willard controversially advocated for a form of Christian socialism and failed to fully embrace racial equality, but she remained the president of the WCTU and a strong advocate for women's rights until her death in 1898 at the age of 58.[106]

Willard's life stands for a simple but profound principle: women should be full and equal partners in American public life. And the social reform movement that she strengthened and multiplied eventually won the passage and ratification of the 19th Amendment, which states simply, "The right of citizens of the United States to vote shall not be denied or abridged by the United States or by any State on account of sex." Her home state of Illinois honored Willard by contributing a statue of her to Statuary Hall at the U.S. Capitol Building (each state selects just two), and her statue was the first statue of a woman to be selected for the collection.[107]

Corrie Ten Boom

Consider Corrie ten Boom (1892-1983), who protected Jews during the Holocaust, paid dearly for her efforts and traveled the world with a message of forgiveness and hope.

At the outbreak of World War II, Corrie was in her late forties and lived with her father Casper and her sister Betsie. The family made a living by watchmaking and, as an expression of their Christian faith, often cared for foster children. After the Nazi war machine rolled through Holland and the *Sicherheitsdienst* (Secret Service or "SS") began rounding up Jews for extermination, the ten Booms decided to act.

They routinely housed 5 to 6 Jews or other fugitives in their home and worked to build a broader network called "the Beje group." Through these efforts, Corrie and her family saved over 800 people from the Nazi death camps.

On February 28, 1944, an informant betrayed the ten Boom family, and SS officers arrested Corrie, Casper, Betsie and other extended family members. Casper died of an illness ten days later in Scheveningen Prison, and Corrie and Betsie were soon deported to the Ravensbrück Concentration Camp.[108]

In a flea-ridden barracks crowded with other prisoners, Betsie encouraged Corrie to turn to Scripture. And the sisters even thanked God for the fleas because the pesky insects kept the guards out of their barracks and away from their prized possession: a Bible.

Together, Betsie and Corrie hung onto the truths of God's Word and ministered to their fellow prisoners in the cold and dark of the concentration camp.[109] Corrie later described the scene in her autobiography *The Hiding Place*:

Like waifs clustered around a blazing fire, we gathered
about it, holding out our hearts to its warmth and light.
The blacker the night around us grew, the brighter and
truer and more beautiful burned the word of God. . . . I
would look about us as Betsie read, watching the light
leap from face to face. More than conquerors. . . . It was
not a wish. It was a fact. We knew it, we experienced it
minute by minute—poor, hated, hungry. We are more
than conquerors. Not "we shall be." We are![110]

Betsie soon met the Author of these truths, for she succumbed to
malnourishment and illness in December of 1944. Soon after, Corrie
was released from German custody and returned to her home in
Holland.

After the war, Corrie began a ministry of hope and reconciliation,
stating confidently "God will give us the love to be able to forgive our
enemies." And she practiced what she preached. She met a former
Ravensbrück guard who begged her for forgiveness; and she tearfully
forgave him for his cruelty and complicity in Betsie's death.

Over the next thirty years, Corrie shared her story and the gospel in
more than sixty countries, proclaiming "Jesus is Victor." In 1983, at
the age of 91, Corrie joined Betsie in the presence of the One who
inspired their stand against the Holocaust and strengthened them in
the dark nights at Ravensbrück.[111]

Masao Yamada

Consider Masao Yamada (1907-1984), America's first Japanese
American chaplain who ministered in a volunteer *Nisei* unit and served
on the front lines in Europe during World War II.

Masao was born in 1907 to an immigrant plantation carpenter on
the Hawaiian island of Kauai. Because schooling options were limited
on the island, his parents sent him to a boarding school on Oahu.
While there, a Pastor named Takie Okumura led Masao to Christ.[112]

After high school, Masao attended the University of Hawaii and
worked as a youth leader for the Young Men's Christian Association
(YMCA). Upon graduation, he applied for a job with the YMCA; but

the position was given to a white applicant at a much higher salary. Indignant, Masao protested the decision to the president of the Honolulu YMCA, a wealthy financier named Frank Atherton. Masao thoroughly impressed Atherton with his bearing, boldness and dedication to fairness, and Atherton suggested that Masao pursue his seminary degree at Auburn Theological Seminary in New York.

After finishing his studies at Auburn and then Andover-Newton Theological Seminary in Boston, Masao returned to Hawaii and became the pastor at Central Kona Union Church. In 1935, he married Ai Mukaida, and they moved to Japan to study the language so they could minister more effectively to Japanese Americans. But the Japanese government quickly labeled them "pacifists" and forced them to leave the country.

Masao was serving a church on his native island of Kauai when World War II broke out, and he helped form and lead an emergency service committee on the island. In 1943, the U.S. Army formed the 442nd Regimental Combat Team, a unit comprised almost entirely of *Nisei* or second-generation Americans of Japanese ancestry (AJAs). When the army assigned Caucasian chaplains to the unit, Masao reached out to the officers in charge. His son later explained his reasoning, "My father knew from experience that the [AJA] boys from Hawaii were going to suffer prejudice when they went to the Mainland, and if he didn't go, there wouldn't be anyone to speak up for them."

Why did Masao think that? Well, he had good reason. On February 19, 1942, President Franklin Delano Roosevelt signed his infamous Executive Order 9066, which commanded the removal of all resident enemy aliens (including Japanese, Italians and Germans) from military areas on the West Coast. The War Department interpreted this broadly and decided that "military areas" should include ports, cities, industrial areas and even agricultural areas. And government officials soon forcibly removed AJAs and resident aliens from Japan from their homes and businesses.

These AJAs and resident aliens were given very short notice, were only allowed the possessions they could carry and were transported to relocation or internment camps in barren parts of the American west. All told, more than 110,000 AJAs and resident aliens from Japan were detained by the U.S. government until late in the war.[113]

Masao knew about these public events, and he volunteered to serve as chaplain for the 442nd despite or perhaps because of the treatment of Japanese Americans. In fact, many of the volunteers in the 442nd left their relocation camps to join the war effort. Masao wrote in his letters to Ai that these young men were ready to die to prove their loyalty to the United States.

In 1944, the 442nd headed to Europe along with the 100th Infantry Battalion (another *Nisei* unit) and then to the front in France. Masao was a noncombatant, but he was often at the front dodging bullets and explosions while praying with soldiers and comforting the dying. On September 1, 1944, Masao was gravely injured when his jeep hit a land mine. The explosion launched the vehicle thirty feet into the air, killed everyone in the jeep except Masao and peppered him with shrapnel. Despite these injuries, he was back with his men by the end of September.

In October of 1944, the 442nd and the 100th were tasked with rescuing the 141st Infantry (formerly part of the Texas National Guard), which was surrounded by German forces in the dense Vosges forest. The *Nisei* units fought a fierce, five-day battle amidst snow and ice and finally rescued the Texans; but not before the 442nd had suffered 1,000 casualties (800 dead and 200 wounded) out of 3,000 men. Texas Governor John Connally later paid tribute to the heroism and sacrifice of the 442nd Regimental Combat Team and the 100th Battalion by making every member of both units honorary Texans.[114] These exploits also earned the 442nd the title "The Purple Heart Regiment" for earning the most purple hearts of any unit in World War II.

Masao was in the midst of this terrible and deadly struggle, and he personally visited five or six hundred wounded men. He later wrote about the difficulty of comforting "the breaking soul" of dying soldiers. Masao served as the chaplain of the 442nd until the end of the war.

When he returned to Hawaii, Masao pastored the Church of the Holy Cross on the island of Hawaii and lobbied the University of Hawaii to build a campus in Hilo. In 1955, he moved to Oahu and became the chaplain for Hawaii State Hospital, which served mentally ill patients. He held that position until his retirement.

When he passed away in 1984, Masao was buried in the National Memorial Cemetery of the Pacific along with other members of the *Nisei* regiments.

President Harry S. Truman captured the impact of the 442nd and Masao when he spoke these words, "You have fought not only the enemy, but you have fought prejudice – and you have won. Keep up that fight, and we will continue to win – to make this great Republic stand for just what the Constitution says it stands for: the welfare of all the people all the time."[115]

The Reverend Doctor Martin Luther King Junior

Consider Reverend Doctor Martin Luther King Junior (1929-1968), the pastor and Civil Rights leader who helped end legal segregation and promoted equal protection and opportunities for black Americans. I have set out his formal name and titles above because many Americans overlook a key word, "Reverend."[116]

King was born in Atlanta, Georgia in 1929. An excellent student, he skipped two grades and entered Morehouse College at the age of 15. While at Morehouse, he experienced a call to ministry, and he pursued his seminary training at Crozer Theological Seminary and then Boston University.

During this period, he was influenced by the nonviolent civil disobedience of Mahatma Ghandi in India and the work of theologian Walter Rauschenbusch, who argued that Christianity addresses the whole human being and not just the eternal soul. After graduation, King and his wife Coretta moved to Montgomery, Alabama, and MLK took his first pastorate at Dexter Avenue Baptist Church.

In the winter of 1955, Rosa Parks refused to give up her bus seat to a white passenger, and she was arrested for her stand by sitting. In response, a group of black pastors formed the Montgomery Improvement Association, elected King as their president and implemented a city-wide bus boycott. King set the tone for the Montgomery Bus Boycott, stating: "We must keep God in the forefront. Let us be Christian in all our actions."

Don't miss how quickly these events transpired. Rosa Parks was arrested on December 1, 1955. King was elected as president of the

MIA on December 5, 1955, and the 26-year old King was immediately thrust into the spotlight on and controversy surrounding the bus boycott.

On January 26, 1956, King was arrested for the first time on a trumped-up driving offense as part of a "Get Tough" campaign to end the boycott. On January 27, 1956, he arrived home late from a lengthy MIA meeting. The phone rang, and he decided to pick it up. The voice on the line snarled a racial slur and then these words: "[W]e are tired of you and your mess now. And if you aren't out of this town in three days, we're going to blow your brains out, and blow up your house."[117]

On that evening, King faced a crisis. His life had been relatively peaceful and quiet up to that point, but everything had changed in the course of a few months. Yes, the discrimination and hatred in Montgomery were very real and needed to be rooted out. But he had a wife and young daughter to consider, a church to lead and a career in ministry to think about.

As King described later, he prayed, "Lord, I'm down here trying to do what's right. I think I'm right. I think the cause that we represent is right. But Lord, I must confess that I'm weak now. I'm faltering. I'm losing my courage. And I can't let the people see me like this because if they see me weak and losing my courage, they will begin to get weak." Then, King had an experience that changed the rest of his life. He explained:

> And it seemed at that moment that I could hear an inner voice saying to me, "Martin Luther, stand up for righteousness. Stand up for justice. Stand up for truth. And lo I will be with you, even until the end of the world." … I heard the voice of Jesus saying still to fight on. He promised never to leave me, never to leave me alone…[118]

This experience steeled King for the fight ahead. During the threats, arrests and violence that followed, King never doubted his purpose or protection and often referred to that midnight meeting with God as the source of his resolute courage. On January 30, King's home was bombed, yet he encouraged the crowd to stay the course on protesting injustice through nonviolent means.

In the fall of 1956, the U.S. Supreme Court ruled bus segregation unconstitutional, and King was one of the first passengers on the integrated buses on December 21, 1956. This victory in Montgomery made King a national figure, and he used that influence to launch the Southern Christian Leadership Conference in 1957. Under his leadership, the SCLC organized protests in major Southern cities, including Albany, Atlanta, Birmingham, St. Augustine and Selma.

During the campaign in Birmingham, Alabama, Police Commissioner Eugene "Bull" Conner arrested King for demonstrating without a permit. And, while sitting in jail, King wrote a powerful response to critical white clergy in Birmingham and called them to assist in the Civil Rights movement. He wrote:

> In the midst of blatant injustices inflicted upon the Negro, I have watched white churchmen stand on the sideline and mouth pious irrelevancies and sanctimonious trivialities. In the midst of a mighty struggle to rid our nation of racial and economic injustice, I have heard many ministers say: "Those are social issues, with which the gospel has no real concern." And I have watched many churches commit themselves to a completely other worldly religion which makes a strange, un-Biblical distinction between body and soul, between the sacred and the secular.

He then reminded these pastors of the church's history and warned them about inaction:

> There was a time when the church was very powerful—in the time when the early Christians rejoiced at being deemed worthy to suffer for what they believed...By their effort and example they brought an end to such ancient evils as infanticide and gladiatorial contests. Things are different now. So often the contemporary church is a weak, ineffectual voice with an uncertain sound...If today's church does

not recapture the sacrificial spirit of the early church, it will lose its authenticity, forfeit the loyalty of millions, and be dismissed as an irrelevant social club with no meaning for the twentieth century.[119]

King's efforts in Birmingham were ultimately successful as stores and other businesses integrated, and this victory became a turning point in the effort to end segregation in the American South. On June 23, 1963, King gave his famous "I Have a Dream" speech to more than 250,000 participants in the March on Washington. And, in 1964, King attended the signing of the Civil Rights Act, which protected black Americans from discrimination in public places and employment.

Later that year, at the age of 35, King became the youngest recipient of the Nobel Peace Prize and *Time Magazine's* first black "Man of the Year." In 1965, King turned his attention to voting rights; and, after protesters were beaten by policemen on the William Pettus bridge in Selma, Alabama, President Johnson announced the Voting Rights Act. This federal law now prohibits racial discrimination in the voting process.

During these efforts, King was threatened, arrested, stabbed in the chest, and even stoned. Still, he marched on.

On April 3, 1968, King delivered his "I've Been to the Mountaintop" speech while in Memphis, Tennessee, to protest the treatment of sanitation workers. He concluded the speech: "Like anybody, I would like to live a long life. Longevity has its place. But I'm not concerned about that now. I just want to do God's will. And He's allowed me to go up to the mountain. And I've looked over. And I've seen the promised land."[120]

The next day, James Earl Ray shot and killed King while he was on the balcony of the Lorraine Motel.

King's funeral was an international event attended by more than 50,000 people. In 1968, the United States declared King's birthday, January 15th, a national holiday. And, in 2011, the Dr. Martin Luther King, Jr. Memorial was dedicated in Washington, D.C.

Dr. Martin Luther King, Jr. is a seminal example of Christian citizenship. His courage and conviction pricked the conscience of the nation and forced Americans to look clearly at the injustice that had played out since the founding—and to do something about it. And he called Christians to look back, look up and lock arms with brothers and sisters in Christ to end segregation and build toward a just and equitable society for all people.[121]

I think often of King's midnight encounter with Jesus during the dangerous and uncertain days of the Montgomery Bus Boycott. Does not Christ say the same thing to us in His Word? "[Insert your name here], stand up for righteousness. Stand up for justice. Stand up for truth. And lo I will be with you, even until the end of the world." May we heed Christ's commands and follow King's example.

Luis Palau

Consider Luis Palau (1934-), the Argentinian-born evangelist and "The Billy Graham of Latin America" who has proclaimed the Good News and built relationships with government officials across the globe. Palau was born in Buenos Aires, Argentina, in 1934. His father was a Christian, having come to Christ through the ministry of a British missionary. In 1947, Palau committed his life to Christ. And, in 1952, he heard evangelist Billy Graham on the radio for the first time.

While listening to Graham, Palau prayed that God would lead him into evangelism. In 1960, a pastor named Ray Stedman invited Palau to the United States, and Palau studied for the ministry at Multnomah School of the Bible in Portland, Oregon. Palau soon married Patricia Scofield, and he served as the Spanish interpreter for Billy Graham's evangelistic crusade in Fresno, California, in 1962.[122]

In 1964, Palau began regular radio broadcasts to the Spanish-speaking world. Next, from 1966 to 1974, he launched major evangelistic crusades in Columbia, Mexico, Honduras, Guatemala, Peru, Nicaragua and Argentina with crowds ranging from 20,000 to 187,000. In 1979, Palau joined up with Billy Graham for a crusade in Sydney, Australia.

In the 1980s, Palau launched crusades in Scotland, England, Singapore, New Zealand, Hong Kong, Peru, and the former Soviet Union. His crusade in the former Soviet Union was especially significant because it was one of the first evangelistic meetings in

Hungary and Russia after the fall of the Iron Curtain. During a message in Leningrad, more than half of the audience responded to a call for salvation.

Palau continued his global efforts in the 1990s with crusades in the United States and around the world. In 1994, while speaking at a crusade, Palau called on Guatemala's President to declare a National Day of Prayer. And, in 1996, Palau met with Honduran President Carlos Roberta Reina to discuss the gospel, governance and economics. After the 9/11 attacks in the United States, Palau attended meetings with President George W. Bush and other religious leaders at the White House.

In 2008, Palau's evangelistic event in Buenos Aires, Argentina, drew a record 850,000 people.

Also, in 2008, the Luis Palau Association launched its first Season of Service as part of a major event in Portland, Oregon. This effort, now commonly known as CityServe, equips local churches to meet key community needs in an effort to point people to Jesus. In 2011, Kevin Palau (Luis' son) appeared on ABC News along with former Portland Mayor Sam Adam to discuss the impact of these partnerships between churches and the city.

In 2014, Luis preached to more than 14,000 people at the Hangzhou Chong-yi Christian Church. And, while in China, he met with the U.S. Ambassador Jon Huntsman; Jr.; Mr. Wang Zuo An, the director of China's State Administration for Religious Affairs (SARA); and other Chinese officials. In these meetings, Palau encouraged the Chinese government to ease restrictions on Christian churches and to see Christianity as a benefit to Chinese society.[123]

Today, Kevin and Andrew, Luis' sons, lead the Luis Palau Association, but Luis still ministers through radio and TV sermons. Palau announced a cancer diagnosis in 2018; but, as of the writing of this chapter, he is still successfully fighting the disease.

In 2019, Palau published his spiritual memoir *Life on Fire*. And, in a recent interview, he addressed his failing health by stating, "So I'm at peace…I can lay back and rejoice that the gospel goes on. We've got all these evangelists all over the world. It's quite exciting."[124]

In sum, Luis Palau has ministered to government officials all over the world, has connected churches to community needs, and has preached the Good News of Jesus Christ to approximately one billion people.[125]

Summary

What do you think of when you hear the phrase "Christian citizenship?" Do you think of slave holders, segregationist lunch counter owners, and wild-eyed Evangelical partisans trying to force a theocracy on the United States? If you listen to the general cultural narrative about Christians and especially Christians involved in public life, you could certainly arrive at that conclusion. And the Christian past does contain some very dark deeds and evil characters. But focusing exclusively on those deeds and characters fails to tell the full, remarkable story of the Christian church down through the ages.

Christians can certainly be charged with whitewashing their history, and this practice is, at best, shortsighted. But, if we only focus on the bad actors in Christian history, we commit the very same error as those that white out the sin-stained chapters. We tell a false tale about Christian citizenship.

We should not tell the story of slaveholding preachers without also telling the story of Equiano, Moore, Wilberforce, Douglass and Tubman. We should not tell the story of colonial missionaries without telling the story of John McKenzie and the worldwide rise of self-government. And we should not tell the story of the church's complicity in the Jim Crow South without also recounting the efforts of Martin Luther King, Jr. and other Christians involved in the Civil Rights Movement. A full and transparent review of the church's history and its impact tells a remarkable story of sacrifice, service and transformation rooted in the Christian gospel.

Have you ever felt nervous or embarrassed to admit that you are a Christian, especially in a public setting? Well, let's get over that. We are followers of Jesus. And we follow in the footsteps of these remarkable Christians who, down through the ages, have protected children, dignified women, helped end chattel slavery, stood up to tyrants, gave their lives and fortunes for the oppressed, and laid the groundwork for the freedom, peace and prosperity of advanced modernity.

In sum, I am a Christian, and I follow in the footsteps of these giants of the faith as they followed Christ. The church's legacy is imperfect but impressive; and we should step into the public square confident of this remarkable past.

5 APPLY TO THE UNITED STATES

W e have reviewed Biblical principles, Biblical examples and historical examples of Christian citizenship. Now, let's apply those principles and examples to our citizenship here in the United States (and, by extension, to citizenship in other participatory democracies).

As we launch into this application section, let's do a brief review of American civics. Since we are applying Biblical principles to American government, we should have a clear understanding of the form of government in the United States.

Some of the readers of this book may roll their eyes at this statement. I mean, what is this—a fourth grade civics class? I understand that question, but American civics education is in crisis. As of 2017, only 25% of American students reached the "proficient" standard on the National Assessment of Educational Progress (NAEP) civics assessment.[126] Further, according to a poll conducted by the Annenberg Public Policy Center at the University of Pennsylvania in 2019, approximately 61% of Americans are unable to name all three branches of government, and 37% of Americans cannot name a single right guaranteed by the First Amendment.[127]

Further, as American citizens, we are constantly bombarded with competing views of the history, structure and purpose of American government. So, let's do a quick refresher.

Here's my summary of American government: We live in a republic that makes us royal and assumes we're righteous. Here's what I mean.

Brief Review of American Civics

We live in a democratic republic. That is the form of government anticipated by the Declaration of Independence and set out in the United States Constitution. The Declaration of Independence primarily explained our reasons for separating from Great Britain but also set out our founding principles. Here's a key concluding statement from the Declaration:

> We, therefore, **the Representatives of the united States of America**, in General Congress, Assembled, appealing to the Supreme Judge of the world for the rectitude of our intentions, do, in the Name, **and by Authority of the good People of these Colonies**, solemnly publish and declare, That these United Colonies are, and of Right ought to be Free and Independent States [emphasis added]...[128]

Note that this declaration was made by the representatives of the various colonies pursuant to the authority of the people rather than a monarch. Further, after experimenting with a weaker form of government called the Articles of Confederation, representatives of the states signed off on the text of the Constitution on September 17, 1787. And the Constitution was ratified by New Hampshire (the ninth state to do so) and became the law of the land on June 21, 1788.

The preamble reads:

> **We the People of the United States**, in Order to form a more perfect Union, establish Justice, insure domestic Tranquility, provide for the common defence, promote the general Welfare, and secure the Blessings of Liberty to ourselves and our Posterity, **do ordain and establish this Constitution for the United States of America** [emphasis added].[129]

Once again, the authority for the Constitution comes from the people as exercised by their representatives at the Constitutional Convention. Further, the Declaration of Independence and the U.S. Constitution both recognize the federal nature of the union—the central (what we often call "federal") government is distinct from the government of the states.

If you look up your state constitution, you will find a similar structure of government. For example, the 1851 Indiana Constitution includes this preamble:

> TO THE END, that justice be established, public order maintained, and liberty perpetuated; **WE, the People of the State of Indiana**, grateful to ALMIGHTY GOD for the free exercise of the right to choose our own form of government, **do ordain this Constitution** [emphasis added].

In sum, as Americans, we live in a democracy in the sense that the people collectively are vested with ultimate authority. And we live in a republic in the sense that we elect representatives from among us to vote on critical issues and to oversee the day-to-day affairs of the nation.

Therefore, we, the citizens of the United States, are "royal." We collectively wield the power once held by the crown, and this makes us citizen sovereigns. The kings and queens of old have nothing on a single mom from inner-city Detroit or a farm hand from rural Nebraska who casts a ballot to determine the direction of the nation.

But this privilege also comes with a critical responsibility for the present and future of the country.

Next, the American experiment assumes we are righteous. In 1788, a democratic republic was a novelty. Most of the nations on the planet still utilized some form of monarchy, which has been the default system of government throughout human history. But the American founders charted a new course and declared that the American people collectively would be better at controlling the destiny of the nation than a line of kings and queens who varied in competence and courage.

But this experiment relied heavily upon a key assumption. The founders assumed the American people could and would govern themselves according to a set of moral principles. They built the experiment around the premise that no autocratic force would be necessary to control American citizens because they would have internal controls and would guide the nation according to a Judeo-Christian moral vision, which was prevalent at the time.

John Adams, who helped engineer the American experiment, stated it this way, "Our Constitution was made only for a moral and religious people. It is wholly inadequate to the government of any other."[130] And, as I noted previously, George Washington stated the following in his Farewell Address: "Of all the dispositions and habits which lead to political prosperity, Religion and morality are indispensable supports."[131]

This point may seem controversial; but I also think it's obvious. Let's step back from the culture wars and divisive political scene right now and just think about the nuts and bolts of the American system. Simply put, an effective system of self-government requires self-control. If we, as citizens, do not control our baser appetites like lust, greed, and pride, our society will soon devolve into chaos, tribalism and brute-force, high-stakes power struggles (sound familiar?).

Democracy works best when we work to control ourselves and order our lives according to a proper moral standard. I used the word "righteous" in this section, and that word may sound a little "high and mighty." But it is an important word. First, according to Proverbs 14:34, righteousness exalts a nation. So, as a Christian, I believe that true flourishing will only come if we order our national affairs according to God's good design.

But, in a more general sense, righteousness simply points to the fact that there is a right and wrong. American culture currently maintains that pluralism must mean relativism, i.e. that the only way we can get along is to deemphasize our deeply held convictions and act as if there is no truth.

This approach is simply insufficient for our increasingly complex and quickly changing world. We need the word "evil" in our vocabulary, and we need a properly ordered sense of right and wrong to navigate the coming years. The founders assumed that American citizens would be armed with these all-important moral concepts and would govern themselves and the nation according to them.

Before I move on, I need to address another growing trend in broader American culture. Many in the media, academia and now the general public paint the United States as inherently evil and racist from its very start and at its very core.[132] And, the argument continues, the entire system should be torn down and rebuilt from the ground up.

What are Christians to make of such a claim? Two thoughts.

First, this view of American history overlooks America's complex but remarkable past. Instead of providing a comprehensive survey of American history, I will simply point out two memorials: The National Memorial for Peace and Justice in Montgomery, Alabama, and the Normandy American Cemetery in France.

The National Memorial for Peace and Justice, which opened to the public in 2018, displays 800 hanging steel monuments in remembrance of black Americans murdered in documented lynchings across the United States. These 800 columns do not represent individuals; rather, they represent the American counties where these lynchings occurred.[133] This memorial powerfully illustrates America's dark history of slavery and racism. So, the next time we are tempted to treat America as God's "almost chosen" nation, we should remember those 800 steel monuments and the thousands of murdered image-bearers they represent.

Next, the Normandy American Cemetery in France contains the graves of 9,385 American soldiers who gave their lives to free Europe from a fascist regime. When we entered World War II in 1941, no country other than the United States had the industrial capacity, manpower and wealth to wage a global war against both Nazi Germany and Imperial Japan. Further, perhaps the most remarkable event in American history is what we did not do after World War II.

From 1945 to 1949, the United States was the only nation on the planet that possessed the atomic bomb.[134] Can you imagine what the world might look like if Hitler or Stalin had developed the nuclear bomb first? Even without unilateral control of the A-bomb, these dictators married political ideology and military technology and murdered millions.

Instead of world conquest, we set out to rebuild Europe and Japan and spent our blood and treasure to protect other nations from an aggressive, atheistic communism that has now led to approximately 100 million deaths in 100 years.[135] These remarkable actions reflected a post-World War II Christian moral consensus and Christ's command to "...love your enemies..." (Mt. 5:44). So, the next time we are tempted to treat America as the "Great Satan" or an intrinsically evil force in history and the world, we should remember those 9,385 graves.

The Christian doctrine of sin is a helpful tool in processing these dueling historical realities. Our human inclination is to see people and institutions as all good or all bad. But, as Scripture tells us, we have all sinned and come short of God's glory (Rom. 6:23). And, at the same time, we have God's law written on our hearts, are made in His image and are capable of great good (Rom. 2:15). Therefore, we have the capacity to be monsters and heroes all at the same time. This is true of our nation as well.

So, looking at the United States through red, white and blue-tinted glasses does not tell the full story. But neither does the dark-tinted, singular focus on America's grave sins. Two things can be true at the same time, and we should understand and tell America's full story. Her history is magnificent and, at times, monstrous, and we should work to build on her better nature and toward a better future.

Second, the current critique of the United States targets more than her history. It targets her principles. I am sure you are familiar with the argument, but many commentators and activists claim that the Declaration of Independence and the U.S. Constitution were nothing more than a flowery cover-up for patriarchal and racist white men and a feint of freedom designed to secure their privilege and power.[136]

As Christians, we should consider America's founding principles in light of Scripture. Let's review the Declaration of Independence and the U.S. Constitution in turn.

The Declaration states, "We hold these truths to be self-evident, that all men are created equal, that they are endowed by their Creator with certain unalienable Rights, that among these are Life, Liberty and the pursuit of Happiness..." A number of the American founders were hypocritical when they signed this document because they owned slaves, and the suffragists later pointed out that the Declaration should have read "...all men and women are created equal."[137] But our founding document sourced rights and human dignity from the same place as Scripture—God's created order (Gen 1:26-27).

Therefore, this founding principle is sound. We should not be surprised when human rulers and movements coopt truth in their quest for power and wealth. But truth has a stubborn way of winning out if properly applied over time.

Even many of the founders recognized this hypocrisy. Thomas Jefferson (who owned slaved) denounced the evils of slavery in the first draft of the Declaration of Independence, and a number of the founders opposed the institution.[138] Further, key advocates like Frederick Douglass and Martin Luther King, Jr. strongly denounced American slavery and racism but always pointed back to the words of the Declaration as an aspirational, guiding truth.[139]

The United States fought a Civil War to end the evil institution of slavery, and we should continue to work toward the fully just and equal society envisioned by the Declaration. The principle that all people are created in the image of God and are worthy of equal treatment and respect is a Biblical and sound one.

Next, what about the U.S. Constitution? Should Biblical Christians be ambivalent about our form of government?

Scripture does not specifically dictate a form of government. Rather, it dictates principles about human government, describes human regimes and explains that Christ will one day return as our just and eternal King. So, in my review of Scripture, we are free to experiment with forms of government as long as our government fulfills its Biblical role and we practice proper submission.

This brings me to one of my favorite descriptions of our republic: the United States is a product of "humble faith and common sense."[140] The founders applied Judeo-Christian principles and modern enlightenment ideas in their design of the U.S. Constitution, but even enlightenment thinkers like John Locke were heavily influenced by Biblical concepts.[141]

If you were given the opportunity to form a government, what form would you choose and what principles would you include? The Old Testament prophet Samuel warned Israel about the dangers and foibles of a human monarchy (I Sam. 8:10-22), and the book of Judges stands as a stark warning against anarchy. No human form of government is perfect, but the American system includes checks and balances to frustrate human greed for wealth and power, accountability of officials to the people they govern, a federal system that devolves power to the states, and protections against government action that violates the consciences and equal dignity of its citizens.

The founders were students of Scripture and of history, and they carefully constructed an ordered liberty to, as I mentioned above, chain our worst instincts and unchain our best ones. And this ordered liberty catalyzed an exponential increase in human ingenuity, productivity and prosperity that has blessed the United States and much of the world.

In sum, I am with Winston Churchill, who said, "Many forms of Government have been tried, and will be tried in this world of sin and woe. No one pretends that democracy is perfect or all-wise. Indeed it has been said that democracy is the worst form of Government except for all those other forms that have been tried...."[142]

Has sin affected the American system? Yes, just like every other institution and system. Have American politicians and the American people, at times, failed to live up to the republic's founding principles? Absolutely. But, the Declaration of Independence grounds our republic on the equal dignity of all people, and the U.S. Constitution stands as a remarkable rethinking of human government.

I recognize that other Christians may land in a different place. But, after a close review of Scripture and America's founding documents, I believe Christians should work to renew the American experiment according to its founding formula of equal dignity, humble faith and common sense.

Application to American Government

Now, let's do our best to put down the banner of our political tribe and apply the principles and examples we have studied thus far to American government.

To begin, we should apply these Biblical principles and examples we have studied to the American republic rather than imperial Rome. The New Testament was written in the context of Roman autocratic rule, and we should absolutely follow the example of Jesus, Paul and members of the early church in their interactions with Roman and Jewish officials. But we should also consider the Old Testament figures who participated in foreign governments.

My argument here is simple: Christians in every nation should carefully study their nation's form of government and apply Biblical principles to that form of government. For example, Chinese Christians should study and understand the Communist Party of China, the National Congress, the Central Committee and the Standing Committee. Since religious worship is being suppressed and even persecuted in China,[143] Chinese Christians should consider the early church in Rome as an applicable example and model.

However, since we, as American citizens, have access and authority due to our constitutional order, we should carefully consider Daniel, Esther and Nehemiah due to their participation in foreign governments.

Because of the complexities of public life, I will set out three conclusions or guiding principles that I have reached after studying these issues and ministering in this space for more than a decade. Feel free to disagree and to apply Biblical principles in your context and according to your conscience. But here are my conclusions: (1) we are Christians, (2) we are Caesar and (3) we are citizens.

We are Christians.

First, we are Christians. You may be thinking, "Wow, Josh. That was insightful. We are followers of Jesus. Slow clap for the brilliant and helpful insight."

Well, just hold on a minute. Remember the stat that approximately 60% of Christians receive little to no "political discipleship" from their churches?[144] Many Christians have been catechized in their political engagement by political parties, their families ("Grandpa voted for [insert favored party], and so should you") and the news media. And Christians have fallen into the same political factionalism as the rest of society. Even more alarming, many Christians are finding their identity in and ordering their lives around their socio-political tribe rather than their Savior.

This is primarily a discipleship and spiritual maturity problem that we must all prayerfully consider. I wrestle with this temptation. I have opinions about politicians (who will best lead my state and nation) and about public policy (what laws will promote justice and true flourishing). But I must remind myself that I am a Christian first. And I must engage with that identity and the church's public witness in mind.

The above analysis is important but has become a bit cliché. I imagine that most of us agree that we should find our identity in Jesus and not a political party. But what does that mean in the context of a two-party system, divisive and important elections and key policy discussions that affect the direction of the nation?

I find it helpful to think of this in the context of marriage. My wife, Carissa, and I are celebrating 13 years of marriage this year. In other words, I am just now learning how much I don't know about the institution and about her. Two people striving to follow Jesus together is not for wimps. At least that is what Carissa says! But we have been ministry partners for 13 years and are looking forward to the rest of the journey. Further, marriage is exactly the example Paul uses in Ephesians 5 to explain the mysterious union between Christ and the church.

With that in mind, I vowed on my wedding day to cherish and honor Carissa and to prioritize that relationship above all other human relationships. I am free to travel, minister, develop appropriate friendships with other people and strenuously engage in my individual calling. But I would violate Scripture and my marriage vows if I prioritized my ministry in a way that significantly neglected my family or valued another relationship above my relationship with my wife (I Tim 5:8; Eph. 5:25-33; 1 Peter 3:7).

The same is true in public life. We should strenuously promote that which is right, true, just and beautiful. We should be active members of our cities, states and nation; and we should bring our best ideas to bear in public life. But if our engagement in politics begins to jeopardize Biblical principles, draws us away from our relationship with Christ or damages our public witness, then politics has dethroned King Jesus and crowned itself the lord of our life. This is a significant betrayal of that all-important relationship.

Our allegiance to Christ is a non-negotiable and should be on public display. My wedding ring is always on, and it is a public reminder of my commitment to Carissa. And, in a similar way, our followers on social media, the leaders of our political parties, our constituents (if an elected official) and the general public should know about our prior and ultimate commitment.

In sum, many Christians are consciously or subconsciously following culture's political play book. Instead, we should be doing politics by the Book. We should prioritize our gospel witness while engaging in public life. We are Christians first.

We are Caesar.

Next, let's review Christ's statement in Matthew 22:21: "Render therefore unto Caesar the things which are Caesar's; and unto God the things that are God's." This verse raises the following question: "In the American context, who is 'Caesar?'" Many American Christians think of "Caesar" as the president, congress, or the Supreme Court. But that is inexact.

Caesar, the Roman emperor, wielded ultimate authority in the Roman state. So, who wields ultimate authority in the American system? As discussed above, we do. We, the citizens of the United States, are collectively "Caesar."

So, does this entitle us to dress up in contrived Roman togas made of bed sheets, don a crown and demand that our families fan us with palm leaves and serve us with grapes? Nope. And we may want to consider how well that worked out for Julius Caesar. Joking aside, we are citizen sovereigns, and that authority comes with responsibility.

Jesus said to "Render therefore unto Caesar the things which are Caesar's..." (Matt. 22:21). So, what does Caesar require of us in the American context? Like the Christian citizens of any government, we owe the state general civic obedience and respect. But the American Caesar requires more of us than that. The American form of government requires our principled participation.

If no one voted or ran for office, the American republic would collapse. And if American citizens do not promote truth, justice and equality in government, our political experiment will quickly devolve into something akin to the self-interested and bloody mob rule of the late Athenian democracy.

The fact that we are Caesar cuts against two common notions about Christian engagement in public life.

First, I often hear church leaders declare that they will be avoiding politics and public life entirely to focus on the gospel. And I understand that sentiment (see point #1 We are Christians). But that declaration overlooks the authority and, therefore, responsibility American Christians have under our constitutional order.

Next, I often hear this statement, "Well, the church always flourishes under persecution." I agree that persecution purifies the church and is to be expected by those that follow Jesus (Mt. 13:21; John 15:20). But we are also citizen sovereigns called to rule with wisdom, justice and mercy (Micah 6:8; Pro. 8:15). For this reason, we should not respond to the growing legal and cultural challenges to the gospel with a resigned tone. Why? Because these challenges are happening in our jurisdiction!

Remember the list of benefits the American experiment has provided to the American church? Here's that list again: tax exemptions, private property rights, an institutional separation of church and state, the rule of law, religious freedom, financial wealth, individual liberty and powerful technologies.

Has God, in his sovereignty, placed us here as American Christians to simply shrug these off and watch them burn down? I do not claim to know exactly how God is working in our times, but the loss of these benefits would greatly disrupt the work of the gospel here and abroad.

Just consider the loss of the minister's housing allowance and property tax exemptions. Many pastors rely on the housing allowance to make their low income stretch just far enough to provide for a family while in full-time ministry. And many churches simply could not afford their property taxes or, at least, would be forced to greatly curtail ministry staffing and activities if taxed without an exemption.

True, the early church flourished under persecution, but Christianity is quickly disappearing in the Middle East as Christians are being killed or are emigrating due to terrorism and other forms of persecution.[145] For these reasons, we should prepare for persecution and even welcome it (Matt. 5:12) if it comes due to developments beyond our control. But, as citizen sovereigns of the United States, we have the authority and, I would argue, the responsibility to attempt to prevent such persecution in our times.

In sum, I consider citizenship a matter of stewardship—just like parenting, health and finances. This means that I should not abandon the task of citizenship simply because it is complex or hard. Imagine telling your child, "You know, parenting is dirty and hard and complicated, so we will be putting you up for adoption." What? Really? Christian citizenship is a tension to be managed rather than a problem to be solved; and now is the time to engage in that role for the glory of God and the good of all people.

We are Christians first, but we are also Caesar.

We are Citizens.

Most Christians are familiar with God's command to the Jewish exiles to seek the *shalom* or peace and prosperity of the polytheistic and diverse city of Babylon (Jer. 29:4-7), but the context of that verse is important. When the exiled Jews reached Babylon, they settled in a Jewish enclave along the river Chebar with the expectation that God would soon intervene and return them to Israel (Ezek. 1:1).

This response is quite understandable from a patriotic perspective. Consider the soul-wrenching grief of national destruction described in Psalm 137:1, "By the rivers of Babylon, there we sat down...we wept, when we remembered Zion." However, despite this pain and tragedy,

God specifically commanded the Jews to leave their "holy huddle" and to seek the peace and prosperity of their new home.

Similar to the Jews in Babylon, we often react from a place of deep sadness and angst over lost cultural influence. In fact, many Christians still long for a return to a perceived golden age with at a least a sense of uniformity around Christian social mores. But I think we can all agree that those days have gone the way of Blockbuster absent a significant spiritual renewal in the United States. At times, I grieve this as well. But that grief can lead to angry, desperate engagement that does little for our future.

Regardless of disagreements on why this happened or how we got here, we are here. We live in an increasingly multicultural society with a primarily secular public square. Even if you live in a small town in the Midwest, you have probably noticed these trends. By way of example, I recently spoke to a pastor who lives in a mid-sized city in Indiana, and he has neighbors on his block from almost every continent.

Given the above, should we attempt to legislate a return to a "Christian" America of yesteryear, thus pegging all people that think, look or worship differently than us as "unAmerican"? No. As we have studied, God did not ordain government to coerce converts or to prefer Christians over non-Christians in the administration of justice. Instead, we need to take a cue from Jeremiah and engage in public life in a selfless, serving way.

I need to acknowledge something here. As a millennial, the above is fairly easy for me to write. By the time I graduated law school, most of these major cultural changes were in full swing. But I have engaged in conversations with my grandparents, my parents, and other brothers and sisters in Christ that have lived through the swift and startling cultural changes of the last fifty to seventy-five years. Their sense of grief and loss over Biblical values, the family unit and the church's influence is understandably deep and raw. If you are a more experienced Christian citizen, please hear me. My generation needs your wisdom, experience and guidance to overcome the significant challenges of our times and to lay the foundation for a better tomorrow.

This leads me to the most important motivation for Christian involvement in the public square: Christ's command to love our neighbors as ourselves (Matt. 22:39). In a participatory democracy, am I truly loving my neighbors if I do not engage on questions of justice, equality, peace and prosperity that directly and significantly impact their lives? Am I truly serving my neighbor if I remain silent about ideas, policies or systems that prevent true flourishing? I think not. We should love our neighbors by engaging in public life.

In other words, we are citizens. We are inhabitants of our towns or cities, and we should work together with other citizens for the common good. We should not be religious jerks while strengthening the barbed wire around our church-shaped bunkers; rather, we should be ambassadors of heaven serving our neighbors and strengthening our cities. This change in motivation is a simple concept, but it has the power to fundamentally alter the church's public witness and future in the United States.

So, let's act like citizens of America, not combatants at the Alamo.

In review, we live in a republic that makes us royal and assumes we're righteous. And we should focus on these three guiding principles as we engage in public life: we are Christians, we are Caesar and we are citizens.

As I promised at the beginning of the book, I have been long on the wind up. My goal has been to build a deep Biblical foundation for Christian citizenship. And that is what we have (hopefully) accomplished in Step #1 – Go Over Your Citizenship. Now, with that foundation established, let's move on to three key action steps.

STEP #2 OFFER PRAYER FOR AND BUILD RELATIONSHIPS WITH OFFICIALS

6 THE RED TELEPHONE

O ur world almost ended on October 27, 1962. As you might recall from a history or civics class, the Cuban Missile Crisis involved a clandestine attempt by the Soviet Union to smuggle nuclear weapons into Cuba in an effort to counter U.S. ballistic missiles in Turkey. And the U.S. responded with a naval blockade around the island.

On October 27th, Cuban forces shot down a U.S. U-2 spy plane, killing pilot Rudolf Anderson, Jr. Then, U.S. ships detected a Russian submarine, and the destroyer USS *Beale* dropped practice depth charges to force the sub to the surface.

The Russian captain Valentin Savitsky assumed his submarine was under a live-fire attack and prepared to launch a nuclear-tipped torpedo at the aircraft carrier USS *Randolph*. Fortunately, the Russian command structure required three senior officers to agree to the use of nuclear weapons. And the second-in-command, Vasili Arkhipov, refused to start the end of the world. The submarine eventually surfaced, and the nuclear exchange was avoided.

Meanwhile, a U.S. reconnaissance plane inadvertently ventured into Soviet air space near Alaska, and Russian MIGs scrambled to intercept it. In response, U.S. Delta Dagger fighters armed with nuclear air-to-air missiles (was everything tipped with a nuclear weapon back then?) lifted off to protect the reconnaissance plane. Fortunately, the opposing fighters never met each other, and World War III was avoided.[146]

No matter how many times I study the Cuban Missile Crisis, I still grow tense while reading about these close scrapes with nuclear Armageddon. Fortunately, these events also rattled the leadership of the U.S. and the U.S.S.R. And the two superpowers developed a line of direct communication rather than relying on slow diplomatic channels.

This line went live in 1963, and it was soon popularized in comics and movies as the "red telephone." Interestingly, the hotline has never taken the form of a telephone, instead relying on technologies such as teletype, fax and email to avoid verbal miscommunication. But the public perception of the hotline as a "red telephone" persists. The hotline still exists today, and American and Russian technicians send emails once an hour to ensure that the line of communication is in working order.[147]

The United States now finds itself in a sort of civil cold war, with increasing polarization and tribalism. The American republic has always been a bit, well, rowdy; but these developments indicate a deep and growing divide among Americans about basic principles and a divergent view of the American future.

For these reasons, we need the cultural equivalent of a "red telephone." We need a line of communication that will allow for much-needed discussion among warring cultural forces. And it just so happens that the New Testament outlines a simple but neglected practice that could have profound impact on our current cultural brinkmanship: the practice of praying for and building relationships with elected officials. Here are some practical pointers on beginning or strengthening that practice.

Pray for Government Officials.

Most Christians are familiar with the command to pray for elected officials in I Timothy 2:1-4, but I find it helpful to review the passage from time to time:

I exhort therefore, that, first of all, supplications, prayers, intercessions, and giving of thanks, be made for all men; [f]or kings, and for all that are in authority; that we may lead a quiet and peaceable life in all godliness and honesty. For this is good and acceptable in the sight of God our Saviour; Who will have all men to be saved, and to come unto the knowledge of the truth.

Let's break that down. We should pray for "...all that are in authority." The most apparent application of this passage is, of course, prayer for elected officials. But, before I move on to that point, who else has authority in the American system? You got it. We do! So, we should pray for each other and for the American people collectively. We all need God's wisdom, courage and strength to guide our nation through these difficult days.

Next, we should pray for our government officials. Easy enough, right? But, before we glance over this, let's participate in an exercise. Think about a politician that you absolutely can't stand. Think about a politician who you believe will cause irreparable damage to your city, state or the country. Have someone in mind? Well, when was the last time you earnestly prayed for him or her? And I do not mean this imprecatory psalm: "Let his days be few; and let another take his office" (Ps. 109:8).

You know this as well as I do, but it is customary in American political life to pillory said politician on social media, question their humanity (or at least sanity) and come up with humorous ways to joke about their villainy and ineptitude.

In light of these tendencies, we should remember that Paul wrote I Timothy 2:1-4 to Christians living under the despotic reign of Nero. Remember that mother-murdering monster (did I just violate my own rule?) who persecuted Christians? Yes, Paul encouraged early Christians to pray for *him*.

That said, this passage raises the following questions: (1) "Why should I pray for elected officials?"; (2) "How should I pray for elected officials?"; and, practically, (3) "How do I find the names and contact information of my elected officials?"

First, this passage tells us to pray for our elected officials for a specific reason—so that we may "...lead a quiet and peaceable life in all godliness and honesty." Simply stated, we should pray for elected officials to effectively punish evil and promote good so we can remain focused on fulfilling the Great Commission and doing good.

Here's the ultimate reason for praying for elected officials: God desires all people to be saved and to come to the knowledge of the truth. In sum, Christians pray for the state so the church can do its work of proclaiming the Good News and doing good works (Matt. 5:16). And this gospel witness draws all people, including those in office, to consider a relationship with Jesus Christ.

Next, if you look closely, I Timothy 2:1 includes four types of prayer: supplications, prayer, intercessions and giving of thanks. Though there is some overlap among these concepts, "supplications" in Scripture were often urgent, emotional requests for a specific need; the Greek word for "prayer" conveys an intentionality or routine practice of communicating with God; "intercession" conveys a closeness to God and petitioning him for a specific request for another and "giving of thanks" conveys the more apparent meaning of gratitude for a person.[148]

So, we should make supplications for, pray for, intercede on behalf of and thank God for government officials.

Over the last few years, I have asked a number of government officials this question, "How may I pray for you?" The most common responses include: wisdom to navigate changing times, humility and strength to resist pride, clarity of thought amidst competing priorities, endurance and stamina despite a grueling schedule, grace to deal with angry opponents and constituents, courage to stand up for what is right and strong relationships with their spouse and family amidst the pressures of public life. Of course, follow God's guidance as you pray for your elected officials, but these pointers can help you start or strengthen this spiritual discipline.

Third, many Americans that I speak to do not know the name of their state representative and even their member of Congress. Here's a resource that can help: https://www.congress.gov/state-legislature-websites. This website will direct you to your state legislature's website, and each website has an address search function that will pull up your current state and federal representatives. Also, many Secretaries of State maintain an interactive election page on their website. For example, if you live in Indiana, you can locate your federal, state and even local officials at https://www.in.gov/sos/elections/2681.htm.

In sum, we are commanded to pray for our elected officials, and the above can help us do that in a consistent and meaningful way.

Build Relationships with Government Officials.

Next, Christians should build relationships with government officials.

But, why? Me, talk to *them*? For starters, it follows that praying for a government official is much more effective if you actually have a relationship with that official instead of just a picture on a website.

Actually, we should be building relationships with government officials so we can manipulate them to do our bidding, build a theocracy and make the Doxology the national anthem. Ooh Hoo Ha Ha Ha! Nah, just kidding.

Why should we build relationships with elected officials? Simple: to minister to them as individuals and to partner with them for the common good. When Ananias understandably hesitated to visit Paul shortly after his conversion, Christ reassured Ananias and described Paul's call as follows: "...for he is a chosen vessel unto me, to bear my name before the Gentiles, and kings, and the children of Israel..." (Acts 9:15). Did you catch that? Paul's ministry mandate included a ministry to kings, and an angel later strengthened Paul in the midst of a shipwreck with the statement that he "...must be brought before Caesar" (Acts 27:24).

As Christians motivated by the Great Commission, we should build relationships with government officials because we endeavor to make disciples of all nations (Matt. 28:16-20). We should care for the poor, the widow and the orphan; but we should not neglect a ministry to government officials. And, as explained in Biblical principle #4 (government guards good works), we should work with government to serve our cities, state and nation.

Of course, much of politics runs on the good-old-boy/girl system, the more modern version of the "smoke-filled room" and other forms of symbiotic relationships. Even in court, as the old saying goes, "A good lawyer knows the law, and a great lawyer knows the judge." So, what distinguishes Christian relationship building with elected officials from every other interest group that is seeking influence? I have already mentioned one: prayer. But there are three additional distinguishing factors, as follows: the Word, worth and wisdom.

First, our relationship with government officials should be built around God's Word. I am sure someone somewhere is screaming "separation of church and state" simply because I wrote that sentence, but I am not talking about particular legislation in this section or trying to coerce government officials into a particular point of view. Rather, I am talking about developing a relationship with a person who happens to be a government official around God's Word.

This is probably not a surprise to you, but public officials have statistics and policy arguments thrown at them all day long. So, as eloquent and informed as we may be, our carefully prepared stats and arguments may go unheeded and even unnoticed because of the sheer volume of information legislators receive. But there is one Resource that comes with a supernatural power and a promise that it will not return void—the Scriptures (Isa. 55:11).

My friend and colleague Greg Baker is remarkable at sharing Scripture with government officials ranging from state representatives to members of Congress. Greg leads the Church Ambassador Network in Iowa as well as a growing network of similar efforts across the country, and his nonpartisan efforts to connect the shepherds of the church and the shepherds of the state have positively changed the "spiritual temperature" at the Iowa Capitol.[149]

Greg came to Christ while serving on a political campaign, and he soon realized that his efforts to impact the political arena for Christ looked much different than his discipleship training at his local church. So, he decided to do ministry at the statehouse like he does ministry at his church and in the community group he leads. He carries a Bible with him and starts every meeting with an elected official with an encouragement from the Word. And, every time I talk with Greg about a meeting with an elected official, his first question is "Did you have an opportunity to sow the Word?"

I am thankful for Greg's powerful example and encouragement in this regard. We often make statements such as "America needs Jesus" and "America needs to turn back to God," but when was the last time we opened a Bible with an elected official? I will note that this is a learned skill, but it is an important one that we should master.

Have I admitted enough times that this book is not about groundbreaking new strategies for engaging in public life? When I set out about a decade ago to study the church's waning influence in the United States, I thought I would discover some novel legal or political strategy that would turn the tide. And I spent a lot of time and money trying to locate said strategy.

Instead, I discovered that many Christians have overlooked the basics, like praying for government officials and building relationships around God's Word. These practices will not solve all of the complex problems facing our nation, but they are a critical foundation to our efforts.

One last thought on this point. I am encouraged that many churches are working to equip Christians to live out their faith as teachers, business leaders, coaches, scientists, and social media influencers, etc. Well, shouldn't we also be equipping Christian public officials with Biblical principles related to their important work?

In sum, we should start and build relationships with government officials based on God's Word.

Next, our relationship with an elected official should focus on that official's inherent worth as a person created in God's image. If you are a church leader, I imagine you feel exploited from time to time, and most church leaders could write a book about being "used" as some form of religious commodity. Perhaps you have heard something like this: "Yea, we like the pastor's preaching a little better at the church down the street, but it's really their coffee—it's just so good. So, thanks for helping train up our kids, helping us through that hard time financially, and walking with us through my cancer treatment. We appreciate it, but we like this new church's flavor of Christianity a bit better. See you around!" Feels like a gut punch, right?

Well, the same is true of government officials. Every meeting is about what she or he can <u>do</u> for constituents. And his or her value and continued service in that role is conditioned on how well she or he produces results for the base. Now, I acknowledge that many elected officials also view constituent meetings with a form of political calculus—they want to stay in office and need votes to do that. But this reality does not change our call to minister to our elected officials as individuals rather than just dispensers of political favors or proxies for us at the state or national capitol. What if, instead of walking into our first meeting with elected officials with a specific request, we actually tried to get to know them as a person and thanked them for their important service. Novel thought, right?

Further, our relationships with government officials should not be contingent on our agreement with their ideology or policy positions or on what they have done for us lately. Why? Because our motivation for such relationships is first gospel ministry, not public policy. We often talk about the need for civility and for building relationships across the partisan divide. Well, who is going to do that if not us? What would motivate such a countercultural effort if not the gospel?

In summary, we should pursue relationships with elected officials because God has called us to love and reach all people, including those vested with the authority of public office. Jesus was constantly blowing up cultural stereotypes and biases as he ministered to individuals like a tax collector and a Samaritan woman. Well, we can do the same if we reach out to officials of both major political parties and treat them as individuals worthy of our time and respect.

The final distinctive in our relationship-building efforts should be wisdom, which I will define simply as the proper application of Biblical principles to life. In Proverbs 8:15-16 (the same text used by Reverend Daniel Foster in his election sermon), wisdom states, "By me kings reign, and princes decree justice. By me princes rule, and nobles, even all the judges of the earth." Solomon, when given the opportunity to ask for anything from God (Aladdin had nothing on this request!), told God, "Give me now wisdom and knowledge, that I may go out and come in before this people..." (2 Chron. 1:11).

As American Christians, we treat most of the issues in public life as if they are simple and straightforward. Now, to be clear, some issues are simply moral or immoral, and we should not overly complicate them.

But many decisions in public life involve a number of factors and even competing moral concerns. For example, should a legislator expand a government program if it provides temporary relief to low-income families that are in dire need but may, in the long term, strip away their dignity and motivate dependency rather than self-sufficiency? These are hard questions, and I do not claim to have all the answers all the time. Government officials are required to make a judgment call on such proposals. Eventually, a vote is called, and they have to choose "yes" or "no." We can philosophize and debate, but they have to decide.

Further, these officials make a crushing number of complicated decisions each year. On average, 109,000 bills are introduced annually in state legislatures alone.[150] And, in 2019, members of Congress formally proposed 8,820 pieces of legislation.[151] So, state and federal lawmakers sort through and decide on a prodigious number of complicated moral and legal questions on everything from foster care to bioengineering to foreign policy. Because of this, I sometimes chuckle at Christians who take to social media, overly simplify an issue and then blast their elected official for their decision on the matter. I absolutely believe such Christians have the right to speak their mind; but, in my opinion, that is not helping solve the nation's problems.

Also, contrary to public opinion, many government officials work very hard for very little pay. For example, a state senator in Indiana is paid $27,204 a year along with mileage and a $184 per diem for official state business. Practically, this means that Indiana legislators have to balance another job or profession while focusing on a legislative session each year. Further, legislators in New Hampshire are paid $100 a year with no per diem. Their last raise was in 1889![152]

Sure, there are some federal representatives that make lucrative careers out of politics, but the vast majority of the more than 500,000 elected officials (counting local, state and federal officials) engage in public life because they care about the future of their communities and the country, not the pay.

So, what if we endeavored to make their jobs easier rather than harder? What if we came alongside government officials with ideas, encouragement and even moral guidance on tough questions? What if we became a wise, trusted friend rather than a yelling foe?

Protests are sometimes necessary, and we should stand up for truth and righteousness. But mobilizing Christian voters to denounce or challenge elected officials that they do not know is a less than ideal solution.

Some of you may be thinking that this approach is too "soft," and some of you may be thinking that this sounds a little underhanded— that I am encouraging Christians to build relationships so they can later manipulate legislators. Hold on. Practiced properly, this approach does neither.

Think of a good friend in your life. In the early stages of the relationship, did that friend challenge your deeply held convictions or poke at sensitive issues? Probably not. But, as your friendship grew, did you come to expect and even request their opinion on difficult choices and bad habits in your life? I hope so. That is exactly what friendship is all about. And I am encouraging Christians to pursue similar relationships with elected officials.

We should have Biblical opinions on tough moral and ethical questions related to public life, and we should not shrink from sharing that opinion when appropriate. This does not mean that elected officials will always agree with us or take our advice. In fact, do you always listen to your own conscience? Probably not. But, if your relationship is built on the Word and prayer and if the elected official knows that you value them because of who they are (fellow image bearer) instead of what they do, your relationship will survive and perhaps even thrive through disagreement. Further, if you follow this approach, you will not compromise Biblical truth for momentary political gain, i.e. you will not become just another self-interested political operative.

In sum, we should become the Biblical, reasonable, wise Christian that our elected officials know. They should know that we love them and will pray with them no matter what. They should know that we will cheer them when they are right and question them when they are clearly wrong. And they should know that, if they have a question, we will be there with a careful, informed and Biblical response to tough issues. In other words, they should know we are different because we value and practice wisdom in public life.

Now, to the nuts and bolts of setting up and participating in these meetings. I have found it fairly simple to arrange meetings with elected officials. In the United States, the halls of power are open to the public. If you want to build a relationship with your elected officials, start with one and reach out to his or her staff to request a meeting. Explain that you would like to meet with your elected official when she or he is not in election season or in a critical week such as the close of session.

Then, during the meeting, share a relevant scripture passage just like you do with others in your life. Here are some of my favorite themes and passages: the need for servant leadership in church and state (John 10:10), relying on God's strength in times of overwhelming crisis (Nehemiah 6:9), the benefits of godly wisdom (Proverbs 8), the fact that elected officials are appointed by God for a purpose (Romans 13), and the Biblical call for justice (Amos 5).

Then, ask how you and your church can assist with key problems, ask how you can pray for them, and ask if they are comfortable with you praying with and for them right then. If they agree (in my experience, officials rarely refuse), pray with them. If the meeting goes well, ask if you can continue the relationship in the coming months with a follow-up meeting.

Alternatively, efforts such as the Church Ambassador Network in Iowa and The Daniel Initiative in Indiana are active in a number of states. And these ministries are working to connect pastors with legislators. So, if you are a church leader and are interested in building such a relationship, feel free to contact me or a similar effort in your state.

Here's a practical example of prayer and relationship building. The U.S. Senate has a little-known, sixty-year old tradition: a bipartisan weekly Bible study and prayer breakfast. In December of 2019, CBS news correspondent Margaret Brennan interviewed Delaware Democrat Chris Coons and Oklahoma Republican James Lankford about this Bible study.[153] When Brennan asked Senator Coons about the breakfast and how his faith influences his politics, he stated:

> One of the great things about having a weekly prayer breakfast is we are not getting together to argue about the issues that are so often used to divide people based on faith. We're not sitting there arguing about gay marriage and abortion and the death penalty. We're frankly sitting there praying with and for each other, singing hymns, talking about our families, and then sharing some stories. We're in a very sharply divided partisan moment. It is hard to find

any space here to be vulnerable, to admit that we don't have all the answers, to admit any sort of lack of certainty or confidence in our party's political views and having a conversation that starts around the most basic questions why are we here? What is it we're trying to do? Having a conversation about those very basic questions rather than a fight about the end point—the application through law—is a good way to have a conversation in a place where we so rarely do that.

When it was Senator Lankford's turn, he said:

Faith should impact who you are. If your faith only affects your weekends, that's not a faith, that's a hobby. A hobby is something you do on weekends. A faith is something that permeates everything you do. And so, when I was elected, when Chris was elected, we weren't elected and said, OK, now go there, now you have to take your faith off when you go. It's still who you are and a part of who I am. Our faith and my faith in particular has the strong belief that people are created in the image of God. They have value and worth. That means people that I disagree with, I should be able to disagree with them in a way that still respects them as a person. That changes the way that I debate, that changes the way that I engage on issues because of my own personal faith.

If Senators Coons and Senator Lankford can pray for and with each other and build relationships in the highly charged environment of Washington, D.C., surely we can do the same in our sphere of influence. Many Christians I speak to lament the changes in our culture, the divisive rhetoric in public life and the widening ideological divide in the United States. But they are unsure of what to do. Well, here's a first practical step: pray for and build relationships with your elected officials.

In conclusion, two warring superpowers once established a line of communication to avoid the destruction of the planet. And it is long past time that we employed a similar strategy to avoid the disintegration of our republic. It's time to pick up our version of the red telephone and start talking.

STEP #3 OFFER SOLUTIONS AND PARTNER WITH GOVERNMENT TO SOLVE PROBLEMS

7 HOWDY, PARTNER!

American Christians spend immense amounts of time and money participating in proverbial gunfights with government. And I agree that some and perhaps even many conflicts over Biblical truth cannot be avoided. But, before the proverbial shooting starts, what if we tried taking our hand away from the holster and swapping an ol' "Howdy, Partner!" with government? We might be surprised by what happens.

I have the privilege of routinely connecting church leaders with state legislators from both major political parties in the state of Indiana. In those meetings, I always ask two questions if given the chance, "What, in your opinion, is the worst problem in your district?" And, "How can the church help?" Due to the white-hot political news cycle and the significant ideological chasm separating many of these public servants, I was surprised by a very consistent response, stated in the same way: "the breakdown of the family." Indiana is a midwestern state with more traditional social mores and strong religious influence. But the dissolution of the family has apparently hit home everywhere, including the heartland.

This leads me to a point that I try to remind myself of on a fairly regular basis. As a Christian involved in public life, I must resist the temptation to focus solely on the hot-button, headline-grabbing issues in Washington and neglect the very apparent, deep needs right in front of me.

Stated differently, as Christians, we spend a lot of time and energy on front-page political issues like abortion, LGBTQ rights, and religious freedom. But this focus neglects foundational cultural problems that are not as apparent or controversial. This is a both/and solution rather than an either/or solution; but, with limited attention, we should be mindful of the dazzling attention bug-zapper known as national politics.

As a reminder, this book is about gospel-centered citizenship. And I am doing my best to set out a checklist or road map of sorts to help church leaders and other committed Christians do the hard work of Christian citizenship. We've reviewed our citizenship according to Biblical principles and examples, and we've studied how to pray for and build relationships with elected officials. Now, let's look at another practical and Biblical step: offering solutions and partnering with government officials to solve key problems

There are two concepts that are foundational to this exercise: (1) the importance of the Good News and good works and (2) the view that church and state should be partners rather than opponents.

First, to be clear, I believe that salvation is by grace through faith and not of works (Eph. 2:8-9). But good works are repeatedly encouraged in Scripture as a means of pointing people to a relationship with Christ (Mt. 5:16; Titus 3:1). In fact, the New Testament's references to the church's gospel witness and especially to the church's relationship to government are replete with a curiously consistent command: "do good."

For example, "Let your light so shine before men that they see your good works and glorify your father which is in Heaven" (Matt. 5:16). "...God anointed Jesus of Nazareth with the Holy Ghost and with power: who went about doing good, and healing all that were oppressed of the devil; for God was with him" (Acts 10:38). "Put them in mind to be subject to principalities and powers, to obey magistrates, to be ready to every good work..." (Titus 3:1). And, "As we have therefore opportunity, let us do good unto all men, especially unto them who are of the household of faith" (Gal. 6:10). Further, in I Peter 2:15, we are commanded to silence the ignorance of foolish men by submitting to government and, you guessed it, doing good works.

In sum, we should proclaim the Good News of salvation through Christ alone. But we should also prove the power and beauty of the gospel through good works. Award-winning journalist turned pastor John Dickerson powerfully explained this concept in his book *Hope of Nations*:

> Our good deeds should never be severed from the Good News, as happened in the American denominations that abandoned the authority of Scripture during the 1900s. Those denominations emphasized good deeds at the cost of the Good News. In retaliation, some sincere and biblical Christians have now moved the pendulum to an opposite extreme. They have sacrificed good deeds in order to re-elevate the Good News. The reality is that these two work in tandem: good deeds demonstrate the power of the Good News.[154]

Amen.

Next, as I explained above, the church and state should be partners rather than opponents. If the state is pursuing its role of punishing evil and promoting good and the church is pursuing the Great Commission and doing good works, there should be opportunities for the two institutions to partner together on tough problems. The state's Biblical puzzle piece of promoting good should fit tightly beside the church's puzzle piece of doing good. And the two institutions working together should produce a powerful picture of truth, justice and human flourishing.

Let's get specific.

When I asked Indiana's governor, Eric Holcomb, about a couple ways churches could assist with key problems in my state, he gave me three ideas: foster care, the drug crisis and jail ministry.

Here are a couple of observations about these three problems: they are pervasive, largely noncontroversial and complex. As I have spoken with or to churches around the country, I have noticed that these problems are pervasive—they affect rural and urban areas coast to coast. Though I will address a number of Indiana-specific efforts in this section, I am confident you will find similar efforts in your location.

Further, these issues are largely noncontroversial. No one or at least very few people yell "separation of church and state!" when Christians jump in to offer solutions to foster care. And these issues are a unique opportunity for the church because they are complex issues with no apparent or at least quick legislative solution.

In my opinion, these problems have been fueled by secular ideologies about the family, our reigning life philosophy of personal autonomy stripped of corresponding responsibility, and the general absence of hope and purpose expressed by so many Americans. Therefore, simply appropriating larger and larger budgets for government agencies and programs will not solve these problems.

And, that, ladies and gentlemen, is the opportunity for the church. If we can propose and model creative solutions to these problems, government officials are all ears. Let's take a closer look at the big three mentioned above.

Foster Care

Scripture reminds us that, "Pure religion and undefiled before God and the Father is this, to visit the fatherless and widows in their affliction…" (James 1:27). Therefore, we should deeply care about orphans and about children in foster care.

On any given day, more than 430,000 American children are in the foster care system.[155] Roughly half of foster care placements quit after their first year or first placement, and a child that ages out of the foster care system has less than a 3% chance of earning a college degree.[156] Further, many of the victims of sex trafficking in the United States are runaways from the foster care system or have aged out of the foster care system.[157]

I practiced family law for a time and even represented parents whose children had been removed by the state due to alleged physical abuse, drug abuse or neglect. So, I know firsthand the complexity and difficulty of this crisis. Further, that experience gave me a deep respect for the men and women who have dedicated their careers to social services. I disagreed with their conclusions and methods from time to time, but I came to respect their motivation and efforts.

In case you are unfamiliar with how this system works, here's a brief overview. When the Department of Child Services (or similar department in your state) is notified of potential child abuse or neglect, the state will consider the severity of the report and, if necessary, investigate the matter. Child abuse and neglect are fairly broad concepts in many state laws and often include sexual abuse, controlled substance abuse, physical abuse, failure to provide necessary food and shelter, and educational neglect. If the state believes a child is in immediate danger or if the state concludes that the allegations of abuse or neglect are true, the state agency will remove the child from the home and will file a juvenile court case through its attorneys.

The state will then work with the parent or parents to address the issues of concern, such as physical neglect or drug use, with the goal of reunification of the family. However, if the parent or parents do not address the reasons for removal, the state may eventually move to terminate parental rights to the child.

As you might imagine, the trauma of removing a child from his or her parent(s) is horrific. Therefore, removal should be a last resort. Further, foster kids are often shuttled between or among placements and sometimes suffer additional abuse in the system.

So, how can individual Christians and ministries solve this problem? They can't—at least not alone. Complex problems require comprehensive solutions; and, in my efforts to figure out the foster care problem, I have spoken with a number of state leaders, including the Director of Indiana's Department of Child Services, and a number of ministry leaders that are focused on different aspects of the problem.

To begin, Doug Weinberg, the former deputy director of the Department of Child Services in Indiana and former Director of the Department of Health and Human Services in Nebraska, championed the CarePortal in Indiana. This program allows the Department of Child Services to notify community partners such as churches with emergency needs like beds, food and clothing in an effort to prevent kids from being removed from their homes. As of the first anniversary of this program in spring of 2020, churches and other community partners working through the CarePortal had kept close to 150 kids out of the foster care system in Indiana.[158]

Next, some ministries focus on providing a home-like environment for children on the day they are removed from their parents. Why? Because these children would normally sit in a DCS office until a placement is found. These ministries attempt to soften the emotional blow of the removal with compassion, a comfortable environment and a grab bag of necessities such as hygiene products.

Ministries like Hands of Hope[159] in Indianapolis and White's Residential and Family Services[160] in Wabash, Indiana, (which has been serving in this space since 1850!) encourage churches to prioritize foster care and then build community around foster care families. For example, an older couple in a church may not be in a position to handle a foster care placement, but that couple can serve the foster care family by providing meals, encouragement and (if properly screened) a brief break like a date night for the foster parents.

Other ministries mentor parents who have had their children removed and help them overcome addiction, find work and procure stable housing so they can be reunited with their children. And, of course, a number of adoption agencies are working to place children with adoptive families.

My point in outlining all of this is not to solve foster care in a couple of pages. The problem is much more complex than that. Rather, my point in sharing this is to highlight foster care as (1) a key issue that Christians should care about and (2) a perfect opportunity for us to roll up our sleeves, offer solutions and partner with government to impact a crisis.

Here's a fascinating stat related to the foster care crisis and the church. As pointed out by Christian singer Jamie Grace, the number of kids that need a loving and safe foster care placement is roughly equivalent to the number of churches in the United States. So, if one family in every church in the United States became a foster care placement, the crisis could be solved or at least greatly reduced.[161] Well, let's get to it. What an opportunity!

The Drug Crisis

According to the National Institute on Drug Abuse, 128 people in the United States die from an opioid overdose each day.[162] And 8 to 12 percent of patients prescribed an opioid develop an addiction to the medication. Further, according to the Centers for Disease Control, "...the total 'economic burden' of prescription opioid misuse alone in the United States is $78.5 billion a year, including the costs of healthcare, lost productivity, addiction treatment, and criminal justice involvement."[163] And, as terrible as these stats are, they don't even include the effects of non-opioids such as cocaine and methamphetamine!

In sum, the misuse of opioids and other drugs is a public health crisis.

When I started my law practice, I served as a public defender for several years. Having been raised in a fairly sheltered environment, I was shocked by the scope of drug use and the potency of these drugs— a single use of some of these controlled substances can alter the human brain and lead to a powerful addiction.[164] During those years, I walked with clients as they faced drug charges and the resulting loss of employment, housing and even their children. I cheered with clients that succeeded in the recovery process, and I grieved the ones that did not.

I also learned that this crisis has grown so acute that it has become a leading priority of many in government. Why? Because it affects the workforce, the criminal justice system, public safety and government budgets. And it seems intractable. Treatment providers increasingly opine that even severe consequences, such as incarceration and the loss of family and children, are not enough to overcome the powerful allure of these substances.[165]

So, how can the church partner with government to impact this crisis? Again, I am not naïve or perhaps optimistic enough to think I can outline a solve-all in this section. But we can do three things. We can address the stigma, help with hope, and provide community.

I recently asked Phil Gabriel, the Executive Director of a successful recovery ministry named Trinity Life Ministry in Lafayette, Indiana, for a key takeaway or action step I could share with churches about the drug crisis. His response was straightforward, "We have to address the stigma."

I will admit that his words convicted me. How many times have I looked at an individual working to recover from an addiction and thought, "Why can't you just get it together? Just develop some self-control and kick that habit!" We can make excuses, but the sad reality is that someone working to overcome an addiction is not quite welcome in "polite" Christian society or in our posh, family-friendly suburban church environment.

Further, this stigma overlooks the vice-like grip of chemical addiction (as described above) and downplays other addictions in our lives. For example, anyone that wrestles with pornography or even habitual overeating should have some empathy for an individual grappling with a drug habit.

Even as Christians, we can be tempted to see these individuals as somehow less than us and to avoid any contact with their problems. Instead, we should see these individuals as people Jesus loves and has called us to reach and encourage.

I recognize the safety concerns that naturally arise in such circumstances, and they should be addressed. But this does not change our call to minister to all of our neighbors. So, as the church, we need to dedicate ourselves to overcoming this stigma and reaching out to our neighbors that are wrestling toward recovery.

Next, in conversations with government officials and ministry leaders about this issue, one particular word comes up time and again: "hope." Many people who turn to drug use lack hope for a better future and lack a sense that their life has deep meaning, purpose and positive momentum.[166] And there's the key. Government can pass legislation to criminalize behavior and to change systems to make life better or easier, but government cannot legislate hope.

So, hope falls in the church's jurisdiction. In contrast to the vision of a new, high-paying job, domestic bliss and other aspects of the American dream that often crumble in real life, the church has a much better and durable source of hope. Paul reminds us that, as believers, we should be filled with joy and peace through the Holy Spirit and that this joy and peace should cause us to "abound in hope" (Rom. 15:13). So, government can help in this area through a number of programs and even legislation. But the church can play an even more pivotal role: the church can help with hope.

Finally, the church can provide community. The Pavilion Churches in North Vernon, Indiana, are a great example of this. This probably sounds like the start of a bad joke, but a Baptist minister, a Wesleyan minister and a Nazarene minister all walked into the city hall of North Vernon, Indiana to start a relationship with their mayor. And these pastors now routinely meet with the mayor to pray together and discuss the needs of the community.

This group of pastors also started a chaplaincy program in a local factory, recently received a $65,000 donation from that factory to build an addiction recovery home and are now running the Potter's House, a faith-based addictions recovery program for men.[167] These pastors have also been tapped by a leading state official to participate in discussions on how best to combat the drug crisis.

Here's a key part of their ministry strategy. These churches regularly schedule meals or fellowships together to meet and encourage the men in the Potter's House program. They build Christian community around these individuals and cheer them on toward recovery. One of the program's graduates, who was formally homeless, now serves on a community board addressing drug addiction and homelessness. I love stories like this! Bravo!

Further, the U.S. Department of Health and Human Services' Center for Faith and Opportunity Initiatives recently highlighted the work of Dan Johnson and the ministry he started, the NewDay Center. This ministry utilizes a nine-month aftercare program designed to build Christian community around graduates. In a publication released earlier this year, HHS highlighted the following:

NewDay Recovery Center practices at the intersection of science and faith. Their full-service treatment center delivers professional counseling and medical services to nearly 1,000 individuals and families, alongside a biblically based curriculum. NewDay founder Dan Johnson will tell you the strength of an individual's long-term recovery is directly related to whether or not that person has been integrated into a compassionate community after treatment.

Specifically, a compassionate community that understands the challenges of SUDs [substance use disorders] and the long-term nature of the recovery process and, perhaps most importantly, "does not see the person's substance use disorder as the individual's primary identity."[168]

The NewDay Center also equips churches to become "transition communities" by (1) equipping congregations with basic information about SUDs and the characteristics of recovery, (2) developing mentors in the church to walk alongside individuals in the program and (3) equipping church leaders to assist individuals transitioning out of treatment and back into the pressures and triggers of everyday life.

Most of us are familiar with the problem of peer pressure in relation to the drug crisis. Many individuals that wrestle with a SUD default back into that lifestyle when they return from treatment to their previous environment. The church can play a vital role in providing an alternate, Biblically based community for these individuals.

In sum, the church can serve in the midst of this public health crisis by overcoming stigma, helping with hope and providing community.

Jail Ministry

In 1976, 440,000 Americans were incarcerated.[169] Today, more than 2.3 million Americans are behind bars.[170] That's more than a 500 percent increase in less than fifty years! Further, more than two-thirds of the individuals released each year will be rearrested within three years. These alarming numbers have caused significant jail overcrowding and sparked calls for criminal justice reform in the United States.

As Christians, we are commanded to remember those that are in prison (Heb. 13:3). And, due to rising incarceration rates, this has become an urgent task for the church and a key opportunity for partnering with government to address a societal problem. Like foster care and the drug crisis, which are interrelated with recidivism, this problem is complex and has no easy fix.

So, how can the church help? I consider Prison Fellowship, a ministry started by Chuck Colson after his arrest and imprisonment over the Watergate scandal, to be one of the leading ministries serving in this space (though there are certainly many other great ministries!). I recently interviewed Mark Frisbie, the director of Prison Fellowship in Indiana, on *The Good Citizen Podcast*.[171] And we discussed this issue at length.

The first hurdle is, once again, the issue of stigma. Outside of a few wrongful convictions, people in prison have committed a crime (just call me Captain Obvious); but they have not forfeited the *imago Dei* and have inherent dignity and worth. Prison Fellowship refers to these individuals as "returning citizens" for this reason and because most of these individuals will return to our cities and neighborhoods at some point.

The issue of prevention should certainly be a priority. Building strong churches, mentoring at-risk youth, instilling strong moral character and giving people hope and purpose will help drive down the crime rate.

But the primary focus of most public officials I speak to is the recidivism rate. These efforts have been complicated by the COVID-19 pandemic, but we should minister to returning citizens while in prison and help them stay out of prison upon their release.

Prison Fellowship and a number of other ministries have Biblically based programs that cover Scripture and basic life skills; attempt to keep returning citizens connected with their families (check out the Angel Tree program if you are not familiar); and work to connect these individuals with strong church communities, housing and employment upon their release.

Because women comprise a small minority of returning citizens, much of the church's attention has historically been on men's ministry in prison. But women have become the fastest-growing segment of the prison population.[172] For this reason, the church should step up its engagement with programs like Prison Fellowship's Academy and their newest program, Create: New Beginnings, which "helps women living in prison explore identity and purpose through art—and create new beginnings inside and outside prison."[173]

College Park Church in Indianapolis, Indiana is a great example of a church that has engaged this issue. College Park adopted a neighborhood in urban Indianapolis and encouraged members to move into the neighborhood. One member, David Palmer, started a furniture-making business named Purposeful Design, and this business now employs a number of individuals that were previously in prison.[174]

Faith-based efforts like Purposeful Design provide an excellent way to partner with the Department of Corrections (DOC) or similar department in your state. By way of example, in his 2020 State of the State Address, Indiana Governor Eric Holcomb shared the story of Amber Campbell. Amber obtained a certification in manufacturing safety, production and maintenance during her five-year prison term and was hired by an automotive lighting manufacturer upon her release.

Governor Holcomb stated, "Because of these new programs and opportunities, our state recidivism rate has dropped 4 percent. But in the spirit of always improving, I have a new challenge for Commissioner Carter and the DOC. By 2022, I want 500 returning citizens annually to have validated job opportunities waiting for them before they walk out of prison, and 3,000 more formerly incarcerated individuals in jobs within five months of their release."[175] As I stated above, this is a ready-made opportunity for churches and people of faith to partner with government to engage the real-life problems right in front of us.

After reading the above descriptions about the foster care crisis, drug abuse, and recidivism, you may sense a bit (or a lot) of overwhelm. I know I do. And this overwhelm raises an important question: "How in the world are we supposed to address all of these problems while keeping a job, serving a church and leading a family?" Here's the good news: we're not. Now, I am not excusing myself or the reader from strenuously serving where God has called us. But we are not God. We have limited time, energy, and abilities, so we should focus our efforts using this question: "Given my skills, opportunities, desires, and resources, how can I best serve God right now?"

The answer to the complexity of these crises is the diversity of Christian calling. God has equipped us with distinct skills and even interests so we can address separate problems. So, I often encourage individuals, small groups and churches to (1) identify natural bridges into a community or a specific issue of interest and to (2) focus attention and efforts in that space. That way, in a major city or even a neighborhood, each Christian and church can prayerfully and strategically focus on a ministry niche. This is what creates a gospel movement that can transform a city.

Note how the first three steps of good citizenship work together. First, we should review our citizenship and dedicate ourselves to engaging public life as a Christian. Second, we should pray for and build relationships with elected officials. And, third, in the course of those relationships, we should ask about key problems, identify solutions and jump in to help solve those problems.

In conclusion, I recently interviewed Indiana Senator Andy Zay, who authored the CarePortal legislation here in Indiana. I greatly appreciate his vision for church/state partnerships. He asks this question: "What if the church could solve 50% to 60% of the problems or needs that require public welfare programs?"[176] What a thought! The church historically served such a role in American society; and, in so doing, showed the power and beauty of the gospel. It's time to reclaim that role by partnering with government officials and working alongside them to impact our communities.

STEP #4 DO THE HARD WORK OF CHRISTIAN CITIZENSHIP IN THE PUBLIC SQUARE

8 FOLLOW THE STAR

I visited Abraham Lincoln's birthplace a few years ago. This national park and monument, which is located in central Kentucky, highlights Lincoln's birth in a one-room log cabin on Sinking Spring Farm in 1809. The monument was completed in 1911 as the nation's first official memorial to Lincoln.[177]

As an American who loves history, I was in a bit of a reverie after walking through the exhibit. I was thinking about Lincoln's days on the frontier, the homespun humor and backwoods stories that served him so well during the dark days of the Civil War, and his iron determination to hold the Union together and end slavery.

So, you might imagine my surprise when I exited the main building and looked up to see a large Confederate battle flag secured in the bed of a well-worn pickup truck with a trailer attached. And this was not just any truck. Rather, this vehicle belonged to the individual mowing the grass of the park!

I am a big fan of free speech, but this certainly struck me as ironic. Nothing like waving the ol' rebel flag while mowing the grass of Old Abe's birthplace! It's only been 155 years since the end of the Civil War, but who's counting?

The irony of that display, however, pales in comparison to another deep irony within the state boundaries of Kentucky—the monument to Jefferson Davis. The first and only president of the Confederacy was also born in Kentucky, and the state maintains a 351-foot obelisk dedicated to Davis that appears to mimic the Washington Monument (which is 555 feet tall).[178]

Now, my point here is not to criticize the Commonwealth of Kentucky or to spark a debate over monuments. Similar head-scratching contradictions can be found throughout the United States. Rather, my point here is to highlight the fact that Kentucky was a border state in the Civil War and that both Lincoln and Davis were born there.

These border states—Delaware, Kentucky, Maryland, Missouri, and West Virginia—were deeply divided by pro-Union and pro-Southern sentiments. A St. Louis woman noted, "There is scarcely a family that is not divided." And Kentucky Senator John J. Crittenden's sons joined opposing sides.[179]

Further, Mary Todd Lincoln (Lincoln's wife) was born in Lexington, Kentucky, to a slaveholding family. And her half-sister Emilie Todd Helm even visited the Lincolns at the White House in 1863. Why was that significant? Well, Emilie's husband Ben Hardin Helm was a Confederate general and was killed at the battle of Chickamauga prior to Emilie's visit.[180]

Such was the soul-rending anguish and loss of our great Civil War, as brother fought brother and more than 618,000 Americans died in the effort to "make men free."[181] Nowhere was that anguish and conflict closer to home than in the border states.

We now find ourselves in a new civil conflict, and it is increasing in intensity year by year. I was recently in Iowa, and I drove through a rural community dominated by Trump/Pence and "Keep America Great" signs and an urban neighborhood dominated by "Biden 2020" signs (Kamala Harris had not been selected yet). The kicker? These communities were separated by no more than a 30-minute drive.

To be clear, our cultural divisions are not as deep or as strident as those in the pre-Civil War years. But they are certainly significant. And some observers are openly fretting about the future of the republic.[182]

In sum, we all live in a "border state" in this new civil cold war. No matter how blue or red your state, families, co-workers, and even churches are divided along partisan lines. And the disagreements are heating up. A single statement can end a relationship or a job. Pastors are seen as too political or not political enough. Thanksgiving has become a skirmish of competing worldviews, and Americans now question the wisdom and even good-hearted motivation of those they disagree with.

For these reasons, I understand the instinct of many Christians to simply withdraw from this maelstrom in an attempt to avoid the conflict. But, as I have argued above, I believe such a withdrawal is an abdication of a Biblical responsibility that reflects a lack of care and concern for our neighbors. Further, no matter how hard we try to hide, the issues in and obligations of public life—tax bills come to mind—are sure to find us. Such efforts to avoid public life remind me of kids that participate in the game hide-and-go-seek by simply closing their eyes and expecting no one else to be able to see them. That strategy just doesn't work.

Practically speaking, there is no effective way to keep silent at all times and on all matters. If we desire to "...do justly, love mercy and walk humbly with our God" (Micah 6:8) and to love our neighbor as ourselves (Matt. 22:39), the more effective approach is to engage in public life for the glory of God and the common good (I Cor. 10:31; Jer. 29).

Here are some pointers for doing just that.

The Platform

First, before we dive into specific issues, let's set out a platform for a Biblically based engagement in public life. Politics in the United States has a terrible habit of setting out false choices framed by the political parties, news media or culture. As a Biblical Christian, I recognize the reality of our two-party system, but I refuse to engage without developing a Biblically based set of principles that will guide my actions in public life.

Some of you have been sweating this discussion all along because you knew it was coming. Well, Jesus didn't promise us a cakewalk, so let's embrace the hard work of discipleship in this area!

That said, please understand that I am doing my best to apply Scripture to one of the most complex areas of the Christian life. I, of course, agree with all of the statements made below (I only occasionally disagree with myself), but I recognize that some Christians will disagree with my conclusions. And I admit that I do not always get it right. So, this chapter is as much about the exercise of applying Biblical principles to public life as it is about my conclusions, though I have prayed over and carefully thought through them.

To begin, part of the problem in public life is complexity. There are so many issues to care about! Further, everyone, including your college roommate's uncle's friend's coworker, who somehow managed to connect with you on social media, has an opinion about what you should care about. So, let's focus on a foundational principle and five key issues that should serve as our personal, gospel-focused platform for engagement in public life.

Please note that faithful Christian engagement in public life may focus on more than these five issues. For example, Wayne Grudem's 601-page *Politics According to the Bible* addresses Biblical principles as they relate to a variety of issues, including tax policy and farm subsidies.[183] I am not saying that Scripture speaks to all of these issues with equal clarity (and neither does Grudem). Rather, my point is that Christians exercising their role as citizen may feel led to engage a number of issues in public life. But, in my opinion, our public witness should focus on at least the five key issues listed below.

After a careful review of Scripture, historical examples and our form of government, I have concluded that our public witness should be star shaped. I chose the star for two reasons.

First, the U.S. flag has fifty five-pointed stars representing the fifty states in our union. The U.S. has the most stars in any national flag, but something like 70 of the 195 nations on the planet have stars in their flags.[184] Why? Perhaps because stars have long symbolized something fixed or eternal and because they guided ancient travelers and mariners.

Next, I chose the star because of its rich Biblical symbolism. A star or the stars remind us of God's glory and majesty (Psalm 8), serve as a symbol for angels or messengers (Rev. 1:20), and pointed the wise men to Jesus (Matt. 2:2). Further, in one of my favorite verses of the Old Testament, we are reminded that those who turn many to righteousness will, "...shine like the stars for ever and ever" (Dan. 12:3). In summary, stars in Scripture always point people to God.

Now, to the particulars. At the center of the star is a basic principle that brightens and connects the five key issues. Here it is: God created humanity in His image and tasked us with His mission (Gen. 1:27-28). In Genesis 1:27, we find this truth: "So God created man in his own image, in the image of God created he him; male and female created he them." Humanity's purpose quickly followed humanity's creation: "And God blessed them, and God said unto them, Be fruitful, and multiply, and replenish the earth, and subdue it: and have dominion over the fish of the sea, and over the fowl of the air..." (Gen. 1:28).

The word for subdue (*kabash*) is a call to creative cultivation. We are to be God's agents, working to build a flourishing and just world. This creation or cultural mandate was not canceled by man's fall into sin or limited to just the Jews (Jer. 29). And, Christ restated this principle in the New Testament in the form of the Great Commission, which commands us to make disciples who are to "...observe all things whatsoever I [Christ] have commanded you: and, lo, I am with you always, even unto the end of the world. Amen." (Matt. 28:20).

As Os Guinness explained in his book *The Call*, our primary calling is to be reconciled to God. But we also have a secondary calling: to be disciples and sub-creators as teachers, engineers, parents, citizens, etc.[185] By living out our faith every day everywhere, we work to renew and redeem our world according to God's good design. Once again, the Good News leads to good works that show God's power and wisdom.

This is, of course, controversial as applied to the American experiment. Secular observers warn of Christian attempts to build a theocracy. And many Christians wrestle with whether or not they should promote laws that reflect Biblical morality. Before we jump into five points of the star, let's look closely at these foundational concerns.

Separation of Church and State, not Religion and Public Life

Since I am writing this book to a primarily Christian audience, I will be straightforward. Of course, we should apply Biblical principles in public life. I mean, what other principles should we be applying? Our own? The ideas of philosophers, political scientists or presidents? We can draw good ideas and sound principles from many sources. But government was God's idea and needs His guidance.

In the United States, the founders separated the institution of the church and the institution of the state but never intended to separate religious prudential guidance from the public life of the nation. Nor is it wise for us to do so today. Jonathan Leeman powerfully illustrates this principle in his book *Political Church: The Local Assembly as Embassy of Christ's Rule*:

> The division between politics and religion, I dare say, is an ideological ploy. Imagine an airport security metal detector standing at the entrance of the public square, which doesn't screen for metal but for religion. The machine beeps anytime someone walks through it with a supernatural big-G God hiding inside of one of their convictions, but it fails to pick up self-manufactured or socially-constructed little-g gods. Into this public square the secularist, the materialist, the Darwinist, the consumerist, the elitist, the chauvinist, and, frankly, the fascist can all enter carrying their gods with them, like whittled wooden figures in their pockets. Not so the Christians or Jews. Their conviction that murder is wrong because all people are made in God's image might as well be a semi-automatic. What this means, of course, is that the public square is inevitably slanted toward the secularist and materialist. Public conversation is ideologically rigged. The secularist can bring his or her god. I cannot bring mine because his name starts with a capital letter and I didn't make him up.[186]

This is first and foremost a cultural problem. Our current approach to pluralism is to privatize all religious principles except secular ideologies and to act as if those secular principles are morally and religiously neutral. Further, even many Christians think the church should have no role in public life.

How is this working for us? In a critical moment in our history, we are forced to dance around the important questions of life and the actual cause of key problems (like the breakdown of the family) and even wonder about the meaning of words. And the only moral consensus we can drum up is the following: it's ok to (1) hate Nazis and to (2) love puppies. That's it! Anything else is a bridge too far and produces finger-pointing from conflicting visions of America. In sum, we are discovering that it is nigh impossible to reach a shared conclusion about what is good if we cannot have a conversation about what is true.

So, let's take off the virtual reality goggles and leave the faux world where traditional religious principles are treated as nonessential and even dangerous; secular philosophical arguments are smuggled in as neutral and handed a monopoly on meaning; and principles like justice, equality and truth are expected to endure despite being cut off from their Judeo-Christian roots. And let's re-engage the real world where everyone sources their morality from an ideology or religion. We need to start asking which idea is best for human flourishing and need to start following the answer regardless of source or motivation.

Some might ask: "isn't the alternate approach worse?" Isn't this just advocacy for some sort of Christian moral regime or a slippery slope toward the religious conflict apparent throughout history and especially in the Thirty Year's War in Europe?

No. I am arguing for the institutional separation of church and state while allowing for religious moral influence in public life because I think such a practice is Biblical. I know such an approach is controversial, but should it be? Every decision we make in public life from foreign policy to immigration to employment law has a moral component, so let's stop acting like it doesn't. Stated differently, as a nation, we legislate someone's morality every time we pass a law. And, if we promote a diverse society, why do we require a sort of secular stop-and-frisk to ensure no religious principles or purposes reach one of the most important areas of our lives?

A better approach is to allow every American citizen, including people of faith, to bring their best principles to bear in the public square. This approach (1) has the potential to shore up the crumbling moral foundation of American public life while (2) respecting differing religious and moral opinions. Politics is a battleground of ideas; and, in an increasingly complex and hollow age, let's let the best idea win.

I recognize the legal complications of this argument. In 1971, the U.S. Supreme Court set out the *Lemon* test, which prohibits government action unless that action: 1. has a significant secular (i.e., non-religious) purpose, 2. does not have the primary effect of advancing or inhibiting religion, and 3. does not foster excessive entanglement between government and religion.[187]

The *Lemon* test raises some key questions. What is "secular" and what is "religious?" How significant does the secular purpose have to be before it "sterilizes" religious motivation? And what is a healthy church-state partnership versus an "excessive" entanglement?

Fortunately, in 2019, the Supreme Court scrutinized and disregarded the *Lemon* test in *Am. Legion v. Am. Humanist Ass'n* (the Blandensburg Cross case). Justice Alito, who wrote the 7-2 opinion, stated, "If the *Lemon* Court thought that its test would provide a framework for all future Establishment Clause decisions, its expectation has not been met. In many cases, this Court has either expressly declined to apply the test or has simply ignored it." Justice Stephen Breyer wrote a concurring opinion, stating that Establishment Clause cases should focus on, "...the basic purposes that the Religion Clauses were meant to serve: assuring religious liberty and tolerance for all, avoiding religiously based social conflict, and maintaining that separation of church and state that allows each to flourish in its separate sphere." Justice Thomas took the next logical step and argued that the *Lemon* test should be overruled.[188]

My argument in this section is fairly straightforward. Promoting Biblical principles in the public square is a far cry from establishing a state religion. So, case law should protect the institutional separation of church and state without barring religion's key influence in national public life.

Which Principles?

Next, which Biblical principles should we advocate for in public life? We have established that we should not push for a Middle Eastern style theocracy (remember the lightsaber), so what principles should we promote in the context of a plural participatory democracy?

Going back to central Biblical principles and Christ's example, we should promote principles that uphold God's created order and that advance the equal dignity and treatment of all people; and we should oppose policies and laws that cut against God's created order and insult or prevent the equal dignity and treatment of all people.

For example, I could not, in good conscience, promote an effort to enforce the first commandment (the command to "...have no other gods before Me." (Ex. 20:3)) through legislation. Why? Because God created humans with a body, mind and soul; and, though Christ desires all people to come to the truth, He did not and does not coerce their conversion (John 3:16).

But Christians should promote legislation that mirrors the 6th and 8th commandments because murder, theft and slavery offend the *imago Dei*. Further, Christians should promote a Biblical view of marriage and sexuality because these truths reflect God's created order and will lead to human flourishing.

I have found this question helpful in thinking through tough issues: "By supporting or opposing this cause or policy, am I promoting the common good of all people by affirming the *imago Dei* and reflecting God's created order?" If the answer to that question is "yes," then I am not "legislating my morality" in a secular public square. Rather, I am promoting God's morality for the good of my neighbor in an institution God created. Further, this question cuts against holding non-Christians to the same standards as church members, promoting self-interest guised in religious terms and working toward a generic civic moralism devoid of the gospel.

In sum, though the *imago Dei* and the cultural mandate do not answer all of the questions raised in public life, they do provide an excellent guiding principle for doing the hard work of Christian citizenship.

Five Key Issues

Now, let's look at five key issues that are sourced from and connected by the *imago Dei*: (1) the sanctity of life, (2) racial unity and justice, (3) the Matthew 25 issues (care for the hungry, care for the poor, care for the immigrant, and care for prisoners), (4) the Biblical sexual ethic, and (5) religious liberty for all people. Note that two of these issues sound liberal and three of these issues sound conservative, but they are all Biblical. Further, the inspiration for these five issues came from the public witness of the early church in Rome.[189]

My purpose in this section is not to provide an exhaustive dissection of these issues. Rather, I intend to set out a brief Biblical foundation for each issue and to encourage Christians to engage these areas according to their conscience.

Sanctity of Life

Once again, I must ask everyone to put down their tribal banners for a moment and simply consider what is Biblical. Few issues are as charged and politicized as abortion in the United States, but the life issue is first a Biblical or moral one.

The Scriptures are clear. Life begins at conception. The Psalmist noted that God covered him in his mother's womb, and he praised God because he was "fearfully and wonderfully made" (Ps. 139:13-16). God told the prophet Jeremiah that he (God) knew Jeremiah before he was conceived and sanctified him while he was in his mother's womb (Jer. 1:5). And, when the angel told Mary that she would conceive in her womb and bear a Son, the angel said, "He shall be great, and shall be called the Son of the Highest: and the Lord God shall give unto him the throne of his father David..." (Luke 1:32). Notice that the angel did not distinguish between Jesus in the womb and Jesus after birth and used personal pronouns throughout the announcement. A straightforward reading of the Bible is clear: life begins at conception.

Further, the science is clear. According to Dr. Micheline Matthew-Ross at the Harvard Medical School: "It is scientifically correct to say that an individual human life begins at conception when egg and sperm join to form the zygote, and this developing human always is a member our species in all stages of life."[190]

I acknowledge that there are competing theological and scientific views on this topic, but the life and personality evidenced by a child during an ultrasound provides compelling, observable proof that a fetus in the womb is a little human. Further, I have found this question helpful: "But for human intervention or some other intervening event (such as a miscarriage), would a zygote eventually be born as a human child?" Since the answer is yes, the zygote isn't just a clump of cells. It's a human being made in the image of God and worthy of protection.

In summary, I believe abortion is the great moral issue of our times. I may be wrong, of course, but I believe our descendants will look back one hundred or two hundred years from now and question the practice of abortion like we question slavery and the holocaust. As an advanced and supposedly enlightened society, the United States has allowed more than 60 million legalized abortions from 1973 to 2018. More than 1.9 billion abortions have been performed worldwide since 1980, and the selective killing of girls and those with Down Syndrome in the womb is well documented.[191]

If we do not stand up and speak up about this critical Biblical issue, what good are our sermons and our pontificating on social media about justice and righteousness? Every person from conception to natural death bears the image of God and is worthy of the protection of our laws.

Racial Unity and Justice

Race-based slavery and racial discrimination are America's original sins. I say sins because such acts are clearly prohibited by Scripture. The sixth commandment bans the stealing and selling of human beings and prescribes the death penalty for anyone who owns such a slave (Ex. 21:16). And the Apostle Paul declared that God has made "of one blood all nations" (Acts 17:26). Further, according to Galatians 3:26-29, Christians are all one in Christ. We are "…all the children of God by faith in Christ Jesus. For as many of you as have been baptized into Christ have put on Christ. There is neither Jew nor Greek, there is neither bond nor free, there is neither male nor female…"

So, we should pursue racial unity and justice. The word "justice" is used a lot these days without much of a definition. So, to be clear, I mean a Biblical concept of justice. A key passage to consider is Amos 5.

In this chapter, God declared His intentions to send Israel into captivity because the Jews refused to practice justice in the gate, the place where government and public affairs were conducted. God set out the evidence against Israel as a just Judge, "For I know your manifold transgressions and your mighty sins: they afflict the just, they take a bribe, and they turn aside the poor in the gate from their right. Therefore the prudent shall keep silence in that time; for it is an evil time... Hate the evil, and love the good, and establish judgment in the gate: it may be that the Lord God of hosts will be gracious unto the remnant of Joseph" (Amos 5:12-13,15).

God continued, stating that He found no delight in the Jew's religious ceremonies, their offerings and even their songs because they failed to practice justice (Amos 5:20-23). Then, He commanded them: "But let judgment run down as waters, and righteousness as a mighty stream." I love the imagery in this verse made famous by Martin Luther King, Jr. Here, God told the Jews to pursue a righteousness that will sweep away all injustice like a relentless and powerful wave of water.

In summary, as gospel-centered citizens, we should care deeply about racial unity and justice grounded in the principle that all people are made in the image of God and are, therefore, of equal dignity and worth.

Earlier this year, I was surprised when I published podcast and YouTube interviews with black church leaders on this topic. Within two days, I received one email calling me a cultural Marxist and another email claiming I did not properly understand the historic evils of slavery and discrimination. Now, I have never thought of myself as a Marxist before. And I did my best in those episodes to simply ask my guests about their perspectives on the deaths of Auhmad Arbery and George Floyd and to set out a Biblical roadmap for engaging this issue.[192]

My big takeaway from those conversations and the feedback is that white Christians and black Christians are as divided as ever on the issues of race and justice. I may oversimplify a viewpoint in the next two sentences, but let me try to summarize what I am hearing. White Christians tell me they are tired of hearing about the race issue, consider it largely addressed and don't want to be called racist. Black Christians tell me that white Christians are not really listening, don't truly understand the church's complicity in the evils of slavery and Jim Crow and often ignore the ongoing effects of those historic and present sins.

With those realities clearly in view, I am still convinced that the church should be leading on the issue of racial reconciliation. And we must find a way over these cultural hurdles to build churches that reflect the growing ethnic diversity of our communities and then impact our communities with a Biblical view of unity and justice. No, we have not figured this out in 400 years. And many church leaders that have been working on this issue for a long time have expressed frustration with the divergent views explained above.

But this is an incredible moment for the Christian church. As a nation, we fought a Civil War over slavery, passed sweeping Civil Rights legislation in the 1960s to address legal discrimination and continue to pass laws addressing racism. But, as evidenced by recent events and the resulting riots and unrest, legal solutions are important but are not enough. These measures have not solved the pride and bias in the human heart. And that is a problem that can only be addressed by the power of the gospel.

So, we should continue to address any inequities in the law and the criminal justice system while working hard to build unity among Christians and then broader society. I am aware of and share concerns about unbiblical solutions to this problem. But, as Christian citizens, we should not use someone else's unbiblical solution to prevent us from engaging with a Biblical one!

In sum, just like we care for the unborn because they are made in the image of God, we should care about racial unity and justice and work toward a society that affords all people equal respect, opportunity and justice.

The Matthew 25 Issues

In Matthew 25, Christ commended his servants who fed the hungry, gave water to the thirsty, clothed the poor, healed the sick, cared for the stranger, and visited the prisoner. And, further, He explained that performing these good works for the "least of these" is the same as serving Him (Matt. 25:34-40). Also, in James 1:27, we find this reminder, "Pure religion and undefiled before God and the Father is this, [t]o visit the fatherless and widows in their affliction, and to keep himself unspotted from the world."

Serving the hungry, the thirsty, the foreigner, the sick, the imprisoned, the widow and the orphan has been a historic role of the Christian church here and elsewhere. For example, ten out of the top ten hospitals in the United States "…began with medical doctors who were trained by Christian universities, and nine out of ten had Christian founders who declared their Christian faith as their motive for establishing the hospital (such as John Hopkins, the Mayo Clinic, Massachusetts General, and others)."[193]

Christians should continue that Biblical tradition in the present. I set out additional Biblical motivations for engaging these issues in Chapter 7 on partnering with government officials. The Matthew 25 issues demand our attention.

The Biblical Sexual Ethic

Oh boy, another controversial issue! But, again, I am doing my best to simply follow Scripture where it leads. And Scripture sets out moral principles on sexuality and directs us to order our lives according to those principles. Here's that sexual ethic in three parts: (1) God created marriage to be a lifelong, exclusive union between a man and a woman (Gen. 2:18-25; Eph. 5:23-32); (2) He created sexual intimacy to be expressed exclusively between a married man and woman (Mark 7:21-22; I Cor. 6:9-10) and (3) He created each of us immutably male or female as an expression of His image and nature (Gen. 1:26-27).

Before I jump into the more controversial aspects of this issue, I must mention the epidemic of pornography and the Christian divorce rate. More than a third of Protestant men who regularly attend church admit to watching a pornographic film in the last year.[194] Pornography clearly leads to the objectification of women and drives up the demand for sex trafficking.[195] And, as of May 2020, seventeen U.S. States had passed resolutions recognizing porn as a public health crisis.[196]

Further, though committed Christians do not divorce at the same rate as the general population (a common misperception repeated endlessly during the same-sex marriage debate), the numbers are still high. According to Professor Bradley Wright at the University of Connecticut, people who identify as Christian but rarely attend church divorce at a rate of about 60%; but regular church attenders divorce at a much lower rate of 38%. So, religious commitment and practice matter, but we still have work to do in creating a strong Biblical counterculture concerning marriage and family. [197]

Now, to the more controversial aspects of this issue. I often hear that Jesus said nothing about homosexuality, but that is not accurate. As Kevin DeYoung explains in his book *What Does the Bible Really Say about Homosexuality*:

> Not only did He [Jesus] explicitly reaffirm the creation account of marriage as the one-flesh union of a man and a woman (Matt. 19:4–6; Mark 10:6–9); he condemned the sin of *porneia* (Mark 7:21), a broad word encompassing every kind of sexual sin. New Testament scholar James Edwards states that *porneia* "can be found in Greek literature with reference to a variety of illicit sexual practices, including adultery, fornication, prostitution, and homosexuality. In the Old Testament it occurs for any sexual practice outside marriage between a man and a woman that is prohibited by the Torah."

Therefore, Christ's audience in Mark 7 would have clearly understood his teaching to mean that same-sex behavior was prohibited along with other expressions of sexual sin.[198]

Because the Biblical sexual ethic is rooted in God's good design, it is a positive prohibition designed to lead to fulfillment and flourishing. Regardless of the controversy surrounding this ethic, these Biblical principles are still true and good—good for us and good for all people. And we should follow these principles and promote them as such.

At the same time, we should treat our neighbors in the LGBTQ community with love and respect. I fully acknowledge that the church has, at times, failed to do so. But we do not make up for that behavior by ignoring or abdicating the truth. Instead, we are to speak the truth in love (Eph. 4:15).

This is, of course, complicated by recent legal decisions. The Supreme Court declared a right to same-sex marriage in *Obergefell v. Hodges*.[199] And, in *Bostock v. Clayton County*,[200] the Court expanded the use of the term "sex" in Title VII of the Civil Rights Act (which prevents discrimination in employment) to include "sexual orientation" and "gender identity." Stated differently, this decision recognized the sexual revolution's distinction between sex as a fixed biological reality and gender as a fluid and subjective construct. These decisions show the dizzying speed of change on the issue and the importance of Christian efforts to recover a Biblical view of marriage and human sexuality.

The family is one of the three key institutions created by God. Therefore, as Biblical Christians, we cannot simply redefine or dispense with the institution any more than we can do away with the church or declare the state extinct. As difficult and controversial as it is, we must promote the Biblical sexual ethic as true and good.

Religious Liberty for All People

Religious liberty, like many other words or terms these days, are thrown around by the political parties and interest groups. Some groups put religious liberty in scare quotes and argue that such freedom is nothing more than a cover for discrimination. And others argue that the First Amendment implies a sort of Christian favoritism over and above other religious groups. Neither of these views is correct.

Here's a working definition of our first freedom. Religious liberty is the right to believe and live out one's deeply held convictions without coercion or mistreatment by the government.

This view of religious liberty is founded on the fact that all people are created in the image of God with a body, mind and soul. And God has left us free to believe in Him or reject Him (John 3:16). According to the Gospels, salvation is a choice and cannot be coerced by a human ruler. In sum, as Paul Marshall says, "The right to follow our conscience lies at the center of human dignity and is the core of every other human right."[201]

Let's look once more to Jesus' teaching in Matthew 22:21: "Render therefore unto Caesar the things which are Caesar's; and unto God the things that are God's." As I mentioned above, government may rightly claim general civic obedience and respect. But the state has no claim to ultimate allegiance and worship. Therefore, the state exceeds its Biblical jurisdiction if it (1) forces an individual to worship the state, its leaders or its preferred religion or (2) violates an individual's deeply held religious convictions.

This principle is not absolute, of course. The classic example is the religious practice of child sacrifice. The state can and should constrain such a practice because it involves physical harm and insults the child's equal dignity and humanity.

Though religious liberty may sound like a more conservative issue, it is actually a key protection for all people in our increasingly plural society. Remember John Leland, the preacher who carted the mammoth, tyrant-defying cheese to Washington, D.C. and paved the way for the First Amendment? His description of religious liberty is powerful, so here it is again: "...Government should protect every man in thinking and speaking freely, and see that one does not abuse another. The liberty I contend for is more than toleration. The very idea of toleration is despicable; it supposes that some have a pre-eminence above the rest to grant indulgence, whereas all should be equally free, Jews, Turks [Muslims], Pagans and Christians."[202]

Religious liberty is critical because it serves as a foundation for civil discussion about important issues while preserving the cherished beliefs that inspire our lives. Therefore, we should be advocates for religious liberty for all people.

In summary, our platform in public life should be star shaped. At the center of the star is the fact that God created humanity in His image and tasked us with His mission. And this foundation strengthens and connects the five key issues: sanctity of life, racial unity and justice, the Matthew 25 issues, the Christian sexual ethic and religious liberty for all people. Here's a graphic depicting this star-shaped platform:

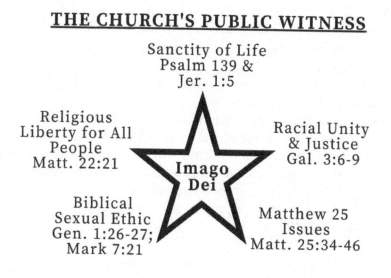

Here's how these five issues work together to build a just and flourishing society. A Biblical view of family and sexuality promotes strong, durable families that are financially self-sustaining and that raise moral and responsible citizens. These citizens are less inclined to be sexually active before or outside of marriage, so the demand for abortion decreases. These families, as part of a local church, are then equipped and encouraged to engage the Matthew 25 issues and to pursue a Biblical vision of racial unity and justice. And these good works, which reflect the power and beauty of the gospel, act as powerful evidence for the value and necessity of religious liberty for all people. This freedom, in turn, allows for a robust exchange of ideas in a diverse society and the promotion of Biblical principles that, if followed, will lead to human flourishing.

Now, let's get practical.

The Practice

In Philippians 1:27, Paul states that our "conversation" or citizenship should be worthy of the gospel. The Greek word for "conversation" or citizenship in Phil 1:27 is *politeuomai* and literally means to "behave as a citizen."[203] So, Paul, under the inspiration of the

Holy Spirit, told the Christians in Philippi to practice their citizenship in such a way that their actions reflected the gospel of Christ. We should do the same in the United States, and here are some pointers for doing that.

This may be an oversimplification, but public life or the public square can be divided into three separate but interrelated arenas: social media, public policy, and elections. Some readers may be surprised that I am beginning with social media or that I am even including social media in this discussion. But many Americans discuss or at least share their political opinions on social media (President Trump's Twitter feed is a key example), so let's start there.

Social Media

I am about to state the obvious; but, twenty years ago, social media platforms like Facebook, Twitter, Instagram, TikTok (and whatever's next) did not exist. So, most Americans did not participate in online sharing and perhaps oversharing of political ideas and opinions. Since we no longer routinely participate in in-person town halls, I suppose this is a healthy development for the free exchange of ideas in our democratic republic. But, as you could probably write a book about, social media can easily turn into a toxic echo chamber and provides a near-constant temptation to engage in behavior that can damage a Christian's individual testimony and the church's public witness.

This is why a gospel-centered engagement in public life must start on social media. Remember the framework I set out in step #1? In review, we should act like Christians, Caesar and citizens on social media.

We should, of course, act like a Christian on social media. I leave this up to your conscience; but, in my opinion, over-the-top political name calling and demeaning memes aren't helpful. If anything, they signal to the watching world that you value your membership in a political tribe more than in the Body of Christ. But those memes get likes, views and shares! True, that is how social media works; but, should Christians really advertise their lack of grace and respect?

I can state the following with certainty. The acquaintances and friends you are trying to reach for Christ (or at least should be) are watching your behavior on social media, so don't let the tone of your political engagement drive them away from the gospel.

Next, engage as Caesar—a fully vested citizen with authority and, therefore, responsibility in the United States. Many Christians do not post about Biblical issues deemed political or controversial by culture, but the watching world should not hear crickets when we are called to be the conscience of the nation.

This is especially difficult for pastors who are leery of being perceived as "too political." We should certainly become "all things to all men" (I Cor. 9:23), and some pastors may want to scale back on their habit of overblowing every other political event as a harbinger of the end of the nation and the church.

But there are some issues (like the five mentioned above) that are primarily Biblical issues rather than political issues. And the church's role is to provide moral guidance to the state and nation. John Stonestreet asks this powerful question, "Does God's morality interfere with God's gospel?" I think not. In fact, the law (in the Biblical sense) is a schoolmaster that points us to Christ (Gal. 3:24-25).

Further, if church leaders are calling the people in their churches and broader communities to full-life discipleship, should they not provide some example in this critical arena? Back to my earlier point about "political discipleship," should we be surprised when Christians engage on social media like frenzied partisans if they are not shown a countercultural, godly example of engagement? In sum, Christians and especially church leaders should be strategic when they engage these issues, but they should not be silent.

Finally, we should engage social media as citizens seeking the common good of our cities, state and nation. Are our posts constantly filled with handwringing about the end of religious liberty, the decline of the republic and inevitable collapse of civilization as we know it? I am, of course, concerned by recent developments. But, repeated digital screams of "the sky is falling!" often fall on deaf ears and do little to solve key problems.

This is why I set out the five key issues above and will set out some ideas in the public policy section below. We should be known as "idea people" who are connecting with others, conversing about problems and creating holistic, Biblically based solutions. Our social media feeds should reflect these efforts as well as the important warnings and news flashes.

Public Policy

Next, the public square is where our culture's values are hammered into the laws that affect our shared lives as citizens. Here are some practical ideas for engaging in this arena with a focus on the five issues set out above.

Sanctity of Life

Concerning the sanctity of life, there is some good news. U.S. abortion rates reached an historic low in 2017.[204] And, when I attended the Walk for Life in 2019, I was struck by one key observation—the crowd was *young*. High schoolers, college students and young adults are providing fresh energy and ideas to the pro-life cause.[205]

That said, we are almost fifty years into the abortion debate; and, despite two new appointments to the U.S. Supreme Court, *Roe v. Wade* and its progeny seem as impregnable as ever. Even if Amy Coney Barrett is confirmed, only one out of eight sitting justices have stated unequivocally that *Roe* and *Planned Parenthood v. Casey* should be overturned.[206] Perhaps that will change; but, to date, Presidents and Supreme Court justices have not significantly changed this issue. And, even if *Roe v. Wade* were overturned, it would simply push the issue of abortion restrictions back to the states. So, from a policy perspective, state legislatures have done the heavy lifting, passing 288 new abortion-related restrictions from 2011 to 2015.[207]

Further, the real catalyst for change on the life issue is the national pregnancy care center movement. Why? Here's a clue. According to a recent comprehensive survey from Notre Dame titled "How Americans Understand Abortion," most Americans don't really "want" abortion. Rather, they prefer that mothers have their babies. But Americans are also very pragmatic about the nature of the relationship between the mother and father, health complications during pregnancy, and the financial and family support system available to a mother after birth.[208]

Pregnancy Care Centers provide the support and community these mothers need and even offer to connect them to an adoptive family in the event of a crisis. These centers have long served as the hands and feet of Jesus on this issue, and they are changing hearts and saving lives one person at a time. So, as Christians, we should remain vigilant about national issues. But we should also track and promote state legislation and, most importantly, support the work of the pregnancy care center down the street.

Racial Unity and Justice

As I stated above, the church should be leading on the issue of racial unity and justice, and we still have much work to do. I have found Dr. Tony Evans' three-step "Kingdom Strategy for Community Transformation" helpful. Here are those three steps: (1) assemble (a community-wide pastor's fellowship which meets regularly and hosts an annual solemn assembly), (2) address (kingdom-minded pastors address cultural events with biblical truth and solutions) and (3) act (pastors mobilize their churches to work together to serve the community and improve underserved neighborhoods).[209]

Notice that Dr. Evans' efforts are focused on cities rather than the entire nation, and a city-based approach is directly in line with the New Testament model for the church. Efforts to promote racial unity and justice may already exist near you or are launching around the country, so I encourage you to get involved. I still have much to learn; but, as of the writing of this section, I am actively involved in such an effort in Indianapolis.

From a policy perspective, I will focus on the issue most relevant to the death of George Floyd: criminal justice reform. I have found the work of Michael Wear and Justin Giboney at the AND Campaign to be helpful in this regard. Michael Wear served as the faith advisor to President Obama, and Justin Giboney is an attorney and political strategist from Atlanta, Georgia. Most importantly, they are both followers of Christ, and they are engaging in public life with a focus on the gospel.

I agree with many though not all of their policy proposals, and they would probably say the same about my work. If you come from a more conservative perspective or background, I encourage you to read Michael Wear's *Reclaiming Hope*[210] and the AND Campaign's new book *Compassion & Conviction*.[211] These books reflect Michael's and Justin's efforts to faithfully apply their Christian faith in public life. Many Christians live in political echo chambers, so we should seek out differing perspectives from time to time.

Before I go further, please understand that I am grateful for the work of the police in protecting and serving communities. According to a recent Bureau of Justice Report, 53.5 million Americans had contact with the police in 2015.[212] And less than 4% of those interactions involved the threat or use of nonfatal force. Further, from June of 2015 to March of 2016, there were 1,348 arrest-related deaths out of more than 50 million police-citizen interactions.[213] So, the actions of a few police officers should not discredit the service or sacrifice of police officers across the country. The proposals in this section are not intended to question the importance or integrity of the many men and women who have dedicated and even given their lives to keep others safe.

Further, I have personal experience in the criminal justice system. I practiced as a public defender for a time and experienced firsthand some of the problems listed below. Biblical Christians can and should support measures to ensure a proportionate use of force during arrests, full transparency in the criminal justice system, adequate legal representation for those accused, fair and proportionate sentencing for convictions and an emphasis on restoration once a returning citizen has paid his or her debt to society. Many cities and states are taking up these matters in the aftermath of the deaths of Auhmad Arbery, George Floyd, and Breonna Taylor, so right now is a perfect opportunity to get involved.

One helpful example at the federal level is the First Step Act, which was authored by Representatives Doug Collins (R-Ga.) and Hakeem Jeffries (D-N.Y.) and supported by organizations such as Prison Fellowship and the Ethics and Religious Liberty Commission of the Southern Baptist Convention. The bill received broad bipartisan support and was signed into law by President Trump in December of 2018.

This law corrected disproportionate sentencing enhancements, allowed federal judges greater discretion in sentencing drug offenses, enhanced access to phone and videoconferencing technologies so families can stay connected, required returning citizens to be held close to their release residence, and added incentives for participating in recidivism-reducing programs (including faith-based programs).[214] Similar efforts should be pursued at the state level where appropriate.

Matthew 25 Issues

In Chapter 7, I set out a number of practical policy ideas related to foster care, the drug crisis and jail ministry. Though these admittedly do not cover all of the Matthew 25 issues, those policy ideas are a good start.

The Biblical Sexual Ethic

Because Congress has not passed legislation such as the Equality Act or on strong religious liberty protections for ministries, both LGBTQ rights advocates and religious liberty advocates have focused their efforts on the federal judiciary. Why? Because, according to the rules of civil procedure, judges have to take up a case filed in their court. In a sense, courts have to do something about these matters once placed on their docket.

During the 2020 U.S. Supreme Court term, the Court handed down a number of key decisions, but I will focus on just two cases that affected religious liberty and LGBTQ rights: *Bostock v. Clayton County* and *Our Lady of Guadalupe School v. Morrissey-Berru.*

In *Bostock*, as mentioned previously, the Court ruled 6-3 to broaden the interpretation of "sex" in Title VII of the Civil Rights Act (which prevents discrimination in employment) to include "sexual orientation" and "gender identity." Justice Gorsuch wrote the opinion, which held: "An employer who fires an individual merely for being gay or transgender defies the law."[215]

Next, in *Our Lady of Guadalupe Schools*, the U.S. Supreme Court re-explained and strengthened the "ministerial exception," a legal principle that recognizes the right of ministries to condition employment on adherence to a ministry's statement of faith and religious practices.

Taken together, what do these cases mean? As predicted by journalist and legal analyst David French, the U.S. Supreme Court appears to be pursuing a judicial version of the "Utah Compromise."[216] In 2015, the Utah legislature passed a law (1) granting anti-discrimination protections to the LGBTQ community and (2) carving out strong religious liberty protections for ministries.

I don't think it is controversial to say that the U.S. Supreme Court is now a political as well as a judicial body in the sense that the Court is sensitive to the cultural mood. And, *Bostock* and *Lady of Guadalupe*, taken together, seem to suggest that the Roberts court is attempting to find middle ground in the clash between religious liberty and sexual freedom. I, of course, do not agree with the *Bostock* decision for reasons stated above; but this approach is certainly preferable to one in which the Supreme Court rules across the board against religious freedom for ministries. This prediction about a judicial "Utah Compromise" may be wrong, but recent decisions seem to point toward its accuracy.

So, how should church leaders and other committed Christians engage this issue? First, we should treat individuals in the LGBTQ community with love and respect while holding to the truths of Scripture. Now is the time to build relationships and have conversations with those that disagree with us.

Next, we should focus on advocating for the right of Christian ministries to hold to a Biblical sexual ethic and on distinguishing such reasonable, good faith beliefs from the unbiblical, racially discriminatory beliefs held by some Christians in the Jim Crow South. In the *Obergefell* case, Justice Kennedy noted that opposition to same-sex marriage, "...long has been held—and continues to be held—in good faith by reasonable and sincere people here and throughout the world."[217]

While maintaining these protections, we should work to build a counter-revolution in our homes, churches and schools. For the moment, we have, quite frankly, lost the cultural argument. That fact does not mean we should stay quiet or abandon the truth. Rather, we need to show our culture rather than just tell our culture why God's design for sexuality and marriage is good, true and beautiful. In summary, we should remain vigilant on the state and national levels, but we should focus on our own hearts, homes and institutions. When secular ideas prove themselves to be bankrupt (and they will), the church will be ready with a contrasting and proven vision for marriage and sexuality.

Religious Liberty for All People

Though I have addressed one aspect of religious liberty above, I will also mention the greatest headline-grabbing religious liberty development in 2020: COVID-19-related church closures. Though these developments have not fully played themselves out as of the writing of this section in late September of 2020, enough has happened to draw lessons from the closures and the church's response.

When COVID-19 cases first surged in March of 2020, most governors issued some form of emergency order that included a lockdown of businesses, schools, churches and other public assemblies. Further, many of these orders contained a list of "essential" and "non-essential" businesses. "Essential" business such as hospitals, grocery stores, hardware stores, gas stations and fast-food restaurants were allowed to remain open; but, most "non-essential" businesses were forced to close. And, in many states, churches were imprecisely categorized as "non-essential."[218]

Most churches initially complied with these lockdown orders in an effort to slow the spread of the virus and to show care and concern for their congregants and neighbors. But, some pastors like Pastor Rodney Howard-Browne in Tampa, Florida, refused to close their churches. Pastor Howard-Browne was arrested and fined for his actions but was quickly released.[219]

Innovative churches turned to drive-in services held in parking lots, but some cities and states even cracked down on these efforts. For example, city officials in Grenville, Mississippi, broke up a drive-in service at Temple Baptist Church and fined the attendees $500 per person. Temple Baptist sued the city, and a federal judge found the ban on drive-in services unconstitutional.[220]

By late May or June, most states had lifted the more stringent meeting bans, and many churches around the country returned to in-person worship services while observing social distancing and other health measures.

However, states like California and Nevada are, at the writing of this section, still prohibiting sizeable in-person or at least in-building worship services.

In California, John MacArthur and Grace Community Church have defied local health orders, and officials have threatened the church with fines.[221] Other churches such as Godspeak Calvary Chapel have actually been held in contempt and/or fined for gathering in defiance of health directives.[222] And, in Nevada, Calvary Chapel Dayton Valley continues to challenge Governor Sisolak's reopening guidelines that allow casinos to open at 50% of their fire code capacity but limit worship services to 50 people.[223]

In two 5-4 decisions that surprised many legal observers, the U.S. Supreme Court declined to provide emergency relief to churches challenging these bans. Chief Justice John Roberts authored a brief opinion in *South Bay United Pentecostal Church v. Newsom* and set out the applicable legal standard: government cannot infringe on the free exercise of religion unless the state has a compelling interest and its actions are narrowly tailored to accomplish that interest.[224] Roberts concluded, "...Similar or more severe restrictions apply to comparable secular gatherings, including lectures, concerts, movie showings, spectator sports, and theatrical performances, where large groups of people gather in close proximity for extended periods of time."[225] In other words, he found that California's restrictions were narrowly tailored to the state's compelling interest in slowing the spread of the virus.

Roberts reached a similar conclusion in *Calvary Chapel Dayton Valley v. Sisolak* (the Nevada case) but did not explain the decision. In both cases, four Justices strongly disagreed, stating that the comparison of churches to other public assemblies is arbitrary or at least overly simplistic. Justice Gorsuch penned this zinging rebuttal in *Calvary Chapel Dayton Valley*, "The world we inhabit today, with a pandemic upon us, poses unusual challenges. But there is no world in which the

Constitution permits Nevada to favor Caesars Palace over Calvary Chapel."[226]

In sum, the Supreme Court weighed in and held that state laws that apply gathering restrictions evenly to churches and other secular public assemblies (such as theaters, etc.) survive scrutiny under the federal constitution, at least in the context of an emergency appeal. The *Calvary Chapel Dayton Valley* case is ongoing, and the Supreme Court may reach a different conclusion if it considers the full merits of the case after the pandemic has passed.

There are many lessons to be drawn from these events, but I will point out two—one about church-state relations and one about the church's intramural disputes.

First, the biggest headline about the pandemic-related shutdowns should be how well most church leaders and most government officials worked together to keep people safe and slow the virus. That said, some government officials treated the church as just one more organization to regulate rather than as a peer or equal institution. This argues for a renewed emphasis on relationship building with elected officials. Further, some state legislators are reviewing the statutes granting emergency powers to governors, and Christians could pursue legislation clearly outlining the procedures for or limiting pandemic-related bans on church gatherings. For example, the Ohio legislature just passed a bill that includes this language, "Notwithstanding any contrary provision of the Revised Code, no public official shall issue an order to close all places of worship in the state or in a geographic area of the state."[227]

Next, a note on our intramural discussions and disagreements. Even Christians strongly disagreed and disagree on whether or not churches should practice civil disobedience in this context. For example, some Christians take John MacArthur's position that civil disobedience is in order, and others hold to Jonathan Leeman's position that churches should continue to follow health directives.[228] I will note that Capitol Hill Baptist Church, which is informally connected with Jonathan Leeman and IX Marks, has sued Washington, D.C. mayor Muriel E. Bowser over gathering restrictions. But, as of the writing of this section, CHBC is still gathering outdoors in Virginia rather than meeting in defiance of local health orders.[229] Such disagreements are common in matters that involve claims of conscience. As Christians, we should extend grace to one another as we navigate these unprecedented developments (Rom. 14). And we should recognize that conscience cases are ultimately about the right of conscience and not just our conscience.

Next, Christians should pay attention to the Religious Land Use and Institutionalized Persons Act (RLUIPA). This law prevents zoning authorities from implementing any regulation that imposes a "substantial burden" on a religious person or assembly unless the regulation is justified by a "compelling interest" and the government agency uses the least restrictive means. Practically, this protects churches and other religious assemblies from being "zoned out" of cities or particular districts or treated disparately because they are religious and tax exempt.[230] Many municipalities will be facing large budget shortfalls due to the pandemic, and these revenue gaps will undoubtably increase scrutiny on tax-exempt properties. Some municipal officials are not well versed on RLUIPA, so Christians should be prepared to point out this legal protection when appropriate.

Please note that the fifth issue is religious liberty *for all people*. This is both Biblical and practical. We should support religious liberty for people of other faiths because, according to Scripture, government steps out of its God-ordained role if it attempts to dictate how a person worships or forces a person to violate his or her conscience (with very rare exceptions, such as child sacrifice).

Further, the law treats all religious organizations alike. So, if we attempt to block the building of a mosque or temple in our cities, we are laying the legal groundwork for Christian churches to be treated in a similar way in the near future. The best strategy, therefore, is to promote religious liberty for all people.

This concludes our brief explainer on practical ideas for engaging public policy related to the five key points set out above. Now, let's move on to some guiding principles for voting and elections.

Elections

How should Christians vote? Now, that's a loaded question! But it should be. The answer to that question will affect the direction of our republic. So, we should give this question careful attention and should approach it with Biblical wisdom.

First, let me clear up a common misperception. I often hear pastors say something along the lines of, "I can't talk about political issues from the pulpit because that will jeopardize my church's tax-exempt status." This is simply incorrect. Let's take a brief look at the actual legal standard.

The IRS prohibits 501(c)(3) organizations, including churches and most ministries, from "directly or indirectly participating in, or intervening in, any political campaign on behalf of (or in opposition to) any candidate for elective public office."[231] You will note that this "Johnson Amendment" (the provision was proposed by Lyndon Johnson) does not prohibit sermons on Biblical issues related to politics. In fact, the IRS' own guidance states: "Also, the ban by Congress is on political campaign activity regarding a candidate; **churches and other 501(c)(3) organizations can engage** in a limited amount of lobbying (including ballot measures) **and advocate for or against issues that are in the political arena** [emphasis added]."[232] Also, this ban does not prevent pastors from campaigning for candidates or running for office in their personal capacity.

In sum, pastors are absolutely free to preach about Biblical issues relevant to public life without concern for their church's tax-exempt status.

I will note that this prohibition is of questionable constitutionality and that the IRS has rarely enforced it. Further, President Trump signed an executive order in 2017 limiting enforcement of the provision. But that executive order could be undone with the stroke of a pen, and the ban has not been amended by Congress. So, the Johnson Amendment is still technically on the books.[233]

That said, I am not a fan of political punditry from the pulpit. Given the political and cultural climate, I see little need to cause division in a church by specifically naming a candidate and telling a congregation to vote for him or her. If a pastor feels specifically led to do so, I defer to that pastor's conscience. But, promoting a candidate can easily be perceived as a commitment to a party or candidate rather than the gospel.

My approach is to preach about Biblical principles and to encourage Christians to vote according to their consciences and as an expression of civic responsibility. Since we are encouraging an allegiance to Scripture and Biblical principles over a political party (would anyone argue the opposite?), why not reflect that in the way politics is addressed from the pulpit? I, of course, defer to pastors in their local context, but the above approach makes practical sense to me.

That addressed, let's move on to a Biblical checklist for choosing candidates. When Moses became overwhelmed with his responsibilities in leading the children of Israel and acting as a judge of their disputes, his father-in-law Jethro encouraged him to appoint officials to help bear the burden of leadership.

Jethro told Moses, "...provide out of all the people able men, such as fear God, men of truth, hating covetousness; and place such over them, to be rulers of thousands, and rulers of hundreds, rulers of fifties, and rulers of tens: [a]nd let them judge the people at all seasons..." (Ex. 18:21).

Here's a summary of those qualifications: we should choose elected officials based on (1) competence, (2) morals, (3) honesty and (4) financial integrity.

First, elected officials should be able or competent in their work. Candidates should evidence the requisite skills and experience to serve the office they seek. Sometimes, Christians overlook this qualification, but we shouldn't. Competence is critical.

Second, elected officials should fear God. In the context of a plural society, I analyze this qualification as follows: a candidate's sense of right and wrong should be based on eternal principles and not the whims of society or their own self-interest. Public officials should understand their role as "God's minister" for our good and that they are ultimately accountable to God for their actions.

I am, of course, aware of and support the constitutional ban on religious tests as a requirement for public office. But I am not referring to formal government action in this section. Rather, I am setting out Biblical principles for Christians as they evaluate a candidate's character and fitness for elected office. If a candidate's moral compass predictably spins toward popularity over principle and power over service, then he or she is not fit for office.

Third, candidates for elected office should display a high degree of and a deep regard for truthfulness. If a candidate has repeatedly or blatantly lied in public or private life, we should not entrust him or her with high office.

And, fourth, elected officials should hate covetousness. Candidates should evidence a deep commitment to serving the common good rather than their own financial interests.

In sum, Christians should prioritize competence, morals, honesty and financial integrity when they choose elected officials. Though other voting guides can be helpful, this Biblical guide should be the first one we consult.

Now, unless Jesus is on the ballot, we will always be voting for the lesser of two or more "evils." Every human being is fallen in some way. So, we should consider these flaws and failures in context and in conjunction with the qualifications set out above. That said, as Christians, we should never spray-paint over such failures as if they are not a problem or, in some cases, sinful. The better approach is to praise a candidate for actions that are in line with Scripture and question faults or actions that are not. Ultimately, we have to decide and cast our ballot, and we should consider all of the above factors when we do.

Further, we should review how we engage with political parties. We should be bending or moving the party platforms back toward God's good design, but Christians in both parties have long been trained to be silent about morality in exchange for electoral victories. For far too long, the parties have assumed the support of Christians without giving more than lip service to Biblical values. That is primarily our fault, or at least it is our fault if we do not operate differently now.

Some Christians have chosen to vote for third-party candidates due to moral concerns with the two major parties or at least their Presidential candidates, and I respect that decision. But, for now, choosing to abandon the two primary parties would mean the forfeiture of almost all meaningful political influence in the United States and would cede control over the country's future to those that hold a different worldview. If we lived in a European country under a proportional electoral system (where voters in minority parties still achieve representation in the legislature) rather than a winner-take-all plurality system, I might agree with the third-party approach. But my current view is that proper stewardship of our democratic republic argues for participation in the two parties.

I imagine that Christians that are members of the Republican party will point out quite forcefully that abortion and religious freedom are key reasons for abandoning the Democratic party. And I imagine that Christians that are members of the Democratic party will point out President Trump's moral track record and Twitter account as reasons enough for abandoning the Republican party. But, just hold on a minute with the tar and feathers. This book is about Christian citizenship. So, as Christians, we should stop thinking about this primarily according to party lines and start analyzing this as members of the Body of Christ.

Respected pollster George Barna has argued that Christian conservatives are largely responsible for the election of President Trump,[234] but he has also noted that "notional" Christians were a "game changer" in the 2016 election. Here's that explanation from Barna:

> While the media have made a big deal about the prolific level of evangelical support won by Trump, the real story may be elsewhere. Barna's research indicates that perhaps the most significant faith group in relation to the Trump triumph was notional Christians. These individuals – who consider themselves to be Christian, typically attend a Christian church, but are not born again – have supported the Democratic candidate in every election since 1996. On average, notionals have given the Democratic candidate 58 percent of their votes. That trend was broken this year as Hillary Clinton took just 47 percent of the group's votes while Trump was awarded 49 percent. Given that notionals are by far the largest of the five faith segments, that transition was a game changer for the Republicans.

In sum, Barna's research shows that conservative Christians helped put Trump in office, but "notional" Christians—religious non-

Christians to be more precise—also played a major if not deciding role.[235]

Further, according to a Pew survey of validated voters in the 2016 election, Christians are deeply divided along racial and partisan lines. In 2016, approximately 96% of Black protestants voted for Hillary Clinton while 77% of White evangelicals voted for Donald Trump. Further, voters of other races (including Hispanics) largely split their votes, with 51% voting for Hilary Clinton and 46% voting for Donald Trump.[236] As noted by historian Thomas Kidd, this is nothing new. Orthodox or traditional Christians have never been politically unified in the United States.[237]

I am always a little leery of stats and figures because they are easily manipulated, and I am sure you are too. But I am confident that the above statistics prove my central premise: the gospel-preaching church in the United States is not politically unified.

With that in mind, we can continue our current approach of questioning the spiritual maturity and even orthodoxy of our brothers and sisters in Christ that vote differently than we do. Or, we can work to encourage each other to follow Jesus and to promote Biblical principles in our sphere of political influence.

Is there a time and place for encouraging fellow Christians to leave a party over unbiblical principles? Yes. Do I have strong opinions about the five key Biblical issues listed above and how they should impact public life? Absolutely. But, let me ask this. What would it take for you to change your political viewpoint on an issue that is not central to the gospel, such as tax policy or welfare programs? I imagine that the pain of death may not be sufficient to change your mind.

So, why do we expect blanket statements on social media outside of the context of a relationship to change a historic and present reality—political disagreements among Christians? A better approach is to encourage Christians in both parties to follow Jesus in how they engage in public life. Political affiliations and positions may change as a result of following Jesus; but I doubt the reverse is true.

I imagine that this section is not quite what you expected when you picked up this book, and my 25-year-old self might be surprised at its contents. But, please hear my heart. As Biblical Christians, we have engaged in a roughly 50-year culture war. Despite these efforts, abortion is still legal, same-sex marriage is the law of the land, religious freedom is under deep scrutiny, riots and protests due to racial injustice just occurred in most major American cities and the American nuclear family is broken.

Please do not read the summary above as a criticism of the faithful and important work of Christians in the public square over the last 50 years. I am deeply grateful for their defense of life and religious liberty and their advocacy for Biblical principles in a quickly changing culture. These efforts are directly responsible for the robust religious liberty protections currently enjoyed by ministries, the right to homeschool, and many other benefits. Further, as I explained in the introduction, I believe we should pursue a Nehemiah approach. We should defend religious liberty (sword) while building strong churches, building partnerships with government officials and seeking the common good (trowel).

So, my summary above is not meant as criticism. Rather, I set it out as a difficult but, I believe, accurate description of where we are today. Given these developments, should we expect to win by playing politics like everyone else? No. We should stand up for truth, justice and righteousness in our times, but we should dedicate ourselves anew to a Biblical strategy.

I don't know about you, but I'm tired of doing church and engaging culture as usual. I'm tired of doing the same thing and insanely expecting different results. Many churches are shifting their focus from drawing crowds to making disciples and are adjusting their methods or at least programs due to COVID-19. Well, let's take a similar approach in public life. Let's recognize the realities of this political and cultural moment. And let's get back to the basics while doing everything possible to proclaim the gospel and impact our communities with Biblical truth.

What if we encouraged Christians to focus on following Jesus and on standing up for Biblical principles no matter the cost? What if, instead of bending with political movements further left and further right, American Christians focused on a unity around Biblical principles and an ordered liberty that reflects God's good design? What if we stopped seeing ourselves primarily as members of political parties and started seeing ourselves primarily as members of God's family?

This, I believe, has the power to revive the church and renew the American Republic.

The above may sound hopelessly naïve; but I promise you my work in the trenches over the last ten years has mercilessly crushed my youthful idealism. I know firsthand the enormity and complexity of the problems that face the church and the nation. So, I am not hopelessly naïve. Rather, I'm just hopeless for our country absent a major move of God in our times. And that will not come from novel political strategies. Rather, it will come by prayer and fasting and by engaging government in God's way. So, let's get to work.

In conclusion, Step #4 is to do the hard work of Christian citizenship in the public square. I will admit to you that I struggled intensely with this chapter. My focus in this book is on Biblical principles, and I have attempted to keep those principles front and center. But I am also aware that simply stating those principles does little to help church leaders and other committed Christians wrestle through the tough issues and decisions in public life. So, in a sense, I went first. I offered my best efforts at explaining Biblical principles, selecting important issues in public life and applying those Biblical principles to those issues as an example.

I am sure some readers will think I went too far, and I am sure others will think I stopped short of key conclusions. That is the danger of saying anything in this climate. But I set out to write a practical field guide for Christian citizenship, not just another book diagnosing the nation's problems with little in the way of what to do about it.

In conclusion, let's look back to that conversation between Pilate and Jesus. Many Christians I meet today observe the complexities of public life and say something akin to, "I am a citizen of Heaven" and "God's kingdom is not of this world" and excuse themselves from meaningful participation in the public square. In so doing, they compare their actions to Christ's statement before Pilate.

But what if that is the wrong or at least an incomplete application? A few years ago, I was listening to a podcast by Russell Moore, and he said something that struck me. He explained that we, as American Christians, are tasked with promoting Biblical principles in public life and that we should not shirk that duty.[238] Then, he remarked that Christians that abdicate their role as citizen are not acting like Jesus.

Rather, he said, they are acting like Pilate. They are washing their hands of a God-given responsibility in the public square.

May that not be said of us.

9 LINCOLN'S WORN LEGACY

President Lincoln's Second Inaugural Address is one for the ages, but the words he wore at that address are perhaps as important as the words he spoke. Here's what I mean. Lincoln wore a long black coat to that famous address, and he wore the same coat to Ford's Theatre on the fateful night of April 14, 1865. After John Wilkes Booth shot Lincoln, doctors removed the blood-soaked garment so they could care for Lincoln during his final hours.

That black coat was custom made at Lincoln's request, and the coat's lining depicts an eagle clutching a banner emblazoned with these words: "One Country, One Destiny."[239]

So, in a sense, Lincoln wore his mission statement and his legacy. He held the Union together. He ended slavery. And he set our young nation on a path toward prosperity and global influence. Those words, "One Country, One Destiny" moved from hope to history due to his efforts and sacrifice.

Now, his legacy is in peril. We are deeply divided. And, as a nation, we have lost our purpose. We are like a professional athlete after his or her final game or match. We are unsure of the purpose of our union. So, we neglect it, use it for our own benefit, or turn to tearing it down.

And, sadly, even many Christians have chalked up America as a lost cause.

So, we must come back to first principles. America is an idea. The founding generation built our republic on an ordered liberty inspired by humble faith and common sense. This idea unified us despite differences in tradition, history, language, ethnicity, and culture. And this idea is America's "secret sauce" that unleashed her potential and transformed her from thirteen out-of-the-way colonies to a world power.

Sadly, we have changed from "One Nation Under God" to "One Nation Over God." And, as a result, America has fractured into the default setting of human history: warring factions seeking their own interests. And, if we are not careful, we will be pulled into this strife. We will be pulled into doing citizenship like everyone else.

This is why we must change our story about citizenship.

As human beings, we are creatures of narrative. We rely on story to measure our success and give our lives meaning. And each of us has an internal story about citizenship in the United States.

Many American Christians have defaulted to the story that they are part of an embattled church that must take America back through ever-more desperate political action. And others have defaulted to the story that they are members of an increasingly exiled church and have no role or responsibility in public life. As explained above, neither of these stories about citizenship is the correct, Biblical one.

So, let's set the story straight. As Christians, our primary citizenship is in heaven. We should deeply care about the United States and serve our fellow citizens. But, our hope, purpose and significance are not bound up in the results of an election or even in the future of our country. The United States is a remarkable nation, but it is one nation among many that have risen and fallen. In sum, we work and care for our country. But we must prioritize God's kingdom.

Here's a powerful explanation of this principle, penned by English journalist Malcolm Muggeridge in 1980:

> We look back on history and what do we see? Empires
> rising and falling, revolutions and counter-revolutions,
> wealth accumulating and wealth dispersed, one nation

dominant and then another. Shakespeare speaks of "the rise and fall of great ones that ebb and flow with the moon."

In one lifetime I have seen my own fellow countrymen ruling over a quarter of the world, the great majority of them convinced, in the words of what is still a favorite song, that, "'God who's made the mighty would make them mightier yet.'" I've heard a crazed, cracked Austrian proclaim to the world the establishment of a German Reich that would last a thousand years; an Italian clown announce that he would restart the calendar to begin his own assumption of power. I've heard a murderous Georgian brigand in the Kremlin acclaimed by the intellectual elite of the world as a wiser than Solomon, more enlightened than Ashoka, more humane than Marcus Aurelius. I've seen America wealthier and in terms of weaponry, more powerful than the rest of the world put together, so that Americans, had they so wished, could have outdone an Alexander or a Julius Caesar in the range and scale of their conquests.

All in one little lifetime. All gone with the wind. England part of a tiny island off the coast of Europe, threatened with dismemberment and even bankruptcy. Hitler and Mussolini dead, remembered only in infamy. Stalin a forbidden name in the regime he helped found and dominate for some three decades. America haunted by fears of running out of those precious fluids that keep her motorways roaring, and the smog settling, with troubled memories of a disastrous campaign in Vietnam...

All in one lifetime, all gone. Gone with the wind.

Behind the debris of these self-styled, sullen supermen and imperial diplomatists, there stands the gigantic figure of one person, because of whom, by whom, in whom, and through whom alone mankind might still have hope. The person of Jesus Christ.[240]

Amen.

Some may say that this dual citizenship makes us poor citizens in the here and now. I disagree. This truth keeps us from some starry-eyed patriotism that can't see evil or failure in the country's past or present. This truth steels us to do the hard work of building a just, equal and prosperous society knowing full well that utopia will elude us until His kingdom comes. And this truth rescues us from despair when all seems lost and culture turns against Biblical principles.

So, yes, we are Christians first; but, we are also citizens of a democratic republic that grants us authority and assumes our principled participation.

But how can we engage in that role without jeopardizing the gospel? Here's how.

First, we should go over or review our citizenship. We should consider Biblical principles, Biblical examples, and historical examples. And we should apply those principles and learn from those examples as we engage as Christian citizens in the United States.

Next, we should offer prayer for and build relationships with elected officials. We should sow the Word, focus on the individual worth of elected officials and provide wisdom in the public square. We should become a wise friend rather than a yelling foe.

Third, we should offer solutions to tough problems like foster care, the drug crisis and recidivism; and we should partner with government officials to solve those problems.

Fourth, we should do the hard work of Christian citizenship in the public square. We should focus on a star-shaped platform with the *imago Dei* at the center and five key issues connected and strengthened by that truth: the sanctity of life, racial unity and justice, the Matthew 25 issues, the Biblical sexual ethic and religious liberty for all people. Then, we should practice our Christian citizenship on social media, in the creation of public policy, and during election season.

If we will take these steps, we can become and remain gospel-centered citizens in a divided America.

I often ask church audiences to think about the year 2050. This date is close enough for us to impact but far enough into the future for us to envision transformative shifts in our culture and nation. So, what will America look like on this date thirty years from now?

One possible American future is powerfully illustrated by a scene in the Amazon original TV series *The Man in the High Castle*, which explores an alternate reality in which Nazi Germany and Imperial Japan won World War II. In the last episode of season three, the Nazis are depicted destroying the Statue of Liberty in a massive, elaborate ceremony designed to celebrate their global ascendency. In a gut-wrenching scene, Lady Liberty slowly crashes from her pedestal, her torch hand breaks free and skips across the water, and the torch slowly, painfully sinks into New York harbor. Heinrich Himmler, the new Fuhrer that follows Hitler in this dystopia, gleefully exclaims: "At long last, her light goes out!"[241]

I watched that scene with raw emotion. I pray that something akin to the destruction of Lady Liberty and all that she represents never happens on our watch. Given our military might, I doubt America will fall to a foreign invader in our lifetime. But I am afraid that, absent a change in America's trajectory, the light of liberty will slowly dim and go out, drowned by neglect, selfishness, greed and division.

But that does not have to be the end of the American story. There is another, Biblical vision for our citizenship and the future of the United States. What if we focus on building strong churches, and those churches make disciples who make a difference? What if those disciples, who just so happen to be good citizens, then renew the promise of the American republic? And, what if, by 2050, we transform our cities, states and nation through the power of the gospel?

That is the vision I can get behind and the vision I have dedicated my life and ministry to.

As American Christians, we should not focus our hope on "great" politicians who will just club the other side of the political aisle and briefly stoke the ever-dimming fires of liberty. This may be a strategy for survival, but it is not a sound strategy for renewal or transformation. Instead, America needs a movement of "good" citizens who will work tirelessly and selflessly for the sake of the gospel and the good of the country.

In conclusion, the legacy Lincoln once wore is now worn. The phrase "One Country, One Destiny" seems like little more than a naïve slogan from a prior age. But it need not remain so. America is not too far gone to renew. God is the governor of the nations, sets up kings and removes them and is working all things according to His will (Ps. 22:28, Dan. 2:2; Eph. 1:11). With Him, all things are possible (Matt. 19:26).

Lincoln once called a crowd at an American battlefield to dedicate themselves to an unfinished work so that "…this nation, under God, shall have a new birth of freedom and that government of the people, by the people, for the people, shall not perish from the earth."[242]

Now, as Christians on the American mission field, Christ is calling us to dedicate ourselves to the unfinished work of the Great Commission and to the hard work of gospel-centered citizenship. The new birth in Christ (Jn. 3:3) is the surest guarantee of a new birth of freedom in our times. But this renewal will not come without the selfless efforts of Christians who, by their good citizenship, point their fellow Americans past the flag and Capitol to the cross and their eternal King.

From division, we can rise to unity around an ordered liberty. And, from lack of purpose, we can rise to promote truth and justice in the growing dark of an uncertain global future. As Christian citizens equipped with God's power, we can once again turn "One Country, One Destiny" from hope into history.

10 BIBLE STUDY GUIDE

Prior to writing this book, I asked a number of pastors about the best way to address Christian citizenship in our charged political environment. The answer was practically unanimous: develop a resource that allows Christians to discuss the topic in the context of small groups or Sunday school classes.

For that reason, I have developed the following Bible study guide designed to allow you and your small group or Sunday school class to work through these principles and action steps and to encourage each other to follow Jesus in this area of your lives.

This study is designed to be an 8-week study, and each session begins with an ice-breaker question and a passage of Scripture followed by the key principles set out in the applicable chapter. I, of course, encourage participants to read the applicable chapter and Scripture passage prior to the class session.

If members of your small group or Sunday school class are citizens of another country, they are still welcome in this study! In fact, their perspective on this topic will provide rich comparisons and contrasts. We are studying Christian citizenship, not just American Christian citizenship.

One last thing before we get started. Due to the sensitivity of this topic, I encourage the group leader to start the study with this statement or something similar:

> Welcome to our Bible study on Christian citizenship. Do you know that people have strong opinions on this topic? Just a few, right? You may have heard someone say, "I don't discuss religion or politics." Well, over the next few weeks, we are studying both! So, let's begin with the purpose of this study.

> At [insert church name], we believe that we are called to proclaim and live out the gospel in every area of our lives, including in our role as citizen (Matt 28:16-20; Phil 1:27). But this is increasingly complicated in our polarized and plural society. The political parties, news media, and even family and friends are quite happy to tell us how to engage in public life, and many Christians have defaulted to the same political habits and practices as everyone else. But we should not follow our culture's political playbook. Rather, we should do public life by the Book. In Philippians 1:27, we are commanded to practice our citizenship in a way that is worthy of the gospel. So, over the next 8 weeks, we will be studying how to do that in a divided America.

> That said, we will not be telling you which party to affiliate with or which politicians to vote for. Rather, the point of this study is to equip you with Biblical principles so you can apply them according to your conscience in the public square.

> But we do hope to engage in meaningful discussions about the issues of our day from a Biblical perspective. And we need to remember that Romans 13 (on government) is followed by Romans 14 (on Christian conscience). I imagine there are a number of different

viewpoints and even political affiliations in this room, but we are one in Christ (Eph. 4:1-6). We often talk about the need for civility in public life. Well, now is our opportunity to practice something better than civility—love. We are to love one another (John 15:17), so let's dedicate ourselves to speaking the truth in love over the next eight weeks. I am looking forward to this study as we learn what Scripture says about this important area of our lives and discuss how best to live out these principles in our cultural moment. With that said, let's dive into the first lesson.

Lesson #1 Review Biblical Principles

Ice breaker: What is your favorite national holiday? Why? (If you are a citizen of another country, feel free to share about a national holiday from your home country.)

Passage: Romans 13:1-7

1. Government is God's Idea. What practical lessons do you draw from this truth? What secular philosophies or ideas have led Christians to see government as entirely secular rather an institution created by God?
2. Government isn't God. Why do you think politics has, at least in some ways, replaced religion in our society?
3. Government needs a guide. How can we serve as the conscience of an increasingly plural society? Where would you draw the line between (1) the church providing moral guidance to the state and (2) violating the Biblical separation between the two institutions?
4. Government guards good works. Why do many Christians see the church and state as opponents rather than partners? What can be done to change this from the church's perspective and the state's perspective?
5. Government will go away. How does focusing on Christ's eternal kingdom make us good citizens of the United States?

What daily habits or practices would help us stay mindful of our dual citizenship?

Lesson #2 Review Biblical Examples

Ice Breaker: What is the hardest/most complicated task you have completed with the help of a YouTube video?

Scripture: Hebrews 11:32-40

1. Pick one Old Testament example citizen and discuss the details of his or her life. What lessons did you learn from this Biblical example?
2. I think Daniel, Esther and Nehemiah are helpful examples for American Christians and other Christians in participatory democracies. Do you agree (it's ok not to)? If so, why?
3. List all of the Herods in order. Just kidding! Instead, discuss the importance of the Herods and the High Priest and Sanhedrin in the Biblical narrative.
4. Pick one New Testament example citizen other than Jesus. Discuss the key events and lessons from that example's life.
5. How can we apply Christ's teachings or example on power, persuasion and public life?

Lesson #3 Review Historical Examples

Ice Breaker: What kind of snob are you? I went first and admitted that I am a coffee snob; so, come on, people. I can't be the only snob out there!

Scripture: Matthew 28:16-20

1. Why is it important to study Christian citizenship across continents and ages?
2. What key lesson did you draw from the early church in Rome?

3. Choose one example citizen from the early church to the 1700s (up to and including Roger Williams). Discuss the events and lessons of that individual's life.
4. Choose one example citizen from the 1700s to the 1900s (up to and including Frances Willard). Discuss the events and lessons of that individual's life.
5. Choose one example citizen from the 1900s to the present. Discuss the events and lessons of that individual's life.

Lesson #4 Apply to the United States

Ice Breaker: Since this chapter is about American history and government, go around the room and ask the participants if they have an interesting ancestor or a family member that participated in an historic event. For example, my grandfather was a Navy pilot and participated in the Korean war.

Scripture: I Peter 2:11-17

1. Do you tend to see the United States as a great nation? Or, do you tend to emphasize the sinful events in America's past? Why?
2. How do the Biblical doctrines of sin and redemption help us acknowledge and learn from the sins of the past but also have hope for the future?
3. How can we be Christians first in a two-party system?
4. Who is "Caesar" in the American system (again, it is ok to disagree with me), and how should we apply that principle in our lives?
5. What are some practical examples of seeking the common good rather than just our own interests in public life?

Lesson #5 Offer Prayer for and Build Relationships with Government Officials

Ice Breaker: Why do you think civility is breaking down in the United States?

Scripture: I Timothy 2:1-4

1. Prior to reading this chapter, did you consistently pray for all Americans in their role as citizen sovereigns? Did you consistently pray for elected officials? If not, how will you practice this discipline in the future?
2. How can we make supplications for, pray for, intercede on behalf of and thank God for government officials?
3. List your state legislators, governor, and members of Congress.
4. Break up into groups of two and practice sharing a passage of Scripture with an elected official.
5. Ask the group to pull out their calendars and schedule a time to meet with or at least communicate with their elected officials via phone, mail or email. Then, plan a time for members of the group to report back on those efforts.

Lesson #6 Offer Solutions and Partner with Government Officials to Solve Key Problems

Ice Breaker: What do you think is the worst problem in your city or neighborhood?

Scripture: Titus 3:1-8

1. How can we do good works without losing our focus on the Good News?
2. How should Christians engage the issue of foster care? Is there a foster care family in your church or neighborhood that you could encourage or support?
3. How can we address the stigma associated with opioid addiction/substance abuse disorder, provide hope, and provide community?
4. How can the church assist returning citizens as they integrate back into society?
5. What are your or your group's natural bridges into your community? What area or issue is God leading you to impact?

Josh Hershberger

Lesson #7 Do the Hard Work of Christian Citizenship in the Public Square

Ice Breaker: Have you noticed the increasing polarization in American politics? What are some examples of that?

Scripture: Philippians 1:23-30

1. What does it mean to practice citizenship that is worthy of the gospel (Phil 1:27)?
2. How should Christians approach politics on social media? Should church leaders engage differently than other Christians?
3. Review the Biblical justifications for the star-shaped platform. Do you agree? Would you substitute or change any of the five points?
4. What is the best way to promote one or two of the five points (select topics of interest to your group)?
5. Note that some of these points sound "conversative" and some sound "liberal." How can we remain focused on Scripture in a primarily two-party system?

Lesson #8 Change Your Story about Citizenship

Ice Breaker: Describe the United States in 2050 if current trends continue.

Scripture: Revelation 22:1-7

1. What does victory in the public square look like to you? What does defeat in the public square look like to you?
2. How will you change your story about citizenship in light of this study?
3. Why do you think God raised up the United States or at least allowed the United States to become a world power? What

193

purpose or mission should we pursue as a nation in the next century?

4. How does looking to the New Jerusalem renew and focus our citizenship now?

5. What step do you need to work on to become or remain a "good" citizen?

ABOUT THE AUTHOR

Josh Hershberger is an attorney, minister and speaker. He leads The Daniel Initiative, a ministry of Indiana Family Institute dedicated to building relationships between the ministers of God and the ministers of government (Rom. 13) with the goal of ministering to those officials and partnering with them for the common good, and The Good Citizen Project, a national ministry dedicated to equipping Christians to be gospel-centered citizens. Josh is licensed to practice law in three states (IN, KY & TN), represents Christian ministries throughout much of the United States, and serves as a teaching pastor at his church in southeast Indiana. He lives in Hanover, Indiana, with his wife, Carissa, and his children, Aryana and Gabriel.

Find out more about The Daniel Initiative and Indiana Family Institute at www.hoosierfamily.org.

Find out more about the Good Citizen Project at www.goodcitizen.us.

Listen to *The Good Citizen Podcast* wherever you download your podcasts.

Additional works from the author (available on Amazon.com):

The Bold Church Strategy: Serving Our Way Back to the Center of the City

Persuasion Points: Practical Responses to Culture's Toughest Questions

DISCLAIMER

The information contained in this book is general in nature and is not intended to provide, or be a substitute for, legal analysis, legal advice, or consultation with appropriate legal counsel. Further, this document is not intended to be a substitute for the analysis or advice of a licensed tax professional, and you should additionally consult with a tax professional. You should not act or rely on information contained in this document without seeking appropriate professional advice. By printing and distributing this resource, Joshua Hershberger is not providing legal advice, and the use of this document is not intended to constitute advertising or solicitation and does not create an attorney-client relationship between you and Joshua Hershberger or between you and any attorney affiliated with Joshua Hershberger.

NOTES

[1] Guinness, Os. *Last Call for Liberty: How America's Genius for Freedom Has Become Its Greatest Threat*. Kindle ed., Downers Grove, Illinois, *Ivp Books*, An Imprint of *Intervarsity Press*, 2018, p. 74.

[2] *Ibid.*

[3] Haberman, Clyde. "Religion and Right-Wing Politics: How Evangelicals Reshaped Elections." *The New York Times*, 28 Oct. 2018, www.nytimes.com/2018/10/28/us/religion-politics-evangelicals.html. Accessed 25 Sept. 2020.

[4] Stetzer, Ed, and Andrew McDonald. "Why Evangelicals Voted Trump: Debunking the 81%." *ChristianityToday.Com*, 18 Oct. 2018, www.christianitytoday.com/ct/2018/october/why-evangelicals-trump-vote-81-percent-2016-election.html. Accessed 25 Sept. 2020.

[5] Hershberger, Josh. *#99 Keys to Gospel-Centered Citizenship with John Stonestreet*. 1 Oct. 2019, www.goodcitizen.us/99-keys-to-gospel-centered-citizenship-with-john-stonestreet/. Accessed 1 Sept. 2020.

[6] Kentucky General Assembly. *Constitution of Kentucky*. 1891, https://apps.legislature.ky.gov/Law/Constitution/Constitution/ViewConstitution?rsn=263.

[7] The Holy Bible, King James Version. Cambridge Edition: 1769; *King James Bible Online*, 2018. www.kingjamesbibleonline.org. All Scripture quotations in this book are taken from the King James Version. Though I consider the inerrancy of

Scripture an essential doctrine, I do not consider the Bible version debate an issue that requires separation from my brothers and sisters in Christ. I routinely work with churches that use a variety of versions but hold to the inerrancy and authority of Scripture.

[8] Colson, Charles. *Kingdoms in Conflict.* New York, Ny, *Zondervan Publishing House,* 1987, p. 114.

[9] Newbigin, Lesslie. *Honest Religion for Secular Man.* 1966. *Wipf and Stock,* 5 Aug. 2011, pp. 56–77.

[10] Noonan, Peggy. *Patriotic Grace: What It Is and Why We Need It Now.* New York, *Harpercollins,* 2008.

[11] WallBuilders. "Sermon - Election - 1790, Massachusetts." *WallBuilders,* 27 Dec. 2016, www.wallbuilders.com/sermon-election-1790-massachusetts/. Accessed 25 Aug. 2020.

[12] Erickson, Erick. "The Church Should Remember This Martin Luther King, Jr. Quote." *The Resurgent,* 4 Apr. 2016, www.theresurgent.com/2016/04/04/the-church-should-remember-this-martin-luther-king-jr-quote/. Accessed 25 Aug. 2020.

[13] Goodrich, Luke W. *Free to Believe: The Battle over Religious Liberty in America.* Colorado Springs, Co, *Multnomah,* 2019.

[14] Washington, George. Farewell Address. *National Archives,* 19 September 1796, https://founders.archives.gov/documents/Washington/99-01-02-00963.

[15] Ashford, Bruce Riley. "Two Reasons Why Religion and Politics Cannot Be Separated." *BruceAshford.Net,* 27 Apr. 2016, www.bruceashford.net/2016/two-reasons-why-religion-and-politics-cannot-be-separated/. Accessed 23 Aug. 2020; Ashford, Bruce Riley. *Letters to an American Christian.* Nashville, Tennessee, *B & H Publishing Group,* 2018, p. 37.

[16] Mark David Hall. *Did America have a Christian Founding? Separating Modern Myth from Historical Truth.* S.L., *Thomas Nelson Pub,* 2020.

[17] Christos Antoniadis. "A Comparison of the Roman and Han Empires." *Medium,* Medium, 10 Apr. 2019, www.medium.com/@christoss200/a-comparison-of-the-roman-and-han-empires-9a8116f5b53c. Accessed 23 Aug. 2020.

[18] Stone, Lyman. "Christianity Has Been Handling Epidemics for 2000 Years." *Foreign Policy,* 13 Mar. 2020, www.foreignpolicy.com/2020/03/13/christianity-epidemics-2000-years-should-i-still-go-to-church-coronavirus/. Accessed 1 Aug. 2020; Stark, Rodney. *The Rise of Christianity: A Sociologist Reconsiders History.* Princeton University Press, 1996, pp. 73–77.

[19] Wright, Ted. "Who Was the Pharaoh of the Exodus?" *Cross Examined.Org | Christian Apologetics Organization | Dr. Frank Turek,* 3 July 2013, www.crossexamined.org/ancient-israel-myth-or-history-part-3c/. Accessed 25 Sept. 2020.

[20] Beegle, Dewey M. "Moses | Hebrew Prophet." *Encyclopedia Britannica*, 15 Dec. 2017, www.britannica.com/biography/Moses-Hebrew-prophet. Accessed 6 June 2020.

[21] Akhilesh Pillalamarri. "The 5 Most Powerful Empires in History." *The National Interest*, 22 Feb. 2015, www.nationalinterest.org/feature/the-5-most-powerful-empires-history-12296. Accessed 25 Aug. 2020.

[22] Sztersky, Subby. "The Story of Esther, Where Sacred and Secular History Meet." *Focus on the Family*, 2018, www.focusonthefamily.ca/content/the-story-of-esther-where-sacred-and-secular-history-meet. Accessed 25 Sept. 2020.

[23] Simpson, Ian. "Cyrus Cylinder, Ancient Decree of Religious Freedom, Starts U.S. Tour." *Reuters*, 7 Mar. 2013, www.reuters.com/article/us-usa-cyrus/cyrus-cylinder-ancient-decree-of-religious-freedom-starts-u-s-tour-idUSBRE9260Y820130307. Accessed 25 Aug. 2020.

[24] Berding, Kenneth. "How Many Herods Are There in the Bible?" *The Good Book Blog - Biola University Blogs*, 2014, www.biola.edu/blogs/good-book-blog/2014/how-many-herods-are-there-in-the-bible. Accessed 1 Aug. 2020.

[25] Sanders, E.P., and Jaroslav Pelikan. "Jesus - Jewish Palestine at the Time of Jesus." *Encyclopedia Britannica*, 2019, www.britannica.com/biography/Jesus/Jewish-Palestine-at-the-time-of-Jesus. Accessed 24 Apr. 2020.

[26] Shurpin, Yehuda. "The Sanhedrin: The Jewish Court System." *www.Chabad.Org*, 2019, www.chabad.org/library/article_cdo/aid/4100306/jewish/The-Sanhedrin-The-Jewish-Court-System.htm#footnoteRef1a4100306. Accessed 25 Sept. 2020.

[27] The Editors of Encyclopedia Britannica. "Sanhedrin | Judaism." *Encyclopedia Britannica*, 2008, www.britannica.com/topic/sanhedrin. Accessed 28 Aug. 2020.

[28] The Editors of Encyclopedia Britannica. "Legion | Military Unit | Britannica." *Encyclopedia Britannica*, 2020, www.britannica.com/topic/legion. Accessed 24 Aug. 2020.

[29] Davis, Paul K. *Besieged: 100 Great Sieges from Jericho to Sarajevo*. Oxford; New York, *Oxford University Press*, 2003, pp. 35–39.

[30] Sherwin-White, A N. *Roman Society and Roman Law in the New Testament*. 1960. Eugene, Or, *Wipf And Stock*, 2004, pp. 144–186.

[31] The Editors of Encyclopedia Britannica. "Civitas | Ancient Rome." *Encyclopedia Britannica*, 2011, www.britannica.com/topic/civitas. Accessed 3 Mar. 2020.

[32] Sanders, E.P. "St. Paul the Apostle - Jewish Law." *Encyclopedia Britannica*, 1 Apr. 2019, www.britannica.com/biography/Saint-Paul-the-Apostle/Jewish-law. Accessed 4 June 2020.

[33] History.com Editors. "Brutus Dies by Suicide." *HISTORY*, 9 Feb. 2010, www.history.com/this-day-in-history/brutus-commits-suicide. Accessed 25 Aug. 2020.

[34] Jackson, Wayne. "A Brief Study of the Word 'Kingdom.'" *Christian Courier*, 2020, www.christiancourier.com/articles/1348-brief-study-of-the-word-kingdom-a. Accessed 11 Sept. 2020.

[35] Aviva and Shmuel Bar-Am. "Berko Park, Aka Ancient Tiberias." *www.Timesofisrael.Com*, 8 June 2013, www.timesofisrael.com/berko-park-aka-ancient-tiberias/. Accessed 11 Sept. 2020. "Berko Park, aka ancient Tiberias: King Herod Antipas unwittingly built Tiberias directly over a Jewish cemetery. Luckily, some 130 years later, Rabbi Shimon Bar Yohai decided to purify the place."

[36] Jerusalem Talmud, Shevi'it 39a, chpt. 9, halachah 5.

[37] Manson, T W. *The Sayings of Jesus, as Recorded in the Gospels According to St. Matthew and St. Luke. With Introd. and Commentary.* 1949. London, Scm Press, 1974, p. 276. "The answer of Jesus is defiant... 'fox'...describes an insignificant third-rate person as opposed to a person of real power and greatness. To call Herod 'that fox' is as much as to say he is neither a great man nor a straight man; he has neither majesty nor honour."

[38] DeYoung, Kevin. "The First Sexual Revolution: The Triumph of Christian Morality in the Roman Empire." *The Gospel Coalition*, 9 Sept. 2019, www.thegospelcoalition.org/blogs/kevin-deyoung/first-sexual-revolution-triumph-christian-morality-roman-empire/. Accessed 11 Sept. 2020.

[39] Gibbon, Edward, and D M Low. *The Decline and Fall of the Roman Empire, an Abridgement.* Book Club ed., London, Harcourt, Brace and Company, 1960, pp. 153–154.

[40] *Ibid.*

[41] Christianity Today Editors. "Constantine." *Christian History | Learn the History of Christianity & the Church*, Christian History, 8 Aug. 2008, www.christianitytoday.com/history/people/rulers/constantine.html. Accessed 23 Aug. 2020.

[42] The Editors of Christianity.com. "Julian the Apostate Couldn't Defeat Christ." *Christianity.Com*, 2007, www.christianity.com/church/church-history/timeline/301-600/julian-the-apostate-couldnt-defeat-christ-11629670.html. Accessed 25 Aug. 2020.

[43] Christianity Today Editors. "Augustine of Hippo." *Christian History | Learn the History of Christianity & the Church*, Christian History, 8 Aug. 2008, www.christianitytoday.com/history/people/theologians/augustine-of-hippo.html. Accessed 25 Aug. 2020.

[44] Smith, James K. A. "How (Not) to Be Worldly: Tracing the Borders of the 'Earthly City.'" *Christianity Today*, 23 Aug. 2012, www.christianitytoday.com/thisisourcity/7thcity/tracing-borders-of-earthly-city.html. Accessed 11 Sept. 2020.

[45] Charmley, Gervase N. "Augustine and 'The City of God.'" *Banner of Truth USA*, 17 Aug. 2015,

www.banneroftruth.org/us/resources/articles/2015/augustine-and-the-city-of-god/. Accessed 25 Sept. 2020.

46 The Editors of Christianity.com. "Bishop Frumentius, Apostle to Ethiopia." *Christianity.Com*, 2007, www.christianity.com/church/church-history/timeline/301-600/bishop-frumentius-apostle-to-ethiopia-11629673.html. Accessed 23 Aug. 2020.

47 Lawler, Andrew. "Church Unearthed in Ethiopia Rewrites the History of Christianity in Africa." *Smithsonian*, Smithsonian.com, 10 Dec. 2019, www.smithsonianmag.com/history/church-unearthed-ethiopia-rewrites-history-christianity-africa-180973740/. Accessed 25 Aug. 2020. Archaeologists now can more closely date when Christianity spread to the Aksumite Empire.

48 The Editors of Encyclopedia Britannica. "Ethiopian Orthodox Tewahedo Church | Church, Ethiopia." *Encyclopedia Britannica*, 3 Jan. 2020, www.britannica.com/topic/Ethiopian-Orthodox-Tewahedo-Church. Accessed 28 Aug. 2020.

49 McInerny, Ralph, and John O'Callaghan. "Saint Thomas Aquinas (Stanford Encyclopedia of Philosophy)." *Stanford.Edu*, 2014, plato.stanford.edu/entries/aquinas/. Accessed 20 Aug. 2020.

50 The Editors of Christianity Today. "Thomas Aquinas." *Christian History | Learn the History of Christianity & the Church*, Christian History, 8 Aug. 2008, www.christianitytoday.com/history/people/theologians/thomas-aquinas.html. Accessed 25 Aug. 2020.

51 Gee, Allison. "Who First Said 'The Pen Is Mightier than the Sword'?" *BBC News*, 9 Jan. 2015, www.bbc.com/news/magazine-30729480#. Accessed 25 Aug. 2020.

52 Koritansky, Peter. "Aquinas: Political Philosophy | Internet Encyclopedia of Philosophy." *www.Iep.Utm.Edu*, 2020, www.iep.utm.edu/aqui-pol/. Accessed 25 Sept. 2020.

53 *Ibid.*

54 Newman, John Henry, et al. "The Works of St. Thomas Aquinas (18 Vols.)." *www.Logos.Com*, 2012, www.logos.com/product/49356/the-works-of-st-thomas-aquinas. Accessed 23 Aug. 2020.

55 "Thomas Aquinas," *Christianity Today*.

56 Thomas, Aquinas Saint. *Treatise on Law: Summa Theologica, Bks I-II, Qq. 90-97.* Chicago, The Great Books Foundation, 1954.

57 The Editors of Christianity Today. "Martin Luther." *Christian History | Learn the History of Christianity & the Church*, Christianity Today, 8 Aug. 2008, www.christianitytoday.com/history/people/theologians/martin-luther.html. Accessed 30 Sept. 2020.

58 Metaxas, Eric. *Martin Luther: The Man Who Rediscovered God and Changed the World.* New York, Penguin Books, 2017, p. 131.

[59] Lawson, Steven. "The Reformation and the Men Behind It." *Ligonier Ministries*, 21 Oct. 2018, www.ligonier.org/blog/reformation-and-men-behind-it/. Accessed 30 Sept. 2020.

[60] Serge, Joseph, and Managing Editor. "Martin Luther and the Holocaust." *The Canadian Jewish News*, 28 Oct. 2019, www.cjnews.com/perspectives/features/martin-luther-and-the-holocaust. Accessed 25 Sept. 2020.

[61] City of Worms. "Welcome to the Nibelungen City on the Rhine! > Stadt Worms." *www.Worms.De*, 2020, www.worms.de/en/tourismus/. Accessed 30 Sept. 2020. "Martin Luther and the Reformation."

[62] Calvin, John, et al. *The Institutes of the Christian Religion*. Lexington, Kentucky, Pacific Publishing Studio, 2011.

[63] Calvin, John. *The Institutes of the Christian Religion*. kindle ed., 2011.

[64] The Editors of Christianity Today. "John Calvin." *Christian History | Learn the History of Christianity & the Church, Christianity Today*, 8 Aug. 2008, www.christianitytoday.com/history/people/theologians/john-calvin.html. Accessed 30 Aug. 2020.

[65] Reid, W. Stanford. "John Calvin: One of the Fathers of Modern Democracy | Christian History Magazine." *Christian History Magazine*, 1986, p. Issue 12, www.christianhistoryinstitute.org/magazine/article/calvin-father-of-modern-democracy. Accessed 30 Sept. 2020.

[66] Barry, John M. "God, Government and Roger Williams' Big Idea." *Smithsonian Magazine*, 2012, www.smithsonianmag.com/history/god-government-and-roger-williams-big-idea-6291280/. Accessed 11 June 2020.

[67] Barry, John M. *Roger Williams and the Creation of the American Soul: Church, State, and the Birth of Liberty*. New York, Penguin Books, 2012.

[68] Leland, John, and L F Greene. *The Writings of the Late Elder John Leland: Including Some Events in His Life*. Lexington, Ken., Forgotten Books; New York, 1845.

[69] Jr, John E. Ferguson. "John Leland." *www.Mtsu.Edu*, 2020, www.mtsu.edu/first-amendment/article/1219/john-leland. Accessed 12 June 2020.

[70] *Ibid.*

[71] Kennedy, Thomas. "Cheese Poetry | c u r i o." *Library.Brown.Edu*, 18 Apr. 2014, www.library.brown.edu/dps/curio/cheese-poetry. Accessed 30 Sept. 2020.

[72] Equiano, Olaudah. *The Interesting Narrative of the Life of Olaudah Equiano or Gustavus Vassa, the African*. edited by Shelly Eversley, New York, The Modern Library, 2004.

[73] Equiano, Olaudah (c.1745-1797). "BBC - History - Olaudah Equiano." *BBC*, 2014, www.bbc.co.uk/history/historic_figures/equiano_olaudah.shtml. Accessed 20 Aug. 2020.

[74] Prior, Karen Swallow. "Hannah More: Powerhouse in a Petticoat." *Christianity Today*, 4 Mar. 2015,

www.christianitytoday.com/ct/2015/march/hannah-more-powerhouse-in-petticoat.html. Accessed 30 Sept. 2020.

75 Foundation, Poetry. "Slavery by Hannah More." *Poetry Foundation*, 31 Aug. 2020, www.poetryfoundation.org/poems/51885/slavery. Accessed 30 Sept. 2020.

76 Karen Swallow Prior. *Fierce Convictions: The Extraordinary Life of Hannah More; Poet, Reformer, Abolitionist*. Nashville, Nelson Books, 2014.

77 Editors of E2bn. "John Newton (1725-1807): The Former Slaver & Preacher: The Abolition of Slavery Project." *E2bn.Org*, 2009, www.abolition.e2bn.org/people_35.html. Accessed 28 Sept. 2020.

78 The Editors of Christianity Today. "William Wilberforce." *Christian History | Learn the History of Christianity & the Church, Christianity Today*, 8 Aug. 2008, www.christianitytoday.com/history/people/activists/william-wilberforce.html. Accessed 30 Aug. 2020.

79 BBC.com. "BBC - History - William Wilberforce (1759-1833)." *BBC*, 2014, www.bbc.co.uk/history/historic_figures/wilberforce_william.shtml. Accessed 30 Aug. 2020.

80 Editors, History com. "Harriet Tubman." *HISTORY*, 8 Feb. 2019, www.history.com/topics/black-history/harriet-tubman. Accessed 30 Sept. 2020.

81 *Ibid.*

82 The Editors of Christianity Today. "Harriet Tubman: The Moses of Her People." *Christian History | Learn the History of Christianity & the Church, Christianity Today*, 8 Aug. 2008, www.christianitytoday.com/history/people/activists/harriet-tubman.html. Accessed 11 Sept. 2020.

83 *Ibid.*

84 Kate Clifford Larson. *Bound for the Promised Land: Harriet Tubman, Portrait of an American Hero*. New York, One World/Ballantine, 2005.

85 Dilbeck, D. H. "The Radical Christian Faith of Frederick Douglass: The Great Abolitionist Spoke Words of Rebuke—and Hope—to a Slaveholding Society." *ChristianityToday.Com*, 21 Dec. 2017, www.christianitytoday.com/ct/2018/january-february/frederick-douglass-at-200-remembering-his-radical-christian.html. Accessed 30 Sept. 2020.

86 *Ibid.*

87 Douglass, Frederick. *Frederick Douglass: Selected Speeches and Writings*. edited by Philip Foner, Chicago, Lawrence Hill, 1999, pp. 188–206.

88 Brown, DeNeen L. "Frederick Douglass Needed to See Lincoln. Would the President Meet with a Former Slave?" *The Washington Post*, 14 Feb. 2018, www.washingtonpost.com/news/retropolis/wp/2018/02/14/frederick-douglass-needed-to-see-lincoln-would-the-president-meet-with-a-former-slave/. Accessed 20 Aug. 2020.

89 Wills, Garry. "Lincoln's Greatest Speech." *The Atlantic*, Sept. 1999, www.theatlantic.com/magazine/archive/1999/09/lincolns-greatest-speech/306551/. Accessed 30 Sept. 2020.

[90] *Ibid.*

[91] D.H. Dilbeck, "The Radical Christian Faith of Frederick Douglass."

[92] Blight, David, *W. Frederick Douglass: Prophet of Freedom.* S.L., Simon & Schuster, 2019.

[93] Brown, Dee. *Bury My Heart at Wounded Knee: An Indian History of the American West* (p. 445). Open Road Media. Kindle Edition.

[94] Andrea Palpant Dilley, "The Surprising Discovery About Those Colonialist, Proselytizing Missionaries," *Christianity Today*, July 8, 2014, https://www.christianitytoday.com/ct/2014/january-february/world-missionaries-made.html.

[95] The World Staff, "There are 28 other monarchies in the world," *The World*, May 18, 2018, https://www.pri.org/stories/2018-05-18/there-are-28-other-monarchies-world.

[96] Northcott, Cecil. "John Mackenzie and Southern Africa | History Today." www.historytoday.com, 1972 Sept. 9, www.historytoday.com/archive/john-mackenzie-and-southern-africa. Accessed 11 June 2020.

[97] Mackenzie, John. *Austral Africa; Losing It Or Ruling It: Being Incidents and Experiences in Bechuanaland, Cape Colony, and England.* 1887. London, Andesite Press, 11 Aug. 2015.

[98] Justin Holcomb, "Theologian Hero to the Nation: The Life and Legacy of Abraham Kuyper" *The Gospel Coalition*, October 18, 2012. https://www.thegospelcoalition.org/article/theologian-hero-to-a-nation/.

[99] John Hendrick de Vries, *Biographical Note to Lectures on Calvinism, by Abraham Kuyper* (1931; reprint, Grand Rapids, MI: Eerdmans, 1994), iii.

[100] Abraham Kuyper, Dutch Theologian and Statesman, https://www.britannica.com/biography/Abraham-Kuyper#ref288098.

[101] Justin Holcomb, Theologian Hero to the Nation.

[102] Bratt, James D. *Abraham Kuyper: Modern Calvinist, Christian Democrat.* Grand Rapids, Mich., Eerdmans, 2013.

[103] *Ibid.*

[104] Jack S. Blocker, Jr., "Did Prohibition Really Work? Alcohol Prohibition as a Public Health Innovation." *American Journal of Public Health,* February 2006, https://www.ncbi.nlm.nih.gov/pmc/articles/PMC1470475/.

[105] "Biography," *Frances Willard House Museum and Archives,* https://franceswillardhouse.org/frances-willard/biography/.

[106] Let Something Good Be Said: Speeches and Writings of Frances E. Willard, edited by Carolyn DeSwarte Gifford and Amy R. Slagell (Urbana and Chicago: University of Illinois Press, 2007).

[107] Frances Willard, *Architect of the* Capitol, https://www.aoc.gov/explore-capitol-campus/art/frances-e-willard.

[108] Washington, DC, United States Holocaust Memorial Museum. "Corrie Ten Boom." Ushmm.Org, 2019,

https://encyclopedia.ushmm.org/content/en/article/corrie-ten-boom. Accessed 12 June 2020.

[109] Corrie Ten Boom, et al. *The Hiding Place*. 1971. Grand Rapids, Mi, Chosen Books, 2008.

[110] Christine Hoover, "'Thank you, God, for the Fleas'—Finding Courage in the Hiding Place," *The Gospel Coalition*, July 1, 2019, https://www.thegospelcoalition.org/reviews/finding-courage-hiding-place/.

[111] "The History of the Museum," Corrie Ten Boom House, https://www.corrietenboom.com/en/information/the-history-of-the-museum

[112] Michael Markrich, "Masao Yamada: America's First Japanese American Chaplain Served America's First All-Volunteer Japanese American Military Unit," *100th Infantry Battalion Veterans*, https://www.100thbattalion.org/history/veterans/chaplains/masao-yamada/2/

[113] "Japanese-American Internment During World War II," *National Archives*, https://www.archives.gov/education/lessons/japanese-relocation.

[114] W.F. Strong, "How the Japanese Americans Who Saved 'The Lost Battalion' Of World War II Became Honorary Texans," *Texas Standard*, May 29, 2019, https://www.texasstandard.org/stories/how-the-japanese-americans-who-saved-the-lost-battalion-of-world-war-ii-became-honorary-texans/.

[115] W.F. Strong, "How The Japanese Americans Who Saved 'The Lost Battalion' Of World War II Became Honorary Texans," *Texas Standard*, March 29, 2019, https://www.texasstandard.org/stories/how-the-japanese-americans-who-saved-the-lost-battalion-of-world-war-ii-became-honorary-texans/.

[116] Russell Lackey, "Martin Luther King, Jr.'s missing title: the reverend," *Des Moines Register*, January 19, 2015, https://www.desmoinesregister.com/story/opinion/columnists/iowa-view/2015/01/19/russell-lackey-reverand-martin-luther-kig/22005793/.

[117] Bob Adelman, editor, *MLK A Celebration in Word and Image*, October 4, 2011. Boston, MA Beacon Press.

[118] Garrow, David J.. *Bearing the Cross: Martin Luther King, Jr., and the Southern Christian Leadership Conference* (p. 58). Open Road Media. Kindle Edition.

[119] The Martin Luther King, Jr. Research and Education Institute at Stanford University, "Letter from a Birmingham Jail," April 16, 1963, https://kinginstitute.stanford.edu/king-papers/documents/letter-birmingham-jail.

[120] The Martin Luther King, Jr. Research and Education Institute at Stanford University, "I've Been to the Mountaintop," April 3, 1968, https://kinginstitute.stanford.edu/encyclopedia/ive-been-mountaintop.

[121] David Garrow, *Bearing the Cross*.

[122] Luis Palau Association, "Ministry History—Proclaiming the Gospel Since 1966," https://www.palau.org/about/history. Accessed 28 September 2020.

[123] "Luis Palau Back in China to Meet with Officials, 14,000 Hear the Evangelist and Rev. James Meeks," *PRNewswire*, March 26, 2010,

https://www.prnewswire.com/news-releases/luis-palau-back-in-china-to-meet-with-officials-14000-hear-the-evangelist-and-rev-james-meeks-89283472.html.

[124] Abdu Murray, A Visit with Luis Palau, Still on Fire for Christ in the Sunset of Life, *Christianity Today*, June 10, 2019, https://www.christianitytoday.com/ct/2019/june-web-only/luis-palau-life-on-fire-memoir.html.

[125] Luis Palau and Paul J. Pastor, *Palau: A Life on Fire*. Zondervan, Grand Rapids, Michigan, 2019.

[126] Amanda Litvinov, "Forgotten Purpose: Civics Education in Public Schools," *NEAToday*, March 16, 2017, http://neatoday.org/2017/03/16/civics-education-public-schools/.

[127] "Annenberg Civics Knowledge Survey," *Annenberg Public Policy Center of the University of Pennsylvania*, https://www.annenbergpublicpolicycenter.org/political-communication/civics-knowledge-survey/.

[128] "'Declaration of Independence,' a Transcription" *National Archives*, https://www.archives.gov/founding-docs/declaration-transcript.

[129] "'The Constitution of the United States:' A Transcription," *National Archives*, https://www.archives.gov/founding-docs/constitution-transcript.

[130] "From John Adams to Massachusetts Militia, 11 October 1798," *National Archives*, https://founders.archives.gov/documents/Adams/99-02-02-3102.

[131] "Farewell Address" *National Archives*.

[132] Jake Silverstein, "Why We Published the 1619 Project," *The New York Times Magazine*, December 20, 2019, https://www.nytimes.com/interactive/2019/12/20/magazine/1619-intro.html.

[133] "The National Memorial for Peace and Justice," *Equal Justice Institute*, https://museumandmemorial.eji.org/memorial.

[134] "Soviet Atomic Program – 1946," *Atomic Heritage Foundation*, June 5, 2014, https://www.atomicheritage.org/history/soviet-atomic-program-1946.

[135] David Satter, "100 Years of Communism—and 100 Million Dead," *Wall Street Journal*, November 6, 2017, https://www.wsj.com/articles/100-years-of-communismand-100-million-dead-1510011810.

[136] Jeffrey Ostler, "The Shameful Final Grievance of the Declaration of Independence," *The Atlantic*, February 8, 2020, https://www.theatlantic.com/ideas/archive/2020/02/americas-twofold-original-sin/606163/.

[137] "The Declarations of Sentiments and Resolution," *National Women's History Museum*, https://www.womenshistory.org/resources/primary-source/declaration-sentiments-and-resolution.

[138] Anthony Iaccarino, *The Founding Fathers and Slavery*, *Encyclopedia Brittanica*, https://www.britannica.com/topic/The-Founding-Fathers-and-Slavery-1269536.

[139] Foner, "Frederick Douglass: Selected Speeches and Writings; '"I Have a Dream,' Address Delivered at the March on Washington for Jobs and Freedom,"

The Martin Luther King, Jr. Research and Education Institute at Stanford,
https://kinginstitute.stanford.edu/king-papers/documents/i-have-dream-address-delivered-march-washington-jobs-and-freedom.

140 Michael Novak, *On Two Wings: Humble Faith and Common Sense at the American Founding,* Encounter Books San Fransisco, 2002.

141 Kim I. Parker, *The Biblical Politics of John Locke*, Wilfred Laurier University Press, 2004.

142 Winston S Churchill, "The Worst Form of Government," *International Churchill Society,* https://winstonchurchill.org/resources/quotes/the-worst-form-of-government/.

143 Lily Kuo, "In China, they're closing churches, jailing pastors – and even rewriting scripture," *The Guardian,* January 13, 2019, https://www.theguardian.com/world/2019/jan/13/china-christians-religious-persecution-translation-bible.

144 Stetzer and McDonald, "Why Evangelicals Voted Trump: Debunking the 81%".

145 "Christianity may disappear from Syria and Iraq—a call for international intervention," *Religion News Service,* October 23, 2019, https://religionnews.com/2019/10/23/christianity-may-disappear-from-syria-and-iraq-a-call-for-international-intervention/.

146 Ben Brimelow, "9 times the world was at the brink of nuclear war — and pulled back," *Business Insider,* April 25, 2018, https://www.businessinsider.com/when-nuclear-war-almost-happened-2018-4.

147 Evan Andrews, "Was there really a "red telephone" hotline during the Cold War?," *History.com* October 19, 2018 https://www.history.com/news/was-there-really-a-red-telephone-hotline-during-the-cold-war.

148 Mahlon Smith, "A closer look at four different types of prayer in I Timothy 2:1," *biblicalexegete,* December 6, 2014, https://biblicalexegete.wordpress.com/2014/12/06/a-closer-look-at-four-different-types-of-prayer-in-1-timothy-21/.

149 Abigail, Robertson, "'Spiritual Temperature' at Iowa 'State Capitol 'At an All-Time High' as Pastors Pray with Lawmakers," *CBN NEWS*, March 28, 2019 https://www1.cbn.com/cbnnews/us/2019/march/spiritual-temperature-at-iowa-state-capitol-at-an-all-time-high-as-pastors-pray-with-lawmakers.

150 Brenda Erickson, "Limited Bill Introductions," *Legis Brief,* Vol. 25, No. 23, June 2017, https://www.ncsl.org/research/about-state-legislatures/limiting-bill-introductions.aspx.

151 Michael Teitelbaum, "Congress saw more bills introduced in 2019 than it has in 40 years, but few passed," *Roll Call,* January 22, 2020, https://www.rollcall.com/2020/01/22/congress-saw-more-bills-introduced-in-2019-than-it-has-in-40-years-but-few-passed/.

[152] "Legislative Compensation Overview," *National Conference of State Legislatures*, July 22, 2020, https://www.ncsl.org/research/about-state-legislatures/the-legislative-pay-problem636360604.aspx.

[153] "Transcript: Chris Coons and James Lankford on "Face the Nation," December 29, 2019," *CBS News*, December 29, 2019, https://www.cbsnews.com/news/transcript-chris-coons-and-james-lankford-on-face-the-nation/.

[154] Dickerson, John S. *Hope of Nations* (p. 219). Zondervan. Kindle Edition.

[155] "The AFCARS Report: Preliminary FY 2018 Estimates as of August 22, 2019 - No. 26," *The Administration on Children, Youth and Families, Children's Bureau*, https://www.acf.hhs.gov/sites/default/files/cb/afcarsreport26.pdf.

[156] Courtney, M., Dworsky, A., Brown, A., Cary, C., Love, K., & Vorhies, V. (2011). Midwest evaluation of the adult functioning of former foster youth: Outcomes at age 26. Chicago, IL: Chapin Hall at the University of Chicago; Cyndi Sorrell, "51 Useful Aging Out of Foster Care Statistics," *National Foster Youth Institute*, https://www.nfyi.org/51-useful-aging-out-of-foster-care-statistics-social-race-media/.

[157] Michael Dolce, "We Have Set Up a System to Sex Traffic American Children," *Newsweek*, January 12, 2018 https://www.newsweek.com/we-have-set-system-sex-traffic-american-children-779541.

[158] "#94 How to Impact the Foster Care Crisis with Doug Weinberg," interview by Josh Hershberger, *The Good Citizen Podcast*, August 27, 2019, https://www.goodcitizen.us/how-to-impact-the-foster-care-crisis-with-doug-weinberg/.

[159] Hands of Hope, "About Us," https://handsofhopein.org/about-us/.

[160] Whites Residential & Family Services, "Josiah White," https://whiteskids.org/about/history/.

[161] Jeannie Law, "Jamie Grace: If every church in America fostered 1 child 'there'd be no more waiting children'," *Christian Post*, November 30, 2019, https://www.christianpost.com/news/jamie-grace-if-every-church-in-america-fostered-1-child-thered-be-no-more-waiting-children.html.

[162] "Opioid Overdose Crisis," *National Institute on Drug Abuse*, May 27, 2020, https://www.drugabuse.gov/drug-topics/opioids/opioid-overdose-crisis

[163] Florence CS, Zhou C, Luo F, Xu L. The Economic Burden of Prescription Opioid Overdose, Abuse, and Dependence in the United States, 2013. Med Care. 2016;54(10):901-906. doi:10.1097/MLR.0000000000000625.

[164] NIDA. 2020, July 10. Drugs and the Brain. Retrieved from https://www.drugabuse.gov/publications/drugs-brains-behavior-science-addiction/drugs-brain on 2020, August 18.

[165] NIDA. 2020, June 3. Why do drug-addicted persons keep using drugs?. Retrieved from https://www.drugabuse.gov/publications/principles-drug-

addiction-treatment-research-based-guide-third-edition/frequently-asked-questions/why-do-drug-addicted-persons-keep-using-drugs on 2020, August 18.

166 David Chapman, "On the Nature of Addiction and the Loss of Hope," *Melissa Killeen Recovery Coaching*, November 5, 2015, https://www.mkrecoverycoaching.com/2015/11/05/on-the-nature-of-addiction-and-the-loss-of-hope/.

167 "Faith leaders join forces to start addiction recovery house," *The Republic*, February 3, 2018, http://www.therepublic.com/2018/02/04/02042018cr_jennings_recovery_house/.

168 "Faith & Community Roadmap to Recovery Support: Getting Back to Work," *The Partnership Center Center for Faith and Opportunity Initiatives U.S. Dept. of Health and Human Services*, 15 https://www.hhs.gov/guidance/sites/default/files/hhs-guidance-documents/2006242561-gw-faith-community-roadmap-to-recovery-support-march2020.pdf.

169 Grayson Pope, "The History of the Prison Fellowship Academy," *Prison Fellowship*, February 2019, https://www.prisonfellowship.org/2019/02/the-history-of-the-prison-fellowship-academy/.

170 Wendy Sawyer and Peter Wagner, "Mass Incarceration: The Whole Pie 2020," *Prison Policy Initiative*, March 24, 2020, https://www.prisonpolicy.org/reports/pie2020.html.

171 "#137 Prison Ministry during the Pandemic with Mark Frisbie," interviewed by Josh Hershberger, *The Good Citizen Podcast*, July 7, 2020, https://www.goodcitizen.us/137-prison-ministry-during-the-pandemic-with-mark-frisbie/.

172 Wendy Sawyer, "The Gender Divide: Tracking Women's State Prison Growth," *Prison Policy Initiative*, January 9, 2018, https://www.prisonpolicy.org/reports/women_overtime.html.

173 "Create: New Beginnings" *Prison Fellowship*, https://www.prisonfellowship.org/about/in-prison/womens-ministry/create-new-beginnings/.

174 Sarah Eekhoff Zylstra, "Why Indianapolis Megachurch Members Are Joining God in the 'Swamp'," *The Gospel Coalition*, https://www.thegospelcoalition.org/article/why-indianapolis-megachurch-members-joining-god-swamp/.

175 Eric Holcomb, "2020 State of the State Address," January 14, 2020, https://www.in.gov/gov/2020stateofstate.htm.

176 "#108 A New Vision for Church/State Partnerships with Senator Andy Zay," interview by Josh Hershberger, *The Good Citizen Podcast*, December 10, 2019, https://www.goodcitizen.us/108-a-new-vision-for-church-state-partnerships-with-senator-andy-zay/.

[177] "Abraham Lincoln Birthplace," *National Park Service*, https://www.nps.gov/abli/index.htm.

[178] "Jefferson Davis State Historic Site," *Kentucky State Parks*, https://parks.ky.gov/fairview/parks/historic/jefferson-davis-state-historic-site.

[179] Amy Murrell Taylor, "The Border States," *National Park Service*, https://www.nps.gov/articles/the-border-states.htm

[180] Doris Kearns Goodwin, *Team of Rivals: The Political Genius of Abraham Lincoln*, Simon & Schuster, New York, 2005, 590-93, 601-2.

[181] Guy Gugliotta, "New Estimate Raises Civil War Death Toll," *The New York Times*, April 2, 2012, https://www.nytimes.com/2012/04/03/science/civil-war-toll-up-by-20-percent-in-new-estimate.html.

[182] Adam J. White, "A Republic if We Can Keep It," *The Atlantic*, February 4, 2020, https://www.theatlantic.com/ideas/archive/2020/02/a-republic-if-we-can-keep-it/605887/.

[183] Wayne Grudem, *Politics According to the Bible: A Comprehensive Resource for Understanding Modern Political Issues in Light of Scripture*, Zondervan, Grand Rapids, 2010.

[184] Katharina Buchholz, "The National Flags with the Most Stars," *Statista*, June 12, 2020, https://www.statista.com/chart/21986/national-flags-with-most-stars/.

[185] Os Guinness, *The Call: Finding and Fulfilling the Central Purpose of Your Life*, Thomas Nelson, Nashville, 2003.

[186] Jonathan Leeman, *Political Church: The Local Assembly as Embassy of Christ's Rule*, InterVarsity Press, Downers Grove, Illinois. 2016.

[187] *Lemon v. Kurtzman*, 403 U.S. 602 (1971).

[188] Amy How, "Opinion Analysis: Justice allow "peace cross" to stand (Updated)," *SCOTUSblog*, June 20, 2019, https://www.scotusblog.com/2019/06/opinion-analysis-justices-allow-peace-cross-to-stand/.

[189] @timkellernyc (Timothy Keller), "The Early Church Christian social project was a unique kind of human community that defied categories. It had at least five elements: "*Multi-racial and multi-ethnic *Highly committed to caring for the poor and marginalized *Non-retaliatory, marked by a commitment to forgiveness *Strongly and practically against abortion and infanticide *Revolutionary regarding the ethics of sex…" *Twitter*, 13 Sept. 2020, https://twitter.com/timkellernyc/status/1305152774523572224?s=21.

[190] Robert C. Cetrulo, *Constitutional Personhood of the Unborn Child*, University Faculty for Life, http://www.uffl.org/pdfs/vol18/Cetrulo_08.pdf.

[191] Daniel Darling, *The Dignity Revolution: Reclaiming God's Rich Vision for Humanity*, The Good Book Company, 2018, 88.

[192] "#128 Running toward Racial Unity with Adrian Burden," interviewed by Josh Hershberger, *The Good Citizen Podcast*, February 23, 2020, https://www.goodcitizen.us/129-running-toward-racial-unity-with-adrian-burden/;

"#132 What Can We Do About Injustice and George Floyd's Death? with Pastor Andrew Hunt," interviewed by Josh Hershberger, *The Good Citizen Podcast*, June 4, 2020, https://www.goodcitizen.us/132-what-can-we-do-about-injustice-and-george-floyds-death-with-pastor-andrew-hunt/; "#133 A Biblical Roadmap for Engaging Racial Injustice with Courtney Montgomery and Pastor Matt Hodge," interviewed by Josh Hershberger, June 12, 2020, https://www.goodcitizen.us/133-a-biblical-roadmap-for-engaging-racial-injustice-with-courtney-montgomery-and-pastor-matthew-hodge/.

[193] Josh S. Dickerson, *Jesus Skeptic: A Journalist Explores the Credibility and Impact of Christianity*, Baker Books; Grand Rapids, Michigan, 2019, pg. 120.

[194] Joe Carter, "FactChecker: Do Christian Men Watch More Pornography?" *The Gospel Coalition*, June 8, 2020, https://www.thegospelcoalition.org/article/factchecker-do-christian-men-watch-more-pornography/.

[195] Marlo Safi, "The Porn Industry and Human Trafficking Reinforce Each Other," *The National Review*, August 1, 2018, https://www.nationalreview.com/2018/08/porn-human-trafficking-reinforce-each-other/.

[196] Kimberly M. Nelson, PhD, MPH and Emily F. Rothman, ScD, "Should Public Health Professionals Consider Pornography a Public Health Crisis?," *American Journal of Public Health*, February 2020, https://www.ncbi.nlm.nih.gov/pmc/articles/PMC6951382/.

[197] Glenn Stanton, "FactChecker: Divorce Rate among Christians," *The Gospel Coalition*, September 25, 2012, https://www.thegospelcoalition.org/article/factchecker-divorce-rate-among-christians/.

[198] DeYoung, Kevin. What Does the Bible Really Teach about Homosexuality? (p. 75). Crossway. Kindle Edition.

[199] *Obergefell v. Hodges*, 576 U.S. 644 (2015).

[200] *Bostock v. Clayton Cty., Georgia*, 140 S. Ct. 1731 (2020).

[201] Daniel Darling, "Why Religious Liberty Matters for Human Dignity," *Fox News*, August 20, 2018 https://www.foxnews.com/opinion/why-religious-liberty-matters-for-human-dignity.

[202] *Ibid.*

[203] "Strong's G4176 – politeuomai," *Blue Letter Bible*, https://www.blueletterbible.org/lang/Lexicon/Lexicon.cfm?strongs=G4176&t=KJV.

[204] "U.S. Abortion Rate Continues to Decline, Reaching Historic Low in 2017," *Guttmacher Institute*, September 18, 2019, https://www.guttmacher.org/news-release/2019/us-abortion-rate-continues-decline-reaching-historic-low-2017.

[205] Kayla McGhee, "Trump is right: Young people are the heart of the pro-life movement," January 24, 2020,

https://www.washingtonexaminer.com/opinion/president-trump-is-right-young-americans-are-the-heart-of-the-pro-life-movement.

[206] *June Med. Servs. L. L. C. v. Russo*, 140 S. Ct. 2103 (2020).

[207] "Last Five Years Account for More Than One-quarter of All Abortion Restrictions Enacted Since Roe," *Guttmacher Institute*, January 13, 2016. https://www.guttmacher.org/article/2016/01/last-five-years-account-more-one-quarter-all-abortion-restrictions-enacted-roe.

[208] Tricia C. Bruce, PHD, "How Americans Understand Abortion : A Comprehensive Interview Study of Abortion Attitudes in the U.S." *University of Notre Dame: McGrath Institute for Church Life*, 2020, https://news.nd.edu/assets/395804/how_americans_understand_abortion_final_7_15_20.pdf.

[209] Dr. Tony Evans, "A Kingdom Strategy For Kingdom Transformation," *Urban Alternative*, https://go.tonyevans.org/hubfs/pdf/KingdomStrategyForCommunityTransformation-1.pdf.

[210] Michael Wear, *Reclaiming Hope: Lessons Learned in the Obama White House About the Future of Faith in America*, Thomas Nelson, Nashville, 2017.

[211] Justin Giboney, Michael Wear, and Chris Butler, *Compassion (&) Conviction: The AND Campaign's Guide to Faithful Civic Engagement*, Intervarsity Press Downer's Grove, Illinois, 2020.

[212] Elizabeth Davis and Anthony Whyde, BJS Statisticians, "Contacts Between Police and the Public, 2015" *Bureau of Justice Statistics*, October 2018, https://www.bjs.gov/content/pub/pdf/cpp15.pdf.

[213] Arrest-Related Deaths Program Redesign Study, 2015-16:Preliminary Findings, *Bureau of Justice Statistics*, https://www.bjs.gov/content/pub/pdf/ardprs1516pf_sum.pdf.

[214] Joe Carter, "What You Should Know about the First Step Act," ERLC, November 16, 2018, https://erlc.com/resource-library/articles/what-you-should-know-about-the-first-step-act/.

[215] *Bostock*, 140 S. Ct. at 1754.

[216] David French, "The Supreme Court Tries to Settle the Religious Liberty Culture War," *Time*, July 14, 2020, https://time.com/5866374/supreme-court-settle-religious-liberty/.

[217] *Obergefell*, 576 U.S. at 657.

[218] Elana Schor, "Are Church Services Considered 'Essential'?: Depends Where You Live," *Christianity Today*, March 24, 2020, https://www.christianitytoday.com/news/2020/march/state-exemptions-church-covid-19-essential-services.html.

[219] Tony Morrero, "Charges dropped against Tampa pastor who held services during stay-at-home order," *Tampa Bay Times*, May 15, 2020,

https://www.tampabay.com/news/health/2020/05/15/charges-dropped-against-tampa-pastor-who-held-services-during-stay-at-home-order/.

220 Ryan Lovelace, "Mississippi church to sue city government for crackdown on 'drive-in' church service," *The Washington Times*, April 10, 2020, https://m.washingtontimes.com/news/2020/apr/10/mississippi-church-sue-city-government-crackdown-d/.

221 Daniel Burke, "California church defies public health orders, holds indoor services for thousands with no social distancing," *CNN*, August 13, 2020, https://www.cnn.com/2020/08/12/us/pastor-macarthur-church-california/index.html.

222 Kathleen Wilson, "Judge holds Godspeak chapel and Pastor Rob McCoy in contempt, orders fine," *Ventura County Star*, August 21, 2020, https://www.vcstar.com/story/news/2020/08/21/covid-ventura-county-church-pastor-held-contempt-health-violations-indoor-worship/5609260002/; Erin Woo, "Coronavirus fines pile up as Santa Clara church continues inside services North Valley," *The Mercury News*, August 30, 2020, https://www.mercurynews.com/2020/08/30/coronavirus-santa-clara-church-continues-in-house-services-despite-county-fines/.

223 *Calvary Chapel Dayton Valley v. Sisolak*, No. 19A1070, 2020 WL 4251360, at *1 (U.S. July 24, 2020).

224 *S. Bay United Pentecostal Church v. Newsom*, 140 S. Ct. 1613 (2020).

225 *Ibid.*

226 *Calvary Chapel Dayton Valley*, 2020 WL 4251360 at *1.

227 "House Bill 272," *The Ohio Legislature*, 133rd General Assembly, https://www.legislature.ohio.gov/legislation/legislation-summary?id=GA133-HB-272&vcrmeid=q3HIfmbviEiFsil7b0gzQ&vcrmiid=eaEWYzdJYUqbsBUATn9u5Q
.

228 Jonathan Leeman, "A Time for Civil Disobedience? A Response to Grace Community Church's Elders," *IX Marks*, July 25, 2020. https://www.9marks.org/article/a-time-for-civil-disobedience-a-response-to-john-macarthur/.

229 Joe Carter, "Capitol Hill Baptist Shows How to Fight for Religious Freedom in a Pandemic," *The Gospel Coalition*, September 23, 2020, https://www.thegospelcoalition.org/article/chbc-religious-freedom-pandemic/.

230 "PLACE TO WORSHIP INITIATIVE—WHAT IS RLUIPA?," *The United States Department of Justice*, November 7, 2018, https://www.justice.gov/crt/place-worship-initiative-what-rluipa.

231 "Tax Guide for Churches & Religious Organizations," *Internal Revenue Service*, https://www.irs.gov/pub/irs-pdf/p1828.pdf.

232 Charities, Churches and Politics, *Internal Revenue Service*, https://www.irs.gov/newsroom/charities-churches-and-politics.

[233] Salvador Rizzo, "President Trump's shifting claim that 'we got rid' of the Johnson Amendment," *The Washington Post,* May 9, 2019, https://www.washingtonpost.com/politics/2019/05/09/president-trumps-shifting-claim-that-we-got-rid-johnson-amendment/.

[234] George Barna, *The Day Christians Changed America,* Metaformation, Ventura, California, 2017.

[235] Barna Research, "Notional Christians: The Big Election Story in 2016," December 1, 2016, *Barna,* https://www.barna.com/research/notional-christians-big-election-story-2016/.

[236] "An examination of the 2016 electorate, based on validated voters," *Pew Research Center,* August 9, 2018, https://www.pewresearch.org/politics/2018/08/09/an-examination-of-the-2016-electorate-based-on-validated-voters/.

[237] Thomas Kidd, "Traditional Christians Have Never Been Politically Unified," *The Gospel Coalition,* August 26, 2020, https://www.thegospelcoalition.org/blogs/evangelical-history/traditional-christians-have-never-been-politically-unified/.

[238] "For God and Country: Russell Moore on Love and Humility in American Politics," *The Table Podcast,* October 22, 2018, https://cct.biola.edu/love-humility-politics-russell-moore/.

[239] "What Lincoln Wore," *Ford's Theatre,* https://www.fords.org/lincolns-assassination/lincolns-clothes/.

[240] Justin Taylor, "All in One Little Lifetime: All Gone with the Wind," *The Gospel Coalition,* November 17, 2012, https://www.thegospelcoalition.org/blogs/justin-taylor/all-in-one-little-lifetime-all-gone-with-the-wind/.

[241] "Jahr Null," *The Man in the High Castle,* Season 3, Episode 10, *Amazon.com.*

[242] Abraham Lincoln, "Gettysburg Address," *National Archives,* 19 November 1963, https://www.archives.gov/historical-docs/todays-doc/?dod-date=1119.